Discover China
走遍中国

主编 齐少艳 谭秋瑜

外语教学与研究出版社
FOREIGN LANGUAGE TEACHING AND RESEARCH PRESS
北京 BEIJING

macmillan education

Introduction

Discover China is a four-level Mandarin Chinese course, specially designed for beginners to intermediate level students studying Chinese in English-speaking countries. It employs a communicative and integrated approach to language learning. Emphasis is placed on communication in real contexts through pair work, group work and a variety of independent and integrated activities to help students become confident Chinese language speakers.

Key features

Discover China's unique communicative course design includes a number of distinctive features:

- **Topic-driven content in real-life contexts** gets students engaged and motivated. The topics in each book are organized around the lives and travel experiences of five young students in China.

- **A truly communicative approach** lets students learn the language by using it in real-life situations, providing them with the tools they need to communicate in Chinese naturally.

- **Structured and effective learning design** based on the sequence "presentation, practice and production", facilitates effective learning of the language with activities moving from controlled practice to personalized tasks.

- **Systematic vocabulary and grammar development** comes through topic-based practice and extension exercises. The lexical syllabus is based on levels 1-4 of the *Hanyu Shuiping Kaoshi* (HSK test) and the grammatical syllabus takes students up to the Vantage level (level B2) of the Common European Framework.

- **Student-centred grammar learning supplemented with detailed grammar reference** allows students to discover the rules for themselves through identifying patterns in the language samples. The grammar reference provides comprehensive and detailed explanations.

- **Meaningful and integrated character writing practice** through grouping characters with common radicals. These high-frequency characters are presented within the context of the unit theme.

- **Insights into Chinese culture**, through "Cultural corner" sections linked to the unit topics, promote a deeper cultural understanding. Fascinating full-colour photos showing the real China, provide visual appeal and draw students into this diverse culture.

- **Simplified Chinese characters** are used to facilitate learning of the written language used by the majority of Chinese speakers.

- **Pinyin matched to the word level** instead of individual characters helps students understand how to write and space pinyin meaningfully. *Discover China* follows the official pinyin orthography.

- **Extra pair work activities** for each unit provide additional communicative speaking practice.

- **Supported by free online resources** including teacher's books, assessment tasks, unit quizzes, extra character writing sheets and more.

Workbook

The Workbook provides extensive consolidation of the language skills and knowledge taught in the Student's Book.

Each Workbook unit features clear language objectives which correspond with the Student's Book unit structure and activities. A wide variety of vocabulary and grammar exercises, as well as extra reading and listening activities, provide practice of the core language presented in the Student's Book. Writing practice sections give students the option to extend their Chinese character writing skills beyond the Student's Book requisites. A self-assessment at the end of each unit using "I can…" descriptors enables students to reflect on their individual progress.

Characteristics of each level

Book 1 and Book 2 cover basic language relating to everyday topics. The focus is on listening and speaking, although there is a writing activity at the end of each lesson 2. Character writing practice is available in both the Student's Book and Workbook to help students learn how to write Chinese characters with the correct stroke order.

Book 1 is for beginners who have not studied any Chinese. To avoid overwhelming students with character reading at the very beginning, pinyin is placed above all Chinese words and characters to provide the necessary language support. However, to help students develop character recognition skills, pinyin does not appear for conversations and passages in the Workbook. Activities in the online unit quizzes, which simulate test questions from the HSK test, have no pinyin.

Book 2 follows on naturally from Book 1. Pinyin is used only in activities with new words and phrases, and the activities in the pronunciation and speaking section of each unit. Most other activities in the book do not carry pinyin. However, versions of all the main conversations and reading passages with pinyin are available for downloading from *Discover China's* free resources website.

Book 3 and Book 4 cover language from school life and the work environment. The focus is on the development of language skills, which is conducted through various approaches including guided writing. The lessons contain activities to further enhance students' language skills in all areas across different contexts and functions. A new guided writing section teaches students how to compose natural texts following authentic-like texts. The conversations and reading passages are longer, and pinyin only appears in each unit's vocabulary boxes.

Storylines

- **Book 1** presents the fundamentals of the Chinese language, following the characters' day-to-day lives in Beijing. From simple introductions to going shopping, eating out or playing sports, students encounter a broad range of situations and learn the basic language skills they require.

- **Book 2** includes "survival Chinese" for travelling and living in China, as the characters hit the road on their winter holidays. They see the Terracotta Warriors in Xi'an and try authentic Sichuan food in Chengdu, make new friends and broaden their knowledge of Chinese to handle typical subjects such as food and drink, hotels, sightseeing and going to the doctor.

- **Book 3** takes a deeper look at China's diverse culture. Steve lands his dream job and is sent on assignment as a photojournalist to exciting places all over China. Amanda pursues her love of Chinese history and takes the Chinese history class. This provides students with rich exposure to the use of Chinese language across various cultural and social contexts.

- **Book 4** prepares students to use Chinese for work-related purposes. Mark takes up an internship at a Chinese company in Shenzhen, and Yeong-min volunteers at a summer camp for international students studying in China. Both gain valuable experience working with different people and dealing with different situations. Encouraged by Wang Yu, Steve showcases his talent in a photo competition themed around Yunnan. Wang Yu herself goes to study in the US, and finds that living abroad gives her a new perspective on the experiences of her overseas friends in China.

Unit structure

Student's Book 4 | Unit 12   No pain, no gain. 有付出，才有收获。

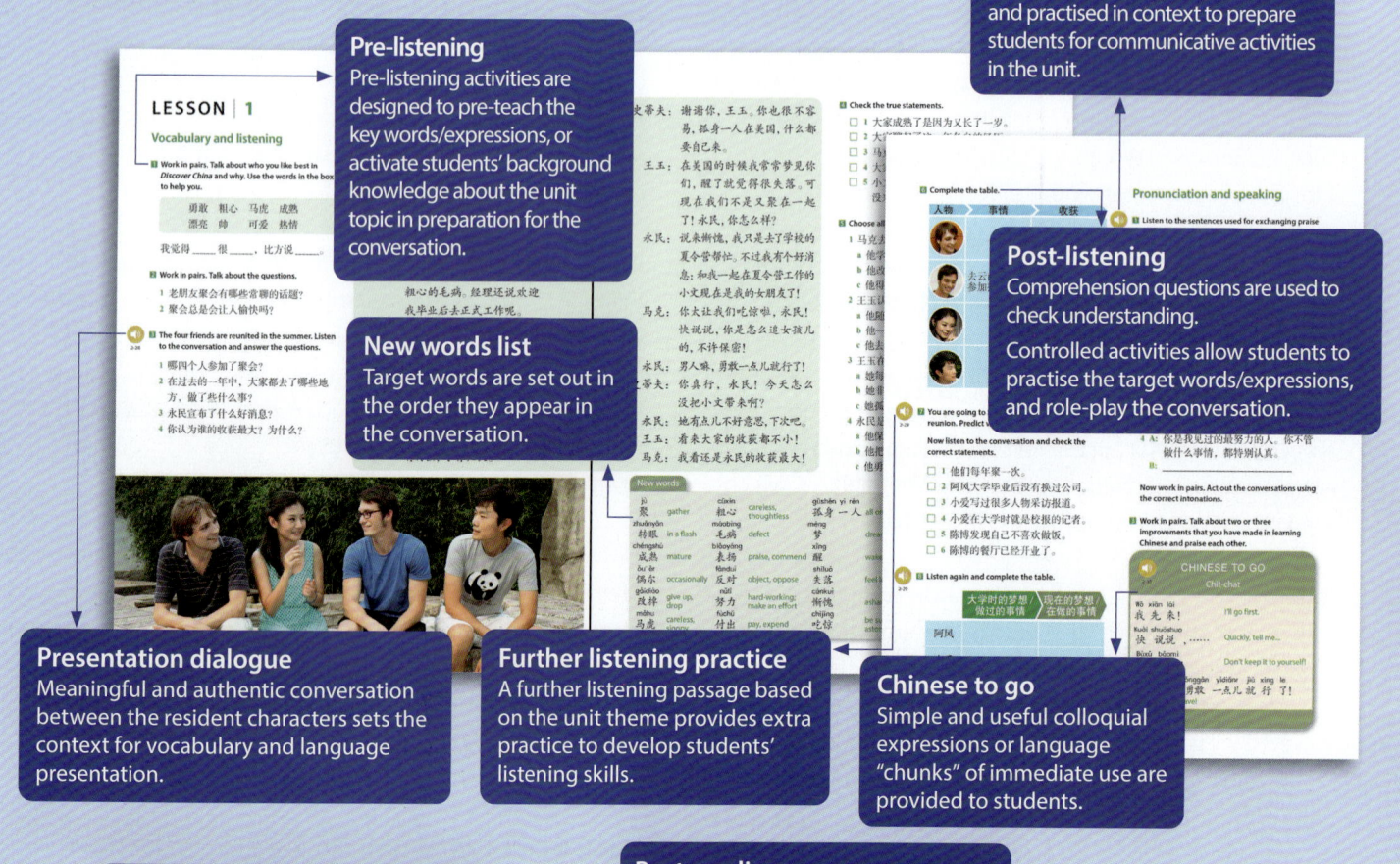

Pre-listening
Pre-listening activities are designed to pre-teach the key words/expressions, or activate students' background knowledge about the unit topic in preparation for the conversation.

Pronunciation
Difficult pronunciation points for English speakers are presented and practised in context to prepare students for communicative activities in the unit.

New words list
Target words are set out in the order they appear in the conversation.

Post-listening
Comprehension questions are used to check understanding.
Controlled activities allow students to practise the target words/expressions, and role-play the conversation.

Presentation dialogue
Meaningful and authentic conversation between the resident characters sets the context for vocabulary and language presentation.

Further listening practice
A further listening passage based on the unit theme provides extra practice to develop students' listening skills.

Chinese to go
Simple and useful colloquial expressions or language "chunks" of immediate use are provided to students.

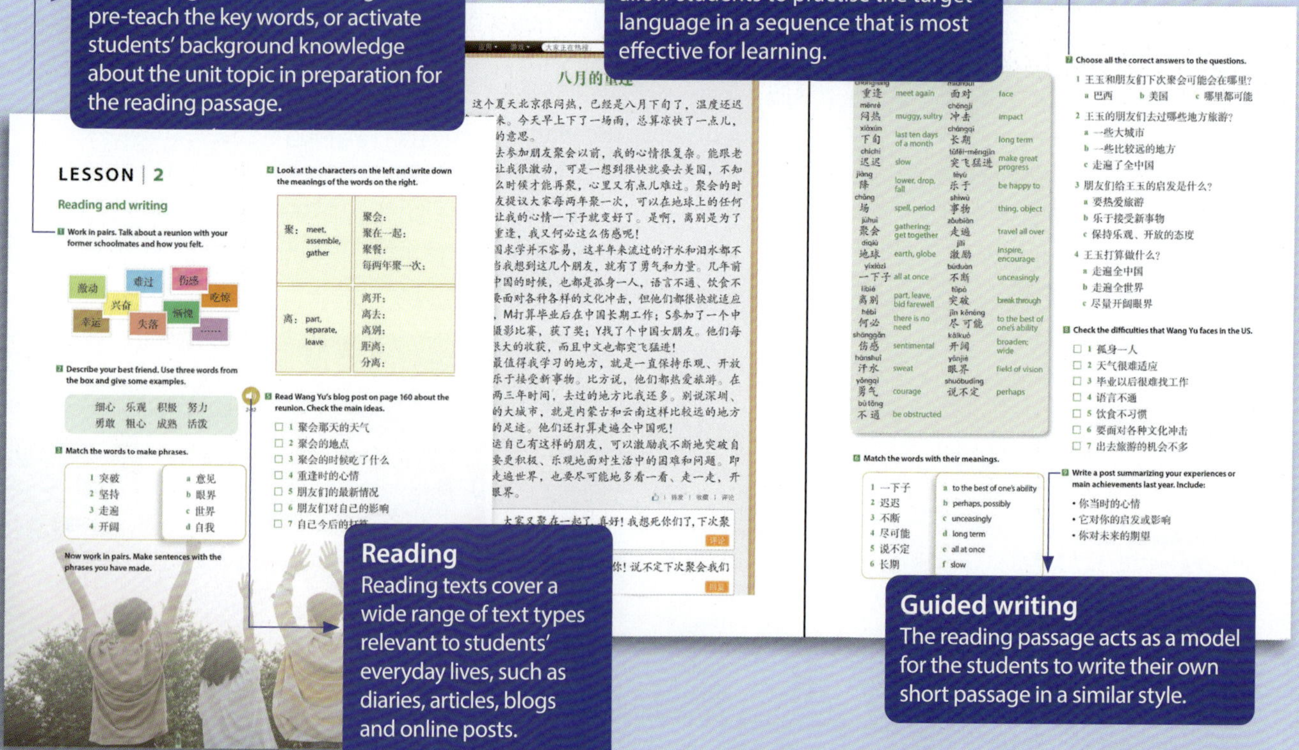

Pre-reading
Pre-reading activities are designed to pre-teach the key words, or activate students' background knowledge about the unit topic in preparation for the reading passage.

Post-reading
Controlled, guided and freer activities allow students to practise the target language in a sequence that is most effective for learning.

Reading
Reading texts cover a wide range of text types relevant to students' everyday lives, such as diaries, articles, blogs and online posts.

Guided writing
The reading passage acts as a model for the students to write their own short passage in a similar style.

4 ❖ Introduction

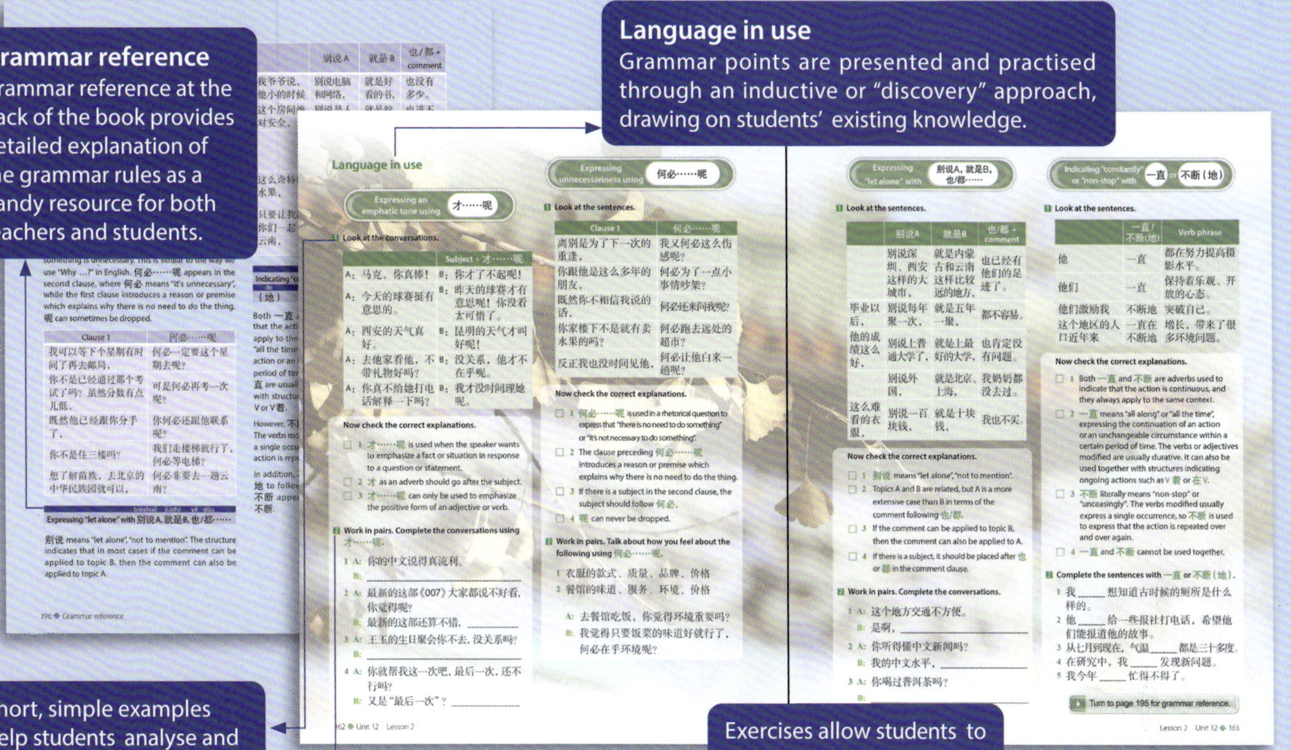

Grammar reference
Grammar reference at the back of the book provides detailed explanation of the grammar rules as a handy resource for both teachers and students.

Language in use
Grammar points are presented and practised through an inductive or "discovery" approach, drawing on students' existing knowledge.

Short, simple examples help students analyse and discover the grammar rules.

Exercises allow students to practise and consolidate the rules.

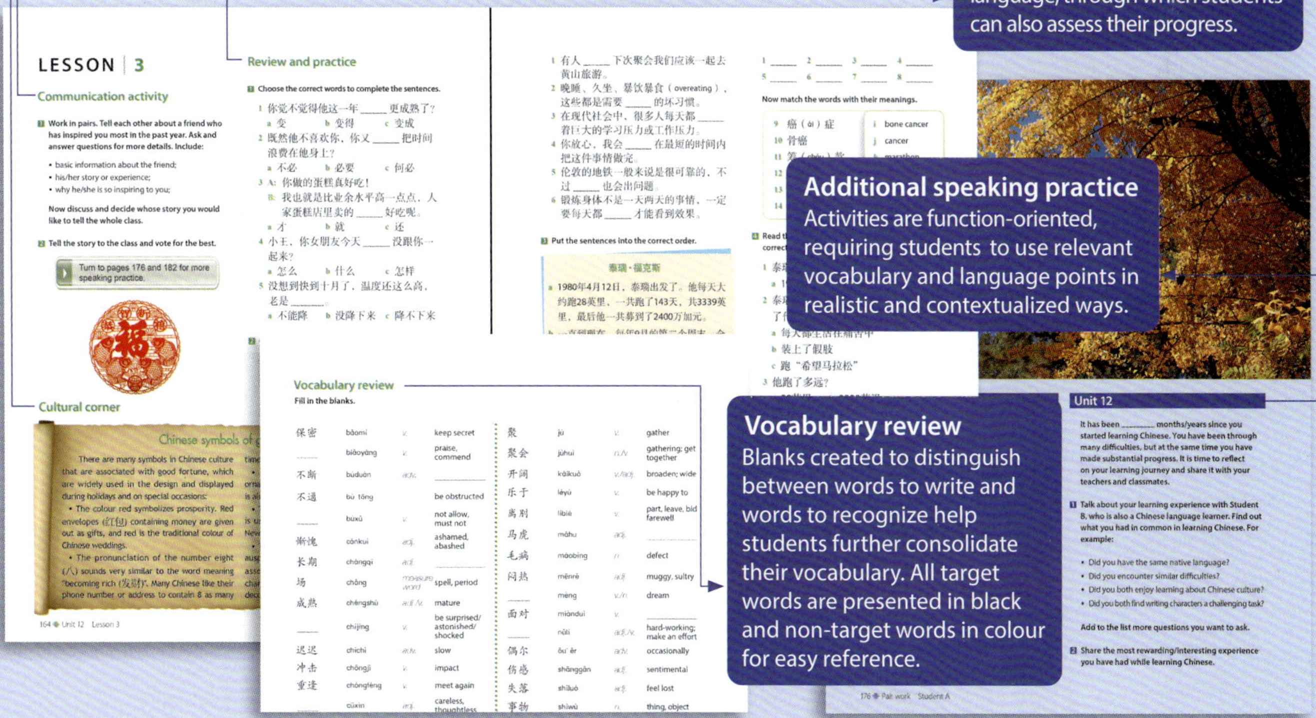

Cultural corner
Cultural points linked to the unit topic enable a greater understanding and appreciation of Chinese life and culture.

Communication activity
Meaningful and realistic communication in relevant contexts is facilitated through role-plays and speaking tasks.

Review and practice
Builds on language acquisition by recycling previously learnt target language, through which students can also assess their progress.

Additional speaking practice
Activities are function-oriented, requiring students to use relevant vocabulary and language points in realistic and contextualized ways.

Vocabulary review
Blanks created to distinguish between words to write and words to recognize help students further consolidate their vocabulary. All target words are presented in black and non-target words in colour for easy reference.

Introduction ◆ 5

Contents

Title	Unit topic	Listening and reading	Speaking and writing
Unit 1 你一定行！ **You can do it!** page 15	Jobs and internships	• Understanding feelings and concerns • Understanding job advertisements	• Asking for information • Giving encouragement • Writing an email asking for more information about a position
Unit 2 你感觉怎么样？ **How did you feel?** page 27	CVs and job interviews	• Understanding key information about a job interview • Understanding difficulties living abroad • Understanding an application letter	• Asking for and giving opinions about a job interview • Talking about difficulties living abroad • Writing an application letter
Unit 3 让您的旅行没有后顾之忧！ **We can help you plan a worry-free trip!** page 39	Planning a trip	• Identifying key information in detailed explanations • Understanding requests and giving responses • Understanding an itinerary	• Asking for and giving clarification about a trip • Writing a simple itinerary
Unit 4 欢迎大家的到来！ **Welcome, everyone!** page 51	Summer camp	• Identifying people's roles • Understanding an opening speech • Understanding rules and regulations • Necessities for a trip	• Chairing an opening ceremony • Welcoming people and giving a brief self-introduction • Writing a short passage about things to notice during a trip
Review 1 page 63			
Unit 5 我一定尽力而为！ **I will try my best!** page 67	Office work	• Understanding expectations • Exchanging opinions • Understanding the basic business writing style	• Showing care and support • Asking for and giving opinions • Writing an invitation card
Unit 6 你们两个配合得很好！ **You two make a good team!** page 79	A business event	• Understanding praise and encouragement • Talking about working experiences • Understanding a speech and protocol at a business dinner	• Showing appreciation and support • Giving humble responses to praise • Showing respect to senior colleagues • Allocating roles for an event

Grammar and vocabulary	Pronunciation	Cultural corner
• Expressing "not at all", "not even one", "not a single …" with 一……都／也＋不／没…… • Emphasizing details of a past action using 是……的 • Showing direction of movement with 回／进／上／下＋来／去 • Introducing an extreme case using 连……都／也…… • Words for job searching and internships	Giving encouragement	Tang poetry
• Indicating a very high degree of something with 不得了 • Repeated actions with 再 or 又 • Expressing "a little bit" using 一下 or 一点儿 • Indicating the beginning of an action or the start of a new state with 起来 • Words for interviews and CVs	Linking words for elaborating tones	Tips for job-hunting in China
• Introducing a new subject using 至于 • Comparative structures using 不如 • Expressing fractions and percentages with ……分之…… • Moderating positive adjectives with 还 • Travel planning	Expressing approximations	Harbin
• "Verb + object" as a separable compound • 通过 as a preposition • Introducing the agent or performer of an action using 由 • Disyllabic words that become monosyllabic in formal style • Welcome speeches and regulations	Welcoming people and giving good wishes	Collectivism vs. individualism
• Concessive clauses with 倒 • Expressing "doing well" with 好好 • Making deductions with 既然 • Stressing an extreme degree with 再……不过了 • Words for office work	Asking for opinions	Nature reserves and wildlife protection in China
• Indicating an extreme degree with ……死了 • Expressing wishes and hopes with 要是／如果……就好了 • Expressing emphasis using 可 • Justifying an opinion or decision using 反正 • Words for business events	Using 就 orally	Humility

Title	Unit topic	Listening and reading	Speaking and writing
Unit 7 顾客永远是对的！ **The customer is always right!** page 91	Dealing with complaints	• Understanding complaints • Identifying a speaker's worries • Understanding a personal letter	• Giving advice • Showing empathy and support • Writing a letter about recent experiences
Unit 8 云南真是个好地方！ **Yunnan is an amazing place!** page 103	Travel and lifestyle	• Understanding unusual experiences • Understanding ideas about lifestyles • Identifying different feelings of the same person travelling to different places	• Showing understanding • Showing appreciation and fondness for a place • Writing a travel journal
Review 2 page 115			
Unit 9 求之不得！ **Only too glad to!** page 119	Participating in a competition	• Understanding encouragement • Identifying worries and concerns • Understanding an announcement of a competition	• Showing care and support • Encouraging people in a competition • Writing an announcement for a competition
Unit 10 这个题目是不是太大了？ **Isn't this topic too broad?** page 131	Topics for speeches and debates	• Identifying agreements and disagreements • Understanding arguments and reasons • Understanding arguments and supporting facts in an essay passage	• Agreement and disagreement • Giving an apology • Writing an argumentative passage with supporting facts
Unit 11 回家的感觉真好！ **It feels so good to be back home!** page 143	A winner's interview	• Understanding people's concerns and recognizing appreciation • Identifying feelings and emotions • Understanding an interview	• Showing empathy and appreciation • Giving support and encouragement • Writing about a person's special experiences
Unit 12 有付出，才有收获。 **No pain, no gain.** page 155	Reunion	• Talking about pains and gains • Understanding retrospection and expectations • Understanding a narrative passage	• Showing disagreement and support • Expressing surprise and joy • Talking about past and future • Writing a narrative passage about past and future
Review 3 page 167			

Pair work activities   pages 171 and 177   **Grammar reference**   page 183

Grammar and vocabulary	Pronunciation	Cultural corner
• Expressing "how come" with 怎么 • Emphasizing an inquiry with 到底 / 究竟 • Minimizing a situation with 不过 / 只不过 / 只 + 是……罢了 • Indicating "not only…, but also…" with 不但 / 不只 / 不仅 / 不光……而且 / 还 / 也…… • Words for business complaints	Comforting someone and showing empathy	The square and the circle
• Comparing 后来 and 然后 • Expressing "no matter what/how/whether" with 无论 / 不论 / 不管……都…… • Expressing tones with adverbs 原来, 果然, 竟然 • Expressing personal judgments with 算（是） • Travelling and lifestyle	Using adverbs for different tones	Yunnan Province
• Expressing "seem to be" with 看起来 • Expressing "nearly" with 差点儿 • Exclamations with 多……（啊） • Expressing "whether or not" with 是否 • Requirements of a competition	Showing confidence and giving encouragement	Four-character idioms in Chinese
• Continual repetition of an action with Verb 来 verb 去 • Indicating a continuing action with the complement 下去 • Talking about disposal of time/money/energy with 把 • Expressing "even if" with 即使……也…… • Argumentative discussions and writing	Showing objection and disagreement	The four great inventions
• Expressing "as one pleases" with 想……就…… • Emphasizing a particular manner of carrying out an action using Verb 1 着 + verb 2 • Emphasizing the reason for a result with 之所以……是因为…… • Expressing "to regard A as B" using 以……为…… • Life experience, feelings and hopes	Comforting and showing understanding	The modern "Marco Polo"
• Expressing an emphatic tone using 才……呢 • Expressing unnecessariness using 何必……呢 • Expressing "let alone" with 别说 A，就是 B，也 / 都…… • Indicating "constantly" or "non-stop" with 一直 or 不断（地） • Pains and gains, retrospection and expectations	Giving praise and showing admiration	Chinese symbols of good fortune

English translations   page 198

Vocabulary list   page 212

Classroom expressions

🔊 Classroom expressions used by teachers
1-2

Qǐng gǎizhèng cuòbiézì 请 改正 错别字。	Please correct the wrong characters.
Zhè liǎng gè zì fāyīn xiāngtóng dànshì yìsi bù yíyàng 这 两 个 字 发音 相同，但是 意思 不 一样。	These two characters sound the same, but their meanings are different.
Zhèlǐ cuò le qǐng zǐxì jiǎnchá yíxià 这里 错 了，请 仔细 检查 一下。	There's something wrong here. Please check it carefully.
Zhè shì fēi zhèngshì / zhèngshì yòngyǔ 这 是 非 正式 / 正式 用语。	This is an informal/a formal expression.
Qǐng zàojù 请 造句。	Please make sentences.
Qǐng fùshù yíxià gùshi / wénzhāng 请 复述 一下 故事 / 文章。	Please retell the story/passage in your own words.
Qǐng kuàisù yuèdú wénzhāng ránhòu jiǎndān èyào de shuō- 请 快速 阅读 文章，然后 简单 扼要 地 说 chū dàyì 出 大意。	Please scan the passage and briefly summarize the main idea.
Qǐng bǐjiào zhǎochū xiāngtóng hé bù tóng zhī chù 请 比较，找出 相同 和 不同 之 处。	Please compare and contrast these two texts.
Nǐ duì zhè piān wénzhāng yǒu shénme gǎnxiǎng 你 对 这 篇 文章 有 什么 感想？	What do you think of the passage?
Qǐng jǔlì shuōmíng 请 举例 说明。	Please give an example.
Nǎ wèi tóngxué néng dàitóu fāyán 哪位 同学 能 带头 发言？	Who would like to speak first?
Nǐ huídá de hěn hǎo xiànzài ràng wǒmen tīngting qítā 你 回答 得 很 好，现在 让 我们 听听 其他 tóngxué yǒu shénme kànfǎ 同学 有 什么 看法。	That's a good answer. Now let's hear what the others say.
Hái yǒu tóngxué xiǎng bǔchōng ma 还 有 同学 想 补充 吗？	Does anyone have anything else to add?
Jiélùn shì shénme 结论 是 什么？	What's your conclusion?
Xiànzài wǒ bǎ jīntiān de kèchéng nèiróng zǒngjié yíxià 现在 我 把 今天 的 课程 内容 总结 一下。	Now I'll summarize the content of today's lesson.

Classroom expressions used by students

Wèi shénme zhèli bù néng yòng zhège cí / zì 为什么这里不能用这个词/字？	Why can't I use this word/character here?
yǒu shénme qūbié ……有什么区别？	What's the difference between…?
Zhè jù huà gāi yòng zài shénme yàng de chǎnghé 这句话该用在什么样的场合？	In what context can this sentence be used?
Qǐng zài duō gěi wǒmen yìdiǎnr zhǔnbèi de shíjiān 请再多给我们一点儿准备的时间。	Please give us a little more time to prepare.
Wǒ néng tántan wǒ gèrén de kànfǎ ma 我能谈谈我个人的看法吗？	Can I state my opinion?
Wǒ néng chā yí jù huà ma 我能插一句话吗？	Can I add/say something?
Wǒ xiān tīngting dàjiā zěnme shuō, ránhòu wǒ zài shuō, kěyǐ ma 我先听听大家怎么说，然后我再说，可以吗？	Could I listen to what the others say before I speak?
Tā shuō de zhèng shì wǒ xiǎng yào shuō de, wǒ tóngyì tā de guāndiǎn 他说的正是我想要说的，我同意他的观点。	What he said is just what I want to say. I agree with his point.
Wǒ bìng bú zhèyàng rènwéi, wǒ juéde 我并不这样认为，我觉得……	I don't agree. My opinion is…
Nín néng xiángxì shuō yíxià zuòyè yāoqiú ma 您能详细说一下作业要求吗？	Can you please explain the details of the assignment?

Places in *Discover China*

Yunnan

云南 (Yúnnán) Province in Southwest China

香格里拉市 (Xiānggélǐlā Shì) Shangri-La Municipality, formerly Zhongdian County (中甸县 Zhōngdiàn Xiàn), renamed after the fictional land of Shangri-La featured in the 1933 James Hilton novel, *Lost Horizon*

梅里雪山 (Méilǐ Xuěshān) Meri Snow Mountains, a mountain range in Yunnan, the highest peak of which, Kawagebo, rises 6740 metres above sea level and is considered sacred by Tibetan Buddhists

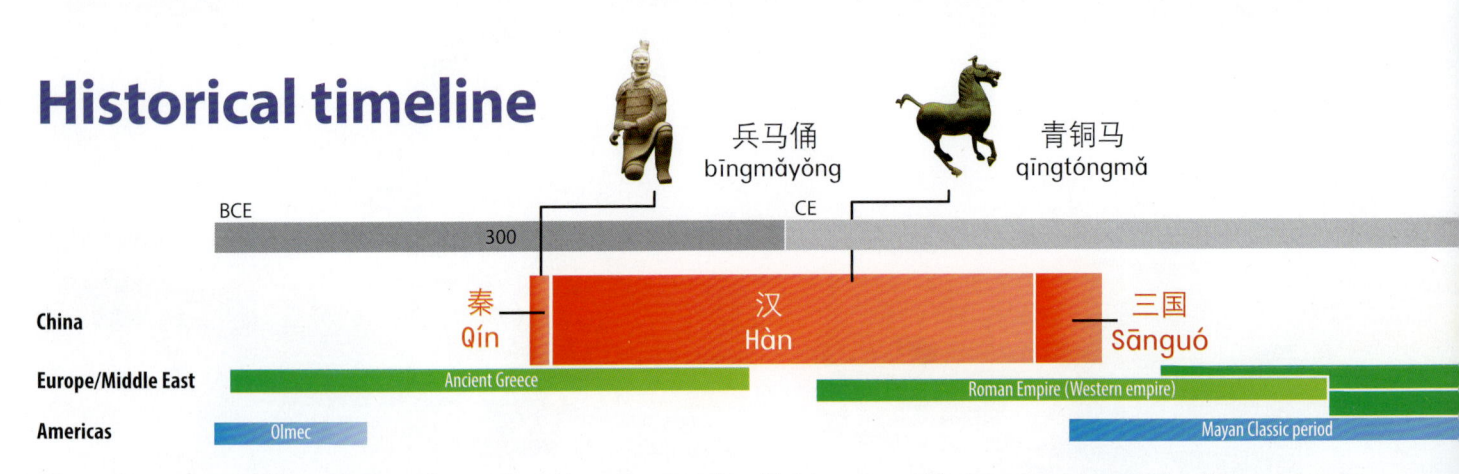

Historical timeline

兵马俑 bīngmǎyǒng

青铜马 qīngtóngmǎ

BCE — 300 — CE

China: 秦 Qín | 汉 Hàn | 三国 Sānguó

Europe/Middle East: Ancient Greece | Roman Empire (Western empire)

Americas: Olmec | Mayan Classic period

* This timeline does not include all dynasties and eras in China's history. The selected eras illustrate some notable contemporaneous periods in China and abroad.

Ha'erbin

哈尔滨 (Hā'ěrbīn) capital city of Heilongjiang Province

冰雪节 (Bīngxuějié) the annual Snow and Ice Festival, featuring grand ice and snow sculptures

Shenzhen

深圳 (Shēnzhèn) in South China

A vibrant international city

唐三彩
tángsāncǎi

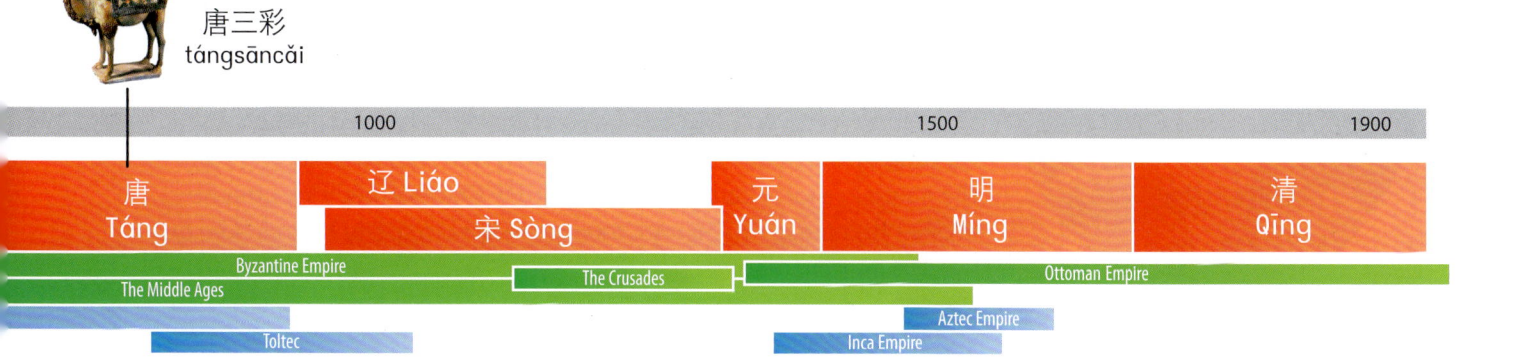

| 1000 | 1500 | 1900 |

唐 Táng
辽 Liáo
宋 Sòng
元 Yuán
明 Míng
清 Qīng

Byzantine Empire
The Crusades
Ottoman Empire
The Middle Ages
Toltec
Aztec Empire
Inca Empire

Meet the characters

Mǎkè
Mark Johnson (马克) comes from Brisbane. Mark went on holiday to China after completing high school, and decided to stay and learn Chinese at a university in Beijing. Mark enjoys the outdoor activities, and he likes surfing and sailing.

Wáng Yù
Wang Yu (王 玉) was born in Beijing. She knows the others from university, where she studies music. She has been learning to play the piano since she was five. She likes cooking and sports such as swimming and tennis.

Āmàndá
Amanda da Silva (阿曼达) is Mark's classmate, from São Paulo. She loves travelling and has a keen interest in history. As well as Chinese language, Amanda is also taking classes in Chinese history at the university.

Shǐdìfū
Steve Brown (史蒂夫), another classmate of Mark and Amanda's, comes from London. He works part-time for a UK-based magazine and is a keen photographer. He enjoys exploring different cultures, and meeting different people.

Jīn Yǒngmín
Kim Yeong-min (金 永民) is also studying Chinese at the university. He comes from Seoul. Like Wang Yu, Yeong-min is a musician, and plays the guitar in a local band. He plans to study Chinese medicine after he finishes his courses in Chinese. Yeong-min likes to spend his free time on reading and listening to music.

UNIT
1

Nǐ yídìng xíng
你 一 定 行！

You can do it!

LESSON | 1

Vocabulary and listening

1 Work in pairs. Talk about your vacation. Use the expressions in the box to help you.

> 假期过得怎么样?
> 假期去哪儿了?
> 你知道吗? ……
> 听说……

2 Match the words to make phrases.

1 招聘	a 经验
2 积累	b 要求
3 申请	c 实习生
4 符合	d 工作

3 Mark and Yeong-min are catching up after the vacation. Listen to the conversation and check the information they talk about.

☐ 1 他们的朋友阿曼达和王玉在哪里
☐ 2 永民假期做了什么
☐ 3 马克下个星期的面试
☐ 4 永民对夏天的计划
☐ 5 他们的朋友史蒂夫在哪儿
☐ 6 永民最喜欢的游戏网站

马克: 永民,假期过得怎么样?
永民: 挺好的。我回韩国去了,看了父母和朋友。在父母身边真幸福,我都长胖了。你呢?假期去哪儿了?
马克: 我哪儿也没去,就在学校学中文。我下个星期有一个面试。
永民: 什么面试?你在找工作?
马克: 只是一个实习生的职位。我想毕业以后留在中国工作,所以想利用暑假实习,积累一点儿在中国的工作经验。
永民: 你真棒,这么早就开始为找工作作准备了。是什么样的公司和职位呢?
马克: 是一家国际贸易公司,他们的客户服务部在招聘翻译。我喜欢跟人打交道,又了解一点儿中国文化,希望能符合他们的

16 ❀ Unit 1　Lesson 1

要求。

永民：你的能力那么强，好好准备，一定没问题。

马克：谢谢你的鼓励。不过，听说申请这个职位的人不少，竞争很激烈，我一点儿信心都没有。

永民：放心吧，你一定行！你是在什么地方看到招聘信息的？

马克：在一个网站上，晚上我把链接发给你。对了，阿曼达回巴西去了，你知道吗？

永民：她给我发邮件了。唉，好多朋友都离开北京了。王玉也去美国留学了。

马克：是啊。不过，可以跟她们网上联系。最近我刚学了一句古诗，"海内存知己，天涯若比邻"。

永民：你真行，连古诗都会了！

New words

xìngfú 幸福	happy; happiness	fúhé 符合	accord with
miànshì 面试	interview	nénglì 能力	ability
shíxí 实习	work as an intern	gǔlì 鼓励	encourage
zhíwèi 职位	position	shēnqǐng 申请	apply for
jīlěi 积累	accumulate	jìngzhēng 竞争	compete
gōngsī 公司	company	jīliè 激烈	fierce
guójì 国际	international	xìnxīn 信心	confidence
kèhù 客户	client	xìnxī 信息	information
zhāopìn 招聘	recruit	wǎngzhàn 网站	website
fānyì 翻译	translator; translate	liànjiē 链接	link

4 Check the true statements.

☐ 1 永民假期回韩国看了父母和朋友。

☐ 2 马克要面试的是一个实习生的职位。

☐ 3 马克想利用暑假实习。

☐ 4 虽然竞争很激烈，可是马克对自己很有信心。

☐ 5 永民不知道阿曼达已经回国了。

海内存知己，天涯若比邻

5 Choose the best answer.

1 马克打算毕业以后 _____。
   a 留在中国工作   b 去美国留学
   c 在贸易公司做翻译

2 马克申请实习主要是为了 _____。
   a 了解中国文化   b 积累工作经验
   c 和客户打交道

3 马克是在 _____ 看到招聘信息的。
   a 学校   b 一个网站上   c 朋友的邮件里

6 Predict what Mark and Yeong-min will do next according to their conversation.

马克：_____   永民：_____

a 去巴西看阿曼达
b 到网上看一看有什么职位可以申请
c 为下个星期的面试做准备
d 申请去美国留学

7 You are going to hear a conversation between two classmates. Look at the words and predict what they are talking about.

世界500强的公司   运气好
校园招聘会   熟人

Now listen to the conversation and write down the three ways to find a job.

找工作的方法
1
2
3

8 Work in pairs. Listen again and check your answers.

Now ask and answer the questions.

1 男同学面试了几次才得到这份工作？
2 女同学让男同学别忘了她，是什么意思？

Pronunciation and speaking

1 Listen to the sentences with a praising or encouraging tone.

1 你真棒，这么早就开始为找工作作准备了。
2 你的能力那么强，好好准备，一定没问题。
3 放心吧，你一定行！
4 你真行，连古诗都会了！

Now repeat the sentences.

2 Complete the conversations with a praising or encouraging tone.

1 A: 我这个学期选了六门课，而且都挺难的。
   B: _____

2 A: 我明天有一个很重要的面试，我很紧张。
   B: _____

3 A: 我刚学了一个新词叫"知己"。
   B: _____

4 A: 我能唱好那首中文歌吗？
   B: _____

3 Work in pairs. Talk about the position you would like to apply for. List your strengths and weaknesses, and encourage each other.

CHINESE TO GO

About me

Wǒ yìdiǎnr xìnxīn dōu méiyǒu
我 一点儿 信心 都 没有。
I have no confidence at all.

Wǒ xǐhuan gēn rén dǎ jiāodao
我 喜欢 跟 人 打 交道。
I am a people person.

LESSON | 2

Reading and writing

1 Work in pairs. Look at the majors in the table below and talk about the potential job prospects.

专业	职位
管理	
英文	
经济	
历史	
新闻	

2 Work in pairs. Match the words with their meanings.

1	互联网	a	link
2	网站	b	website
3	链接	c	home page
4	首页	d	current page
5	搜索	e	print
6	当前位置	f	search
7	打印	g	Internet

Now write down the meanings of the words.

网址：_____

网页：_____

3 Look at the meanings of the two-character words and complete the sentences.

经历：experience 简历：résumé 历史：history	The meaning of 历 is _____.
能力：ability 压力：pressure 风力：wind power	The meaning of 力 is _____.
表演：perform 表现：display 表达：express	The meaning of 表 is _____.
专业：speciality 行业：industry 职业：profession	The meaning of 业 is _____.
过程：process 全程：the whole journey 行程：itinerary	The meaning of 程 is _____.

4 Mark is considering an internship at a company. Read the two web pages he has found and check the true statements.

☐ 1 马克要申请的职位工作地点在北京。

☐ 2 马克要申请的这家公司主要进出口儿童玩具和服装产品。

☐ 3 实习生没有工资。

☐ 4 申请人发送简历以后会在一周内收到通知。

☐ 5 马克要申请的职位需要经常出差。

☐ 6 只有经济专业的学生可以申请这个职位。

Lesson 2   Unit 1   19

网页一
https://yashenzhaopin.com

首页　职位搜索　公司搜索　打印

▶ 当前位置　**亚深国际贸易有限公司**

行　　业：进出口贸易	亚深国际贸易有限公司是一家专门从事儿童玩具和服装产品进出口的公司。公司成立于2000年，在北京、重庆和深圳都设有分公司。
公司规模：100—150人	
所在地区：中国	

基本信息

职位名称	1. 客服实习生（2人） 2. 分公司销售经理（1人）	工作地点	深圳 重庆	发布日期	3月28日 3月15日

网页二
https://yashenzhaopinshixisheng.com

首页　职位搜索　公司搜索　打印

▶ 当前位置　**亚深国际贸易有限公司客户服务实习翻译（2人）**

工作地点	深圳（需要经常出差）
工作内容	协助接待欧美客户，全程中英文口译 协助安排客户工作行程和参观游览活动
申请要求	在校大学生，英语专业、经济专业、管理专业优先 有较强的沟通、表达能力 有英汉翻译或文秘工作经历者优先
工资待遇	公司提供免费住宿和实习工资（面议） 实习期间表现优秀者，毕业后可正式进入公司工作
申请方式	请发简历到公司邮箱wenjing@yashen.com，一周内通知是否进入面试
联系人	文小姐

---

5 Complete the passage with the words in the box.

> 招聘　从事　口译　优先　待遇
> 表达　免费　进出口

　　亚深国际贸易有限公司主要_____儿童玩具和服装的_____贸易。现_____中英文_____实习生两名，要求申请人有比较强的沟通和_____能力，有工作经历者_____。_____包括_____住宿和实习工资。

6 Read the flyer Yeong-min found on the bulletin board and check the true statements.

☐ 1　国际交流中心为冬令营招聘实习生。
☐ 2　工作内容是协助夏令营的组织和管理工作。
☐ 3　除了免费吃、住、行以外，也提供生活补助。
☐ 4　其他学校的留学生也可以报名。
☐ 5　申请表应该用电子邮件发给王老师。

国际交流中心招聘暑期志愿者

招聘人数：2名

工作项目：第四届国际中学生夏令营

工作时间：7月15日—8月15日

工作地点：北京，哈尔滨

工作内容：协助国际交流中心完成国际中学生夏令营的组织和学生管理工作

工作待遇：夏令营期间的吃、住、行费用由国际交流中心承担；另有每日生活补助

申请要求：本校学生，国籍不限；需中英文流利，有较强的沟通能力

申请方式：请在3月30日前到国际交流中心203室找王老师填申请表；4月20日前通知面试

联系电话：62351234

7 Write an email to a student who worked as a volunteer last summer for the summer camp in Activity 6. Mention the following:

1. Your basic background information;
2. Why the position interests you;
3. That you want to know more details about the workload, duties, benefits, etc.

New words

shǒuyè	首页	home page
sōusuǒ	搜索	search
dǎyìn	打印	print
dāngqián wèizhì	当前 位置	current page
yǒuxiàn gōngsī	有限 公司	limited company
hángyè	行业	industry
jìn-chūkǒu	进出口	import and export
guīmó	规模	scale
zhuānmén	专门	specially
cóngshì	从事	be engaged in
értóng	儿童	children
wánjù	玩具	toy
chǎnpǐn	产品	product
chénglì	成立	set up
Chóngqìng	重庆	Chongqing
Shēnzhèn	深圳	Shenzhen
fēngōngsī	分公司	branch company
xiāoshòu	销售	sell
jīnglǐ	经理	manager
dìdiǎn	地点	place
fābù	发布	release
xiézhù	协助	assist
jiēdài	接待	receive (clients)
quánchéng	全程	the whole journey
kǒuyì	口译	interpret; interpreter
ānpái	安排	arrange
xíngchéng	行程	itinerary
yóulǎn	游览	tour
zhuānyè	专业	speciality
guǎnlǐ	管理	administer
yōuxiān	优先	have priority
gōutōng	沟通	communicate
biǎodá	表达	express
wénmì	文秘	secretary
jīnglì	经历	experience
dàiyù	待遇	remuneration
zhùsù	住宿	get accommodation
qījiān	期间	period
zhèngshì	正式	formal
jiǎnlì	简历	résumé
tōngzhī	通知	notify; notice
shìfǒu	是否	whether
xiàlìngyíng	夏令营	summer camp
bǔzhù	补助	subsidy
bú xiàn	不限	with no limit
liúlì	流利	fluent

Lesson 2 Unit 1 21

Language in use

Expressing "not at all", "not even one", "not a single" with 一……+都/也+不/没……

Emphasising details of a past action using 是……的

1 Look at the sentences.

	Subject	一……	(Noun)	都/也	不/没……
明天的面试，	马克	一点儿	信心	都	没有。
昨天，	他	一点儿	东西	也	没吃。
晚会上，	小李	一个	人	都	不认识。
刚到北京的时候，	他	一句	中文	也	不会说。
这些衬衫，	我	一件		也	不喜欢。

Now check the correct explanations.

- [ ] 1 一……+都/也+不/没…… is used to express "not at all", "not a single" or "not even one".
- [ ] 2 Both nouns and adjectives can appear before 都/也.
- [ ] 3 一点儿 modifies uncountable nouns while 一 + measure word precedes concrete nouns.
- [ ] 4 Sometimes, a noun or noun phrase can be moved to the beginning of the sentence in order to emphasise it.

2 Answer the questions using the words given.

1 你觉得哪门课最轻松？（一点儿压力也……）
2 感冒特别严重的时候，你是什么感觉？（一点儿力气也……）
3 深夜的公园是什么样的？（一个人都……）
4 你去过广州吗？（一次都……）

1 Look at the sentences.

1 你是什么时候来上海的？
2 他是在哪儿上的大学？
3 他是两年前跟她结婚的。
4 是我同屋帮我买的票。
5 马克打车去的机场。

Now check the correct explanations.

- [ ] 1 是……的 is used to emphasise the details of an action that took place in the past.
- [ ] 2 是……的 can emphasise the time, place, manner, purpose and agent of a particular action.
- [ ] 3 What the speaker wants to emphasise should be put between 是 and 的.
- [ ] 4 If there is an object of the verb, it can only follow 的, not precede it.
- [ ] 5 是 can be omitted, but 的 cannot.

2 Work in pairs. Talk about the most recent trip. Highlight the following information using 是……的.

- Where did you go?
- Who did you travel with?
- How did you get there?
- How did you book the tickets and hotel?

A: 你是怎么订的票？
B: 我是在网上订的票。

Showing direction of movement with 回/进/上/下+来/去

1 Look at the sentences.

	Verb	Object	Directional complement	
阿曼达已经	回	巴西	去	了。
她还会	回	中国	来	吗？
上课了，你们快	进	教室	去	吧。
你住几层？我可以	上	楼	去	找你。
你别站在那么高的地方，快	下		来	。

Now check the correct explanations.

☐ 1 回/进/上/下 can be combined with either 来 or 去 to show the direction of movement.

☐ 2 来 and 去 serve as directional complements.

☐ 3 The location or destination is placed after 来/去.

☐ 4 来 indicates the action moves towards the speaker while 去 indicates the action moves away from the speaker.

2 Complete the conversations using directional complements.

1 A: 你在几层？
   B: 我在十二层，你可以坐电梯_____。
   A: 保安不让我_____，你能_____吗？我在楼下等你。
   B: 给我五分钟，我马上就_____。

2 A: 我就不_____了，只有几句话，我说完就走。
   B: 都到门口了，怎么能不_____呢？快_____吧。

3 A: 儿子，你几点能_____吃饭？
   B: 我九点才能_____，别等我了。

3 Work in pairs. Talk with directional complements about when you will pay your next visit to home and how long you will stay there before coming back to school.

Introducing an extreme case using （连）……都/也……

1 Look at the sentences.

	（连）	Extreme case	都/也	Verb
你真行！	（连）	京剧	都	学会了。
学中文的人越来越多，	（连）	我奶奶	也	想学几句。
在北京三年了，可是我	（连）	一次长城	也	没去过。
她每天都去图书馆，	（连）	假期	都	去。
你听不听歌呀？怎么	（连）	这首歌	都	不知道？

Now check the correct explanations.

☐ 1 （连）……都/也…… means "even" and expresses surprise at unexpected events or information.

☐ 2 In order to talk about unexpected or surprising events, an extreme case is placed between 连 and 都/也.

☐ 3 In this structure, 都/也 can be omitted.

2 Complete the sentences using （连）……都/也…… to show that your friend is an expert about China.

1 我的朋友中文特别棒，她_____（古诗）

2 她什么中国菜都吃过，_____（云南菜）

3 中国的很多地方她都去过，_____（我没听过的地方）

4 她对中国的传统文化和艺术非常了解，_____（古老的戏剧）

▶ Turn to page 183 for grammar reference.

LESSON 3

Communication activity

1 Work in pairs. Choose three summer plans from the list below. Talk about the pros and cons.

暑期计划	好处	坏处
去某大公司实习		
去小学生夏令营工作		
在快餐店打工		
去中国学中文、旅游		
去医院当志愿者		
在家休息		
其他 _____		

2 Work with another pair. Ask them about your choices, learn about more pros and cons, and choose a plan.

3 Report your plan to the class and vote for the best one.

> Turn to pages 171 and 177 for more speaking practice.

Review and practice

1 Complete the passage with the words in the box.

> 积累　安排　符合　激烈　信心　打交道
> 经历　职位　流利　招聘　搜索　游览
> 表达　通知　简历

　　真没想到两个月的实习这么快就过去了。半年以前，我在网上_____暑期实习信息的时候，看到了这家国际贸易公司，他们当时正在_____口译员。我把_____发给他们以后，很快就收到了面试_____。虽然我以前没有工作_____，竞争也非常_____，可是由于我的中文很_____，沟通和_____能力也比较强，所以经理觉得我_____他们的要求。最后我很顺利地得到了实习_____。我的工作，除了当翻译以外，也得协助经理_____客户的参观_____活动。这次实习让我_____了很多跟客户_____的经验。我有_____，以后我一定会做得更好。

Cultural corner

Tang poetry

Taken from a poem by the early Tang dynasty poet Wang Bo (约650年—约675年), 海内存知己，天涯若比邻 is often quoted by Chinese people at farewell parties. The line means that one can feel the presence of a close friend as if they lived next door, even if they live on the other side of the world. During the Tang Dynasty (618–907), poetry played an important part in Chinese cultural life, and a proliferation of poets and poems helped Tang poetry become established as an important influence in Chinese literature, culture and history. The legacy of the Tang poetry is still felt in daily life in China today. Reciting Tang poems remains a part of Chinese children's education. You can always find a Tang verse in different occasions, able to evoke a precise atmosphere or mood.

2 Choose the correct words to complete the sentences.

1 你还要在图书馆看书吗？你打算几点 _____ 啊？
   a 回去宿舍   b 回宿舍去   c 去宿舍

2 每到考试他都非常紧张，连听最喜欢的音乐 _____ 不能让他的压力小一点儿。
   a 就   b 还   c 都

3 现在找工作越来越难了，不管是什么职位，竞争都特别 _____ 。
   a 激烈   b 严重   c 强

4 为了让孩子变得更有信心，父母应该多 _____ 孩子。
   a 表达   b 沟通   c 鼓励

5 学校安排留学生这个周末去山东 _____ 大明湖。
   a 旅游   b 游览   c 观看

3 Work in pairs. Discuss the three pieces of advice for trainee below and rank them in terms of importance.

_____ 先努力工作再谈待遇
_____ 从小事做起
_____ 主动问问题

Now read the online discussion and answer the questions.

1 为什么方先生认为实习生不应该一开始就问实习工资？
2 很多实习生不愿意做小事的原因是什么？
3 张先生认为主动问问题跟工作进步有什么关系？

★ 我们喜欢这样的实习生 ★   收藏 评论

先努力工作再谈待遇   举报 ▼ | 回复

方先生
人事主管

经常有这样的大学生，来我们公司面试，第一句话就问："实习工资有多少？"一个没有经验的学生，什么都还没开始做，就问待遇怎么样，这样的大学生，我不太喜欢。

从小事做起   举报 ▼ | 回复

王小姐
项目经理

很多实习生觉得实习期间我们给他们安排的工作没有意思，学不到东西。其实，不应该这样想。事情一定会有，只是有大有小，不能因为是小事就不愿意做。如果因为事情很小就不愿意做，或者不好好做，那么谁会放心让他们做重要的事情？

主动问问题   举报 ▼ | 回复

张先生
客户代表

很多实习生都不喜欢问问题。可是，如果你不知道公司的工作方法，也不知道怎么跟客户打交道，有的时候你连要找的人的联系方式都不知道，不问怎么能行呢？不明白的一定要问，没有谁一开始就什么都知道。在工作中，你问得越多，进步得越快。

4 Write a reply to the following post with your own suggestions.

我想利用暑假在学校打打工，赚点儿学费，也可以增加一点儿工作经验。可是我刚来不久，所以不太清楚去什么地方找打工的机会，也不知道我的中文够不够好。另外，打工的时候我应该注意些什么？你能不能给我一些建议？谢谢！

💬 我也说一句

Vocabulary review

Fill in the blanks.

安排	ānpái	v.	_____
	biǎodá	v.	express
不限	bú xiàn		_____
补助	bǔzhù	n.	subsidy
产品	chǎnpǐn	n.	
	chénglì	v.	set up
从事	cóngshì	v.	_____
打印	dǎyìn	v.	
待遇	dàiyù	n.	remuneration
当前位置	dāngqián wèizhì		current page
	dìdiǎn	n.	place
儿童	értóng	n.	children
发布	fābù	v.	release
翻译	fānyì	n./v.	translator; translate
分公司	fēngōngsī	n.	branch company
符合	fúhé	v.	accord with
	gōngsī	n.	company
沟通	gōutōng	v.	communicate
鼓励	gǔlì	v.	encourage
管理	guǎnlǐ	v.	_____
规模	guīmó	n.	scale
国际	guójì	adj.	international
行业	hángyè	n.	industry
积累	jīlěi	v.	accumulate
激烈	jīliè	adj.	fierce
简历	jiǎnlì	n.	résumé
接待	jiēdài	v.	receive (clients)
进出口	jìn-chūkǒu		import and export
经理	jīnglǐ	n.	_____
经历	jīnglì	n./v.	experience
竞争	jìngzhēng	v.	compete
客户	kèhù	n.	
口译	kǒuyì	v./n.	interpret; interpreter

链接	liànjiē	v.	link
流利	liúlì	adj.	fluent
面试	miànshì	v.	_____
	nénglì	n.	ability
期间	qījiān	n.	period
全程	quánchéng	n.	the whole journey
申请	shēnqǐng	v.	apply for
实习	shíxí	v.	work as an intern
	shìfǒu	adv.	whether
	shǒuyè		home page
首页			
搜索	sōusuǒ	v.	search
通知	tōngzhī	v./n.	notify; notice
玩具	wánjù	n.	_____
网站	wǎngzhàn	n.	website
文秘	wénmì	n.	secretary
夏令营	xiàlìngyíng	n.	summer camp
销售	xiāoshòu	v.	sell
协助	xiézhù	v.	assist
	xìnxī	n.	information
信心	xìnxīn	n.	confidence
行程	xíngchéng	n.	itinerary
	xìngfú	adj./n.	happy; happiness
优先	yōuxiān	v.	have priority
游览	yóulǎn	v.	tour
有限公司	yǒuxiàn gōngsī		limited company
招聘	zhāopìn	v.	recruit
正式	zhèngshì	adj.	_____
职位	zhíwèi	n.	position
住宿	zhùsù	v.	get accommodation
专门	zhuānmén	adv.	specially
	zhuānyè	n.	speciality
重庆	Chóngqìng	n.	Chongqing
深圳	Shēnzhèn	n.	Shenzhen

26 ❖ Unit 1　Vocabulary

UNIT 2

Nǐ gǎnjué zěnmeyàng
你 感觉 怎么样?

How did you feel?

LESSON | 1

Vocabulary and listening

1 Check the meanings of the words in the box and think about how you would use them.

> 心情　　　　吃不惯
> 对……满意　　适应
> 困难　　暂时　　复杂

Now work in pairs. Talk about how you felt when you were away from home for the first time.

第一次离开家的时候，我的心情很复杂。我很兴奋，但也很想家。……

2 Mark and Wang Yu are having a video chat to catch up. Listen to the conversation and answer the questions.

1 马克对上个星期的面试感觉怎么样？
2 马克介绍了几段工作经历？
3 王玉对在美国的生活感觉怎么样？
4 马克是怎么鼓励王玉的？

王玉：马克！上次你说的那家公司的面试准备得怎么样了，要不要我再帮你练习一下？

马克：不用了，王玉，谢谢你。面试上个星期三就结束了，我正在等结果呢。

王玉：你感觉怎么样？

马克：还行吧，我对自己的表现还算满意。

王玉：他们都问了你一些什么问题？

马克：他们最感兴趣的是，我作为一个外国人，为什么想留在中国工作。然后让我介绍一下以前的工作经历，还问了我将来的打算。总之，没有问特别复杂的问题。

王玉：你是怎么介绍工作经历的？

马克：我说我帮同学翻译过一些文件；在澳大利亚上高中的时候在一个养老院做过志愿者。

王玉：你有没有强调你的适应能力强、工作态度认真？

马克：我没直接说，但是他们应该能感觉到吧。面试快结束的时候，他们已经跟我谈到实习期间的待遇了。

王玉：应该没问题！对了，你拿

的是学生签证，可以在中国工作吗？

马克：哎呀，我忘了问，你一提醒我又想起来了。明天我再写邮件问问吧。别光说我的事了，你对在美国的生活感觉怎么样？

王玉：还是不太适应。我很想家，想得不得了。我这个中国胃吃不惯美国菜，加上学习压力大，英文又不够用……总之，心情挺复杂的。

马克：别担心，这些困难都是暂时的。我刚来北京的时候跟你现在的感觉差不多，后来不是挺好的？我交了很多新朋友，也爱上了中国菜，现在都想留下来工作了。我想你一定能很快适应新生活！

New words

mǎnyì 满意	be satisfied	tíxǐng 提醒	remind
zuòwéi 作为	as	bùdéliǎo 不得了	extreme
jiānglái 将来	future	wèi 胃	stomach
zǒngzhī 总之	in a word	chī bu guàn 吃不惯	not get used to eating
fùzá 复杂	complex	jiāshàng 加上	moreover
yǎnglǎoyuàn 养老院	home for the aged	xīnqíng 心情	mood, feelings
qiángdiào 强调	emphasise	kùnnan 困难	difficulty; difficult
shìyìng 适应	adapt to	zànshí 暂时	temporary
tàidù 态度	attitude	hòulái 后来	later on
tándào 谈到	talking about	jiāo péngyou 交朋友	make friends
qiānzhèng 签证	visa	àishang 爱上	fall in love
wàng 忘	forget		

3 Check the true statements.

☐ 1 王玉以前帮马克练习过面试。

☐ 2 马克正在等面试结果。

☐ 3 面试时，马克直接强调了自己工作态度认真。

☐ 4 马克已经问过签证的事情了。

☐ 5 虽然王玉很想家，但是她很快就适应了美国的生活。

Lesson 1 Unit 2 29

4 Choose the best answer.

1 马克的面试是什么时候结束的？
   a 这个星期三 b 上个星期三
   c 三个星期以前

2 公司对马克的什么最感兴趣？
   a 以前的工作经历 b 将来的打算
   c 想留在中国工作的原因

3 面试快结束的时候，公司和马克谈到了什么？
   a 面试的结果 b 实习期间的待遇
   c 签证的事情

5 Match the people with the facts.

1 马克
2 王玉

a 帮同学翻译文件
b 学习压力大
c 吃不惯美国菜
d 爱上中国菜
e 在养老院做过志愿者
f 出国后心情很复杂
g 交了很多新朋友
h 英文水平还不够好

6 You are going to hear a telephone conversation. Look at the words and predict what the conversation is about.

应聘　广告　行业　心理学　专业
推销　门票

Now listen to the conversation and put the topics in the order you hear them.

____ 工资待遇
____ 面试结果
____ 自己的优点
____ 以前的工作经历
____ 专业和职位的关系

7 Work in pairs. Listen again and check your answers.
Now ask and answer the questions.

1 李天亮觉得心理学专业和广告行业的关系大不大？
2 李天亮为什么要说推销门票的事情？

Pronunciation and speaking

1 Listen to the sentences. Notice how the underlined words help emphasise the tone.

1 还是不太适应。我很想家，想得不得了。我这个中国胃吃不惯美国菜，<u>加上</u>学习压力大，英文<u>又</u>不够用……<u>总之</u>，心情挺复杂的。

2 我刚来北京的时候跟你现在的感觉差不多，后来不是挺好的？我交了很多新朋友，<u>也</u>爱上了中国菜，现在<u>都</u>想留下来工作了。我想你<u>一定</u>能很快适应新生活！

Now repeat the sentences.

2 Work in pairs. Tell each other how you feel about learning Chinese. Use the underlined words in Activity 1 to make your sentences natural.

CHINESE TO GO
After an interview

Nǐ gǎnjué zěnmeyàng
你 感觉 怎么样？
How do you feel (about…)?

Hái xíng ba
还 行 吧。
Not too bad.

Yīnggāi méi wèntí
应该 没 问题！
I think you have a pretty good chance of success!

30　Unit 2　Lesson 1

LESSON 2

Reading and writing

1 Work in pairs. Talk about three jobs you could be good at, and explain why.

我认为我能胜任……的工作，因为……
- 我过去……，锻炼了……能力。
- 我曾经……，养成了……的好习惯。
- 我多次……
- 我的专业是……
- 我富有……

2 Look at the words on the left and write down the meanings of the words on the right.

同情：sympathize	
责任：responsibility	同情心：_____
幽默：humorous	责任感：_____
心：heart	幽默感：_____
感：sense	
帮助：help	
于：towards, to	有助于：_____
求：ask	
申请：apply for	求职信：_____
推荐：recommend	申请信：_____
职位：position, job	推荐信：_____
信：letter	感谢信：_____
感谢：thank	

3 Work in pairs. Read Mark's résumé and guess what information will be in another section of the résumé.

个人简历

马克
Mark Johnson

联系我

电话：136XXXX4321
邮箱：Markjohnson@bfsu.com

基本资料

性别：男
国籍：澳大利亚
年龄：21
学历：在校本科生
学校：北京外国语大学
专业：中文
兴趣爱好：旅游，冲浪，中国功夫

4 Read Mark's application letter for the internship on page 32 and check the true statements.

- [ ] 1 马克的专业是经济学，明年毕业。
- [ ] 2 马克常常为同学做商务口译。
- [ ] 3 马克在养老院做志愿者的时候，工作主要是照顾老人。
- [ ] 4 马克认为自己在中国的学习、生活经历对他的工作会很有帮助。
- [ ] 5 马克有一些从事商务的朋友。

求职信

尊敬的文小姐：

您好。感谢您抽时间阅读我的求职信。

我叫马克，来自澳大利亚，是北京外国语大学的留学生，将于明年毕业。我希望毕业以后留在中国工作，所以想利用暑假积累一些相关的工作经验。我对贵公司客户服务翻译实习生的工作很有兴趣，我认为自己可以在短时间内适应并胜任这份工作。

我的母语是英语，目前的专业是中文，辅修经济学。在过去的两年里，我多次帮助我的同学翻译各类文章。尽管我没有做过正式的商务接待工作，但是我澳大利亚的朋友来中国进行商务考察时，我曾经帮助他们安排在中国的行程。

我性格开朗，热爱运动和旅行，喜欢和各种各样的人打交道，富有同情心和责任感。上高中时，我曾经在布里斯班的一家养老院做过两年的志愿者，主要帮助他们整理资料、做会议记录，并且组织了很多活动。在这份工作中，我锻炼了自己的策划、组织和沟通能力，养成了做事认真、仔细的好习惯。在中国学习、生活的这几年，我既学到了中国历史文化方面的很多知识，也对东西方文化上的差异有了更深的理解。我认为这些都有助于我胜任贵公司客服翻译的工作。

我非常希望能够得到贵公司的这份实习工作。随信附上个人简历一份。

期待您的答复。

此致

敬礼！

申请人：马克

2023年4月2日

5 Answer the questions.

1. 马克为什么要申请这份工作？
2. 马克是学什么的？
3. 马克有哪些工作经历？
4. 什么事情能说明马克富有同情心和责任感？
5. 养老院的工作经历对马克来说重要吗？为什么？
6. 在中国的这几年，马克的收获大不大？

New words

xuélì 学历	academic background	zérèn 责任	responsibility		
qiúzhíxìn 求职信	application letter	céngjīng 曾经	once		
gǎnxiè 感谢	be grateful	Bùlǐsībān 布里斯班	Brisbane		
chōu shíjiān 抽时间	make time	zhěnglǐ 整理	sort out, clean		
guì 贵	(your) honourable	huìyì 会议	meeting, conference		
shèngrèn 胜任	be competent at (a job)	jìlù 记录	record		
mǔyǔ 母语	mother tongue	bìngqiě 并且	and		
mùqián 目前	present moment	zǔzhī 组织	organize		
fǔxiū 辅修	minor	cèhuà 策划	plan		
guòqù 过去	past	yǎngchéng 养成	cultivate (habits)		
duō cì 多次	many times	zǐxì 仔细	careful		
wénzhāng 文章	article	jì……yě…… 既……也……	both… and…		
jǐnguǎn 尽管	even though	chāyì 差异	difference		
kǎochá 考察	investigate	suí 随	go with		
kāilǎng 开朗	sanguine	fù 附	attach		
fùyǒu 富有	be full of	qīdài 期待	look forward to		
tóngqíng 同情	sympathize				

6 Complete the passage with the words in the box.

> 热爱　将于……毕业　富有　认为
> 目前　有助于　曾经　进行　考察
> 并且　来自　多次

　　马克是一位 _____ 澳大利亚的留学生。他性格开朗，_____ 运动和旅行，_____ 同情心和责任感。上高中时，他 _____ 在布里斯班的一家养老院做过志愿者。_____ 他正在北京外国语大学学习。在过去的两年中，他 _____ 帮助他的同学翻译各类文章，_____ 协助他的朋友来中国 _____ 商务 _____。马克 _____ 2024年 _____。为了积累工作经验，他申请了一家公司的实习翻译职位。马克 _____ 自己的知识、经历和能力都 _____ 他胜任这份实习工作。

7 Read about Mark's work experience.

工作经历

2018年3月—2020年3月
澳大利亚，布里斯班，养老院
志愿者，整理资料、做会议记录、组织活动

2020年6—8月
澳大利亚，布里斯班，快餐店
收银

2021年3月—2023年3月
中国，北京
翻译各类文章，笔译

2022年12月—2023年1月
中国，北京
协助澳大利亚的朋友进行商务考察，安排行程

Now answer the questions.

1. 在这些工作经历中，哪一个是马克在求职信中没有谈到的？他为什么没有强调这个经历？
2. 你认为马克协助他的朋友进行商务考察，这算不算他的工作经历？能不能写在简历中？

8 Write your own résumé. Use Mark's résumé in Activities 3 and 7 to help you.

Lesson 2　Unit 2　33

Language in use

Indicating a very high degree of something with 不得了

1 Look at the sentences.

	Adj. / Verb	得	不得了
广州的夏天	热	得	不得了。
暑假大家都回家了，我一个人留在宿舍里，	寂寞	得	不得了。
快到春节的时候，大大小小的商店都	热闹	得	不得了。
我想我妈妈做的饭	想	得	不得了。
他喜欢这个新游戏	喜欢	得	不得了。

Now check the correct explanations.

☐ 1 不得了 is used to indicate a very high degree of something.

☐ 2 得 preceding 不得了 introduces 不得了 as a complement.

☐ 3 As a complement, 不得了 can be used to modify either an adjective or an emotional verb.

☐ 4 The adjective or verb that is modified by 不得了 should express negative not positive meaning.

2 Work in pairs. Talk about the following topics using 不得了.

A: 你还记得你小时候最喜欢的玩具吗？
B: 我小时候有一个熊猫玩具，我喜欢它喜欢得不得了，每天睡觉都要抱着它。

1 你们学校附近的餐馆，哪家最好吃？
2 你这个学期选的课中，哪门课最难？
3 你觉得什么饮料最好喝？

Repeated actions with 再 or 又

1 Look at the sentences.

	再/又	Verb phrase	
我可以	再	帮你模拟一下面试。	
你得	再	给那家公司打个电话。	
你们下次	再	来香港，	一定要跟我联系。
我昨天	又	去了学校附近的那家中餐馆，	所有的菜都好吃得不得了。
你怎么	又	买了一件白衬衫？	
明天	又	是星期六了。	

Now check the correct explanations.

☐ 1 Both 再 and 又 can serve as adverbs meaning "again", thus indicating the repetition of an action or activity.

☐ 2 再 refers to a future event. It indicates that an action will occur, and it will be a repeat of an earlier action.

☐ 3 If there is a modal verb in the sentence, 再 should be placed before the modal verb.

☐ 4 又 indicates that the repeated action has already taken place, it can also be used to indicate an action which can be expected to recur in the future.

2 Complete the sentences with 再 or 又.

1 这部电影，我两年以前看过一遍，去年暑假 _____ 看了一遍，我打算今年暑假 _____ 看一遍。

2 我第一次去北京是高中毕业的时候，去年和我姐姐一起 _____ 去了一次，要是将来有机会，我还想 _____ 去一次。

3 中文课上个星期五刚考完试，这个星期五 _____ 要考试了。

Expressing "a little bit" using 一下 or 一点儿

1 Look at the sentences.

	Verb	一下/一点儿	Object	
请你	介绍	一下	你的专业。	
我能不能	看	一下	那个电脑?	
你太累了，好好	休息	一下		吧。
我早上	吃了	一点儿	东西，	所以现在不太饿。
他	听说过	一点儿	你哥哥的事。	
你们想	喝	一点儿	什么?	我有咖啡和可乐。

Now check the correct explanations.

☐ 1 一下 and 一点儿 can both be used to moderate a statement to mean "a little bit".

☐ 2 一下 is often used to make a suggestion, a request or an order.

☐ 3 一点儿 can be used as a qualifier to modify the object of the verb and denote that the action performed on it was minor.

2 Complete the sentences with 一下 or 一点儿.

1 这件事情，你再给我 _____ 时间，让我再想一想。
2 你不知道布里斯班在哪儿，上网搜索 _____ 就知道了。
3 我今天忘了带手机，能不能借用 _____ 你的手机？我想给我父母打个电话。
4 我去超市买了 _____ 蔬菜和水果，刚回来。
5 我今天早饭吃得很少，只吃了 _____ 面包，喝了 _____ 牛奶。

3 Work in pairs. Ask your partner for help by making three requests using 一下.

我不认识这个字，你能不能帮我看一下这是什么字？

Indicating the beginning of an action or the start of a new state with 起来

1 Look at the sentences.

	Verb 起（object）来/Adj. 起来
他们一见面就	吵了起来。
你一说我就	想起来了。
看见巧克力没有了，那个孩子	哭了起来。
她走进卧室	听起音乐来。
外面	下起雪来了。
过了四月，天气就慢慢地	热起来了。

Now check the correct explanations.

☐ 1 起来 is used after an action verb or an adjective to indicate the beginning of an action or the start of a new state.

☐ 2 If the verb takes an object, the object can be inserted between 起 and 来 or be placed before 起来.

☐ 3 Even though 起来 still serves as a complement, its literal meaning of "upward movement" as a directional complement has been lost.

2 Work in pairs. Ask and answer the questions using 起来.

1 你小时候最怕什么动物？看见这种动物，你会怎么样？
2 你有没有一想起来就生气的事情？
3 你很难过的时候，有什么办法可以让你高兴起来？
4 在你的家乡，到了几月天气会慢慢冷起来？过了几月，天气又会慢慢热起来？

▶ Turn to page 184 for grammar reference.

Lesson 2　Unit 2　35

Lesson 3

Communication activity

Choose a job ad below. Apply by revising your résumé in Activity 8, Lesson 2 accordingly.

招聘

职位：暑期小学英文老师 2名
工作地点：阳光小学
工作时间：七月初至八月底，周一至周五上午8点到下午3点
申请人要求：英文专业或英语为母语，喜欢孩子，有教学工作经验

具体工作待遇及工作内容，请联系刘小姐，132××××2022

诚聘

因本公司业务发展需要，现招聘以下人员：
1. 中英翻译 1名
2. 客户服务专员 3名
3. 市场经理 1名

要求本科学历，有相关经验

以上人员一经录用，待遇从优

联系人：钱先生，132××××2021

诚聘

梦飞国际教育公司

经理助理 1名
女性，年龄35岁以下，办事认真，责任心强，有文秘工作经验，懂英文且会开车者优先

清风国际旅行社
因业务发展 **急招**

销售代表 3名
男性，要求沟通能力强，会英文、有销售工作经验者优先，需经常出差

导游 5名
高中或大学毕业，形象好，中英文流利，喜欢旅游，有责任心

Now work in pairs.

- Prepare a list of interview questions for the position your partner is applying for.
- Act out the job interviews.

> Turn to pages 171 and 177 for more speaking practice.

Review and practice

1 Choose the correct words to complete the sentences.

1 你 _____ 宿舍的条件满意吗？
  a 为　　b 对　　c 让

2 她从小就 _____ 戏剧和表演，希望自己将来能当一名演员。
  a 热爱　　b 爱上　　c 有兴趣

3 我 _____ 在国际交流夏令营做过两年的志愿者。
  a 经常　　b 从来　　c 曾经

4 他妹妹性格活泼 _____，喜欢跟各种各样的人打交道。
  a 开心　　b 开放　　c 开朗

5 上高中的时候，我住在家里，每天早睡早起。可是上了大学以后，我慢慢 _____ 了晚睡晚起的习惯。
  a 养成　　b 造成　　c 变成

Cultural corner

Tips for job-hunting in China

The days are long gone when it was easy for someone from overseas to find a desirable position in China, and when there was a big gap between the salaries of nonnationals and local Chinese employees. Whilst expatriates can still expect to easily find jobs teaching or tutoring English, if you are looking for a corporate job, be prepared for fierce competition, a low entry-level salary, and high living expenses in big cities like Beijing, Shanghai and Guangzhou, where jobs are concentrated. If you have a special skill or work experience in China, you have a competitive edge. Knowledge of Chinese language and culture may not be a requirement, but is definitely a major advantage.

2 Complete the passage with the words in the box.

| 复杂 | 作为 | 认真 | 满意 | 组织 |
| 强调 | 感觉到 | 一点儿 | 一下 | 流利 |

大家都知道，_____留学生，在中文还不是特别_____的时候，要用中文进行面试是很不容易的。在这里我可以跟大家谈谈我的_____经验。首先要写好简历和求职信。然后可以请朋友帮你模拟_____面试。到面试的时候，你就不会紧张了。我在面试中，一共回答了四个问题，都不是很_____。我主要介绍了自己做志愿者时_____过的各种活动。这些例子既可以说明我做事_____、仔细，也可以让他们_____我的策划、沟通能力很强。另外，我也_____了自己很有责任心。总之我对自己的表现还算_____。

3 Read the sentences and work out the meanings of the underlined words.

1 这本书的<u>开头</u>很有意思，可是越看越没有意思，<u>结尾</u>我已经不想看了。
2 你昨天发给我的邮件，怎么只有你的姓名和联系方式，没有<u>正文</u>啊？
3 我应该<u>称呼</u>她"王秘书"还是"王小姐"？
4 那家公司正在招聘英语翻译，什么专业<u>背景</u>的人都可以申请，英语好就行。

开头 _____ 结尾 _____
正文 _____ 称呼 _____
背景 _____

Now read the essay

怎样写求职信

一封好的求职信会给招聘的人留下很好的印象，所以在工作申请中常常起到很大的作用。写求职信的目的是让对方了解自己、相信自己可以胜任工作。

信的开头要向收信人问好，称呼应该正式，然后清楚地说明自己想申请的职位。

信的正文可以从自我介绍开始，可以介绍专业背景、专业和申请的职位有什么关系、你的兴趣等等。也可以说明你为什么想申请这个职位，或者这个职位对你将来的发展有什么好处。除了自我介绍和申请原因以外，正文的主要内容还应该包括你过去的工作经历。要选择和你申请的职位相关的工作经历，并且要强调你的工作能力、态度、责任心等等。总之，要让招聘的人感觉无论是你的专业知识还是你的工作经历，都让你能够胜任你申请的职位。

信的结尾要表达你非常希望得到这个工作机会，希望对方阅读你的简历，并表示期待对方的答复。

最后写上"此致""敬礼"，还有你的名字和日期。

4 Complete the table according to the essay in Activity 3.

开头	称呼，问好
正文	自我介绍（专业背景、个人兴趣等）
结尾	希望得到工作机会
最后	此致，敬礼，名字，日期

5 Choose one position from the Communication activity on page 36 and write an application letter.

Vocabulary review
Fill in the blanks.

爱上	àishang		fall in love	母语	mǔyǔ	n.	mother tongue
并且	bìngqiě	conj.	___	___	mùqián	n.	present moment
不得了	bùdéliǎo	adj.	extreme	期待	qīdài	v.	look forward to
策划	cèhuà	v.	plan	签证	qiānzhèng	v.	visa
___	céngjīng	adv.	once	强调	qiángdiào	v.	emphasise
差异	chāyì	n.	___	求职信	qiúzhíxìn	n.	application letter
吃不惯	chī bu guàn		not get used to eating	胜任	shèngrèn	v.	be competent at (a job)
抽时间	chōu shíjiān		make time	___	shìyìng	v.	adapt to
多次	duō cì		___	随	suí	v.	go with
辅修	fǔxiū	v.	minor	态度	tàidù	n.	___
附	fù	v.	attach	谈到	tándào		talking about
复杂	fùzá	adj.	___	提醒	tíxǐng	v.	remind
富有	fùyǒu	v.	be full of	同情	tóngqíng	v.	sympathize
___	gǎnxiè	v.	be grateful		wàng	v.	forget
贵	guì	adj.	(your) honourable	胃	wèi	n.	stomach
过去	guòqù	n.	___	文章	wénzhāng	n.	article
	hòulái	n.	later on		xīnqíng	n.	mood, feelings
	huìyì	n.	meeting, conference	学历	xuélì	n.	academic background
记录	jìlù	n./v.	record	养成	yǎngchéng		cultivate (habits)
既……也……	jì…yě…		both … and …	养老院	yǎnglǎoyuàn	n.	home for the aged
加上	jiāshàng	conj.	moreover	暂时	zànshí	adj.	temporary
将来	jiānglái	n.	___	责任	zérèn	n.	responsibility
交朋友	jiāo péngyou		make friends	整理	zhěnglǐ	v.	sort out, clean
	jǐnguǎn	conj.	even though		zǐxì	adj.	careful
开朗	kāilǎng	adj.	sanguine	总之	zǒngzhī	conj.	in a word
考察	kǎochá	v.	investigate	组织	zǔzhī	v.	organize
困难	kùnnan	n./adj.	___	作为	zuòwéi	prep.	as
满意	mǎnyì	v.	be satisfied	布里斯班	Bùlǐsībān	n.	Brisbane

38 ❖ Unit 2 Vocabulary

UNIT 3

Ràng nín de lǚxíng méiyǒu hòugùzhīyōu!
让 您 的 旅行 没有 后顾之忧!

We can help you plan a worry-free trip!

LESSON 1

Vocabulary and listening

1 Look at the words and their meanings.

购	purchase	卧铺	berth
处	place	团体	group, team
务	matters, affairs		

Now work out the meanings of the words in the word map.

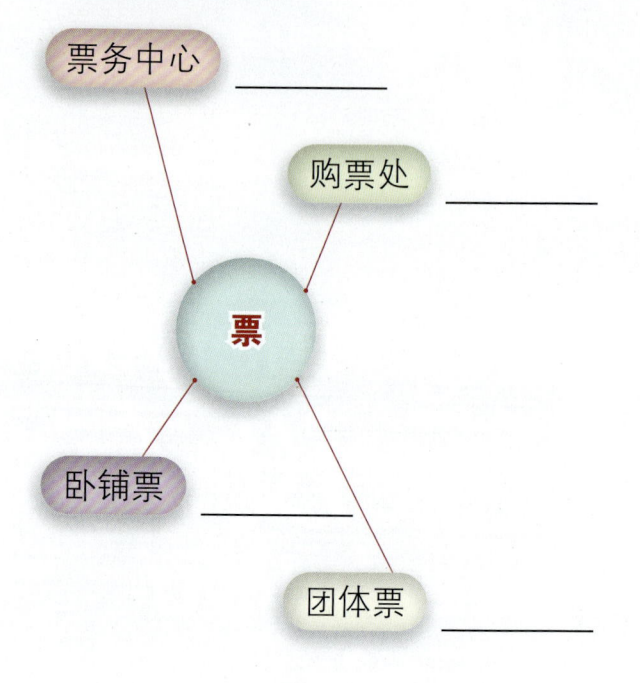

- 票务中心 _____
- 购票处 _____
- 票
- 卧铺票 _____
- 团体票 _____

Now write down more words with 票.

_____

2 Yeong-min is checking with a travel agent about tickets to Harbin for the summer camp. Listen to the conversation and answer the questions.

1 永民问了哪些问题？
2 最后客服把永民的电话转给谁了？
3 你觉得这家旅行社的服务怎么样？

客服： 您好。清风旅行社票务中心。有什么可以帮您？

永民： 您好，我是北京外国语大学的。我们学校有一个十五人左右的团要在七月中旬从北京去哈尔滨。我想问一下那个时候的机票和火车票大概都是多少钱。

客服： 您稍等，我查一下。请问您贵姓？

永民： 我姓金。

客服： 金先生，因为七月是旅游旺季，所以机票基本上是全价。至于火车票，选择就比较多了。您可以选普通列车或者高铁列车，卧铺票或者座票。

永民： 不好意思，能不能麻烦您详细解释一下？

客服： 金先生，是这样的：普通列车从北京到哈尔滨需要10到19个小时不等，卧铺票价大约是硬座票价的两到三倍。硬座当然不如卧铺舒服，但是价钱便宜多了。高铁列车是高速列车，最快的不到5个小时就能到哈尔滨。高铁列车只有座票，不过座位比普通列车要舒服。高铁列车一等座的票价差不多是飞机票全价的一半，二等座还要比一等座便宜大约三分之一。

3 Check the true statements.

☐ 1 永民给旅行社打电话是为了给自己买票。
☐ 2 七月去哈尔滨的机票比较贵。
☐ 3 从北京到哈尔滨的普通列车可能需要12个小时。
☐ 4 永民已经决定买火车票了。
☐ 5 这家旅行社不但可以订票，而且可以安排食宿。

永民：火车票还真不贵。不过我要跟领队商量一下。另外，我们买团体票有没有折扣？

客服：金先生，我建议让我们的旅游顾问来帮您。他们会根据您的要求制订最经济、合理的旅游方案，包括车票、食宿和全部行程安排，让您的旅行没有后顾之忧。您看要不要我把您的电话转给我们的旅游顾问？

永民：那太好了，谢谢你！

New words

lǚxíngshè 旅行社	travel agency	sān fēn zhī yī 三分之一	one third
tuán 团	group	lǐngduì 领队	group leader
shāo děng 稍等	wait a minute	shāngliang 商量	discuss
wàngjì 旺季	peak period	tuántǐpiào 团体票	group ticket
quánjià 全价	full price	zhékòu 折扣	discount
zhìyú 至于	as for	gùwèn 顾问	consultant
lièchē 列车	train	zhìdìng 制订	formulate
gāotiě 高铁	high-speed railway	jīngjì 经济	economical
wòpù 卧铺	berth	hélǐ 合理	reasonable
xiángxì 详细	detailed	fāng'àn 方案	plan
bùděng 不等	varying	shísù 食宿	board and lodging
yìngzuò 硬座	hard seat	quánbù 全部	all, whole
bèi 倍	time (multiply)	hòugùzhīyōu 后顾之忧	disturbance in the rear
gāosù 高速	high-speed	zhuǎn 转	transfer
yī děng 一等	first-class		

Lesson 1　Unit 3　41

4 Choose the best answer.

1 永民可能订什么时候的票？
  a 7月2号   b 7月17号   c 7月25号

2 永民打电话给旅行社是想_____。
  a 咨询票价
  b 找旅游顾问
  c 咨询制订行程服务

3 客服为什么建议永民跟旅游顾问联系？
  a 客服不想给永民折扣。
  b 客服希望永民选择旅行社更多的服务。
  c 客服不知道可不可以给永民折扣。

5 You are going to hear a conversation about different methods of travelling. Look at the descriptions and match them with the methods.

1 跟团游	a 旅行社会为你订机票、火车票，安排住宿和行程。
	b 什么都自己选择，自己决定。
2 自由行	c 旅行社安排交通和住宿，没有导游，想玩哪个景点、玩多长时间都自己决定。
	d 可以住青年旅社。
3 自助游	e 景点都是旅行社安排好的，跟着导游游览参观。

Now listen to the conversation and check your answer.

6 Listen again and complete the table. Write A (for agent) or S (for yourself).

	订票	住宿	景点	吃饭
跟团游				
自由行				
自助游				

Pronunciation and speaking

1 Listen to the sentences. Underline the words expressing approximation.

1 卧铺票价大约是硬座的两到三倍。
2 七月是旅游旺季，所以飞机票基本上是全价。
3 一等座的票价差不多是飞机票全价的一半。

Now repeat the sentences.

2 Complete the conversations using approximations.

1 A: 明天旅行团几点出发？
  B: 我也不确定，_____是早上8点吧。
2 A: 你看见马克了吗？
  B: 我_____半个小时以前见过他，但不知道他去哪儿了。
3 A: 这本书在网上买是不是比较便宜？
  B: 是啊，_____便宜三分之一呢。

3 Work in pairs. Talk about the questions using approximations.

1 从你住的地方到学校怎么走，需要多长时间？
2 你们国家最有名的旅游城市是哪个？那里的旅游旺季是什么时候？
3 你最想去哪里旅游，打算什么时候去？

CHINESE TO GO

Booking tickets

Néng bu néng máfan nín xiángxì jiěshì yíxià
能 不 能 麻烦 您 详细 解释 一下？
Could you please explain more details?

Wǒmen mǎi tuántǐpiào yǒu méiyǒu zhékòu
我们 买 团体票 有 没有 折扣？
Is there any discount for group tickets?

LESSON | 2

Reading and writing

1 Match the photos with the tourist attractions in Harbin.

1. 龙塔
2. 中央大街
3. 圣·索菲亚教堂
4. 松花江

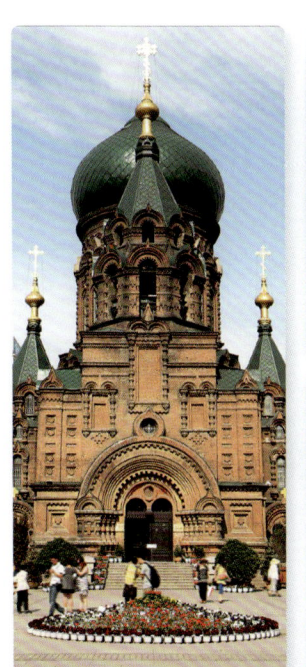

a.
b. 
c. 
d. 

Now work in pairs. Talk about the attractions you would like to visit and why.

A: 要是去哈尔滨，你最想看哪个景点？
B: 我想去看看中央大街，因为它的路看起来很特别。

2 Work in pairs. Tell each other about a recent trip.

Now complete the table with your partner's information.

出发时间、地点	
目的地	
交通工具	
住宿	
早餐/中餐/晚餐	
费用	

3 Decode the words and work out the meanings of the new words.

	First character	Second character	Word meaning	New word
防晒	prevent	suntan, sunburn	sunblock	防晒霜
避暑				避暑胜地
自费				自费项目
欧式				欧式建筑

4 Yeong-min is checking information about Harbin online. Read the itinerary he has found on page 44 and answer the questions.

1. 这个团什么时间出发？一共几天时间？
2. 旅行社的价格不包括哪些费用？
3. 哈尔滨有名的景点有哪些？
4. 夏天去东北旅游要注意什么？

旅游在线

| 联系我们 | 关于我们 | 收藏本页 |

首页　　　　国内游　　　　出境游

北京出发　暑期哈尔滨四日游

价格	￥2000元★	出发日期	7月1日—9月15日，每周二、周五
往返交通	火车		
当地交通	空调大巴	出发地	北京
		目的地	哈尔滨

夏日哈尔滨旅游注意事项：

1. 东北地区早晚温差很大，请注意带好衣物，预防感冒。
2. 夏日阳光强烈，请注意防晒。

第一天　从北京火车站乘车到哈尔滨。

第二天
- 登上亚洲第一高的钢塔——龙塔，俯瞰哈尔滨。
- 游览圣·索菲亚教堂和广场，参观哈尔滨市建筑艺术馆。
- 逛亚洲最长的商业步行街——中央大街。踩在石头路面上，欣赏欧式建筑，感受百年历史。

第三天
- 参观黑龙江省博物馆，了解中国东北的历史和文化。
- 下午自由活动。可在松花江边散步，欣赏"哈尔滨之夏"音乐会的表演；也可去市区购物，品尝当地美食。

第四天
- 游览国家AAAAA级旅游风景区、避暑胜地——太阳岛。可自费参观亚洲最大的室内冰雪艺术馆，欣赏美丽的冰灯和雪雕。
- 晚上乘火车，第二天早上回到北京。

★ 费用包括交通、住宿、每日早餐、每日中餐、景点门票和导游。费用不包括自费旅游项目、每日晚餐、旅游意外保险。

5 Read the questions from a customer and put them in the correct categories.

旅游在线　在线提问

您好，我看了北京到哈尔滨的四日游介绍后，还有一些问题不太明白：

1. 这个"四日游"实际的游玩时间只有三天，是吗？
2. 你们的价格包括给导游的小费（tip）吗？
3. 住宿的条件是什么样的？
4. 第三天下午自由活动之后怎么回宾馆？
5. 注意事项说"早晚温差很大"，带什么样的衣服合适？

a 交通　＿＿＿＿

b 费用　＿＿＿＿

c 行程安排　＿＿＿＿

d 住宿　＿＿＿＿

e 注意事项　＿＿＿＿

New words

shìxiàng 事项	item, matter	guǎngchǎng 广场	square	pǐncháng 品尝	taste
wēnchā 温差	difference in temperature	jiànzhù 建筑	architecture	měishí 美食	cuisine
yùfáng 预防	prevent	guàng 逛	stroll	bìshǔ shèngdì 避暑胜地	summer resort
yángguāng 阳光	sunshine	shāngyè 商业	commerce	Tàiyáng Dǎo 太阳岛	Sun Island
fáng shài 防晒	prevent sunburn	bùxíngjiē 步行街	pedestrian street	shìnèi 室内	indoor
chūfā 出发	set off	cǎi 踩	tread on	bīngdēng 冰灯	ice lantern
dàbā 大巴	bus	xīnshǎng 欣赏	enjoy, appreciate	xuědiāo 雪雕	snow sculpture
mùdìdì 目的地	destination	Ōushì 欧式	European style	fèiyong 费用	expense
dēng 登	climb	gǎnshòu 感受	experience; feeling	zìfèi 自费	pay one's own expenses
Lóng Tǎ 龙塔	Dragon Tower	zìyóu 自由	free; freedom	yìwài 意外	accident
fǔkàn 俯瞰	overlook	Sōnghuā Jiāng 松花江	Songhua River	bǎoxiǎn 保险	insurance
Shèngsuǒfēiyà Jiàotáng 圣·索菲亚教堂	Saint Sophia Cathedral	sànbù 散步	take a walk		

6 Complete the passage with the words in the box.

避暑　　感受　　艺术
欣赏　　热情　　了解

　　哈尔滨是中国东北地区著名的旅游城市。这里四季分明，冬天可以_____冰灯雪雕、滑冰滑雪；夏天可以_____休闲。在这座历史文化名城，你不但可以充分_____中国北方的历史和文化，还可以欣赏到不同国家的建筑_____。在每年夏天的"哈尔滨之夏"音乐会上，你更可以_____到这座城市的_____和活力。

Now read the passage again and match the expressions with their colloquial meanings.

1 四季分明	a 样子和感觉很特别
2 度假胜地	b 四个季节很不一样
3 风格独特	c 在历史上、文化上很有名的城市
4 历史文化名城	d 度假的好地方

7 Recommend a tourist destination of China to a friend. Write an introduction to the place. Use Activity 6 to help you.

Now suggest a three-day trip for your friend. Use Activity 4 to help you.

Language in use

Introducing a new subject using 至于

1 Look at the sentences.

Previous statement	至于 + new subject matter	Further comment
要买食品，这家超市很不错；	至于衣服，	还是不要在这里买了。
去哈尔滨的机票不便宜；	至于火车票，	选择比较多，也便宜多了。
周末咱们一起去看电影吧，	至于看什么电影，	等我查好了再告诉你。
面试我已经尽力了，	至于结果，	不是我能决定的。
上次去西安，我们的确是跟旅行社去的，	至于选的哪家旅行社，	我就想不起来了。

Now check the correct explanations.

☐ 1 至于 as a preposition means "as to" or "with regard to", and is used to introduce a new subject.

☐ 2 The new subject must be related to the topic of the previous statement, or be a new aspect of it.

☐ 3 Only noun phrases can serve as a new subject following 至于. Verb phrases cannot.

☐ 4 There should be a further comment following 至于 and the new subject matter.

2 Work in pairs. Talk about the following topics using 至于.

1 出去旅游，哪些事情比较重要，哪些不太重要？（去什么地方、什么季节去、跟谁一起去）

2 你的学校条件怎么样？（图书馆、宿舍、教室、校园、体育场）

3 工作一定要跟专业相关吗？你怎么看？（能力、学历、专业、工作经验）

4 你喜欢跟什么样的人打交道？（性格、脾气、长相、能力）

Comparative structures using 不如

1 Look at the sentences.

Context	A	不如	B	Adj.
她的中文说得那么好，	硬座	不如	卧铺	舒服。
	我学习	不如	她	努力。
	他们跑得	不如	我	快。
	我	不如	她	。
	看电视	不如	看电影	。

Now check the correct explanations.

☐ 1 The comparative structure using 不如 means "A is not as … as B".

☐ 2 The adjectives or verb phrases in the comparison using 不如 must be words with a negative connotation.

☐ 3 If the adjective appears at the start of the sentence, it can be omitted at the end.

☐ 4 If there is no specific adjective mentioned, the default meaning of "(not as) good" applies.

2 Work in pairs. Talk about the following topics using 不如.

1 如果去不太远的地方旅行，你选择坐飞机还是坐火车？为什么？

2 你最喜欢的男明星和女明星是谁？跟你同伴的答案一样吗？你怎么看他/她喜欢的明星？

3 你喜欢夏天还是秋天？为什么？

Expressing fractions and percentages with ……分之……

1 Look at the sentences.

1 二等座比一等座便宜大约三分之一（1/3）。
2 经常锻炼的人占总人口的四分之一（1/4）。
3 就算只有万分之一（1/10000）的机会，我也要试一试。
4 我们班差不多三分之二（2/3）的人看过这部电影。
5 食品花费占家庭收入的百分之三十四点七（34.7%）。
6 他说的话，你最好不要百分之百（100%）地相信。

Now check the correct explanations.

☐ 1 ……分之…… is used to express fractions or percentages.
☐ 2 When expressing a fraction, the numerator precedes 分之 while the denominator follows 分之, e.g. 3/4 is read 三分之四.
☐ 3 A 占 B 的……分之…… is often used in formal and written expression.
☐ 4 When expressing a percentage, the specific percentage always comes after 百分之, e.g. 25.9% is read 百分之二十五点九.

2 Count the pink boxes.

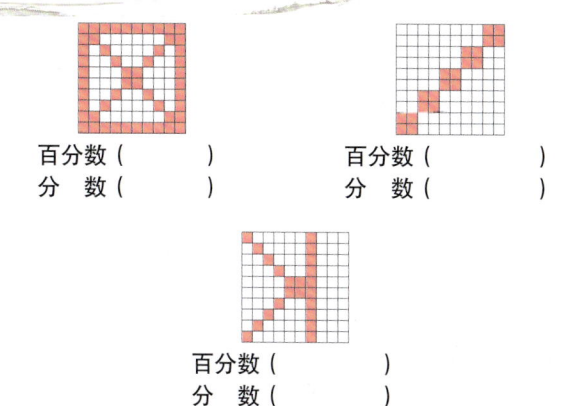

百分数（　　）
分　数（　　）

百分数（　　）
分　数（　　）

百分数（　　）
分　数（　　）

Moderating positive adjectives with 还

1 Look at the sentences.

	还	Positive adjective
我对那家宾馆的印象	还	可以。
那家饭店的火锅	还	不错。
火车票	还	真不贵。
他的中文说得	还	比较流利。
没想到宿舍的床	还	挺舒服的。

Now check the correct explanations.

☐ 1 还 as an adverb is used to moderate or reduce the positive tone of an adjective.
☐ 2 In such expressions, the meaning of 还 is similar to "quite" or "reasonably" in English.
☐ 3 If there are other adverbs of degree modifying positive adjectives, they are placed before 还, rather than after it.
☐ 4 Although 还 appears to moderate or reduce the positive tone of an adjective, the speaker is in fact conveying a positive comment.

2 Work in pairs. Talk about the following topics using 还.

1 你认为学校周边哪个餐馆值得推荐？为什么？
2 在你去过的城市中，哪个给你的印象还不错？为什么？

> Turn to page 185 for grammar reference.

Lesson 2　Unit 3　47

LESSON 3

Communication activity

1. Work in pairs. Choose a city that you think is attractive to Chinese tourists and make a travel plan for them.

   - **Student A:** Write a brief introduction to three tourist attractions of the city.
   - **Student B:** Research prices and schedules of transportation from one major Chinese city (such as Beijing, Shanghai or Guangzhou) to the destination city.

2. Put together a sample itinerary, using Lesson 2 to help you.

3. Present your itinerary to the class. Vote for the two best ones.

> Turn to pages 172 and 178 for more speaking practice.

Review and practice

1. Choose the correct words to complete the sentences.

   1. 关于去哈尔滨旅游的信息，你可以上网 _____ 一下。
      a 检查　　b 找到　　c 搜索

   2. A: 您好，后天从上海到广州的飞机票大概多少钱？
      B: _____，我查一下。
      a 麻烦您　　b 很抱歉　　c 请稍等

   3. 你刚才说的话我不太明白，能不能再说得 _____ 一点儿？
      a 认真　　b 详细　　c 合适

   4. 选专业这么重要的事情，你还是跟父母 _____ 一下比较好。
      a 咨询　　b 建议　　c 商量

   5. 我可以帮您 _____ 电话 _____ 我们的客服经理。
      a 把, 转给　　b 用, 打到　　c 把, 打到

Cultural corner

Harbin

Harbin is the capital city of Heilongjiang, a province situated in the northeastern region of China. Harbin has a cold climate, with an average annual temperature of only 4.6 degrees Celsius. It has the longest winter among the major Chinese cities, earning it the nickname "the Ice City". Harbin is famous throughout the world for its annual International Ice and Snow Sculpture Festival, where magnificent ice sculptures are built and decorated with colourful inbuilt lights. Representing more than 90% of the population, Han people are the largest ethnic group in Harbin, with the Hui, Mongolian and Manchu peoples making up the remainder. There is also a heavy Russian influence on the culture, cuisine and architecture of Harbin. Harbin's major industries include agriculture, transportation, and a substantial power generation industry.

2 Complete the passage with the words in the box.

> 认为　后顾之忧　不如　还
> 三分之一　折扣　至于　要求

很多人觉得，出去旅游，行程安排很重要，吃得怎么样也很重要，_____ 住得怎么样，他们却不关心。我的想法和他们不一样，我 _____ 住在哪里也是非常重要的。我的 _____ 是既要住得舒服，又不要太贵。我一般会选普通的酒店，它们的设施虽然 _____ 高级酒店好，但价钱不贵；而且在有 _____ 的时候，价钱可能只是平时的一半甚至 _____。其实，很多普通酒店的条件也 _____ 不错，只是没有游泳馆、健身房什么的。我觉得住得好、睡得好才能让旅游没有 _____。

3 Read the passage and answer the questions.

1 滨海路是不是很快就能游览完？什么时间去景色比较美？
2 "金石滩"的"金"和"石"是什么意思？
3 "人到广场看风景，人也和广场一起成为了风景"是什么意思？
4 "小吃"是什么意思？"焖子"是一种小吃还是海鲜？
5 大连最早的电车出现于哪一年？

Now match the five activities with the purposes.

1 游览滨海路	a 感受古老的浪漫
2 踩一踩金色的沙滩	b 了解城市的文化
3 看广场	c 感受大海
4 吃海鲜、小吃	d 看美丽的风景
5 坐老式电车	e 品尝当地美食

到大连旅游必做的五件事

如画的风景，金色的沙滩，百变的广场，丰富的海鲜，浪漫的都市——这就是大连。到大连旅游，有五件事，你一定要做。

1 游览滨海路：这条路一边是山、一边是海，水天相连，风景如画。路上有十二个景点，每个景点都值得停下来好好游玩。不过，如果你的时间不太多，那就乘车游览吧。不同的时间来，你会看到不同的美。

2 踩一踩金色的沙滩：大连的金石滩度假区是国家AAAAA级旅游风景区。这里有金色的沙滩、蓝色的海水，还有千奇百怪的石头。在这里，你可以冲浪、潜水、游泳、打沙滩排球，喜欢什么就玩什么。就算这些你都不想做，你也要在沙滩上踩一踩，感受一下大海。

3 看广场：要是你想了解大连，就去看看它的广场。这座城市有八十多个广场，人们常去的也有十几个。在中国，没有哪个城市有这么多广场。人到广场看风景，人也和广场一起成为了风景。

4 品尝海鲜、吃小吃：到了大连，不吃海鲜可不行。这里的海鲜种类丰富，又新鲜又美味。大大小小的餐馆，一样的海鲜可以做出不一样的味道。除了海鲜以外，也别忘了尝一尝当地的小吃，比如焖子（mènzi），会让你一吃难忘。

5 坐老式电车：大连最早的电车出现于1909年，现在的201路电车线还有几辆老式电车。在到处都是高楼大厦的现代城市里，坐在老式电车里，感受"古老的一公里"，这不是很浪漫吗？

4 Think about one city that you are familiar with and outline five great things to do there.

Now write a post to recommend the city.

Vocabulary review

Fill in the blanks.

保险	bǎoxiǎn	n.	insurance
倍	bèi	measure word	_____
避暑胜地	bìshǔ shèngdì		summer resort
冰灯	bīngdēng	n.	ice lantern
不等	bùděng	adj.	varying
步行街	bùxíngjiē	n.	pedestrian street
踩	cǎi	v.	tread on
____	chūfā	v.	set off
大巴	dàbā	n.	bus
____	dēng	v.	climb
方案	fāng'àn	n.	_____
防晒	fáng shài		prevent sunburn
____	fèiyong	n.	expense
俯瞰	fǔkàn	v.	overlook
感受	gǎnshòu	v./n.	experience; feeling
高速	gāosù	adj.	high-speed
高铁	gāotiě	n.	high-speed railway
顾问	gùwèn	n.	consultant
广场	guǎngchǎng	n.	_____
逛	guàng	v.	stroll
合理	hélǐ	adj.	_____
后顾之忧	hòugùzhīyōu		disturbance in the rear
建筑	jiànzhù	n.	architecture
____	jīngjì	adj.	economical
列车	lièchē	n.	_____
领队	lǐngduì	n.	group leader
旅行社	lǚxíngshè	n.	travel agency
美食	měishí	n.	cuisine
目的地	mùdìdì		_____
欧式	ōushì		European style
____	pǐncháng	v.	taste
全部	quánbù		_____
全价	quánjià	n.	full price

三分之一	sān fēnzhī yī		one third
散步	sànbù	v.	take a walk
____	shāngliang	v.	discuss
商业	shāngyè	n.	commerce
稍等	shāo děng		wait a minute
食宿	shísù	n.	board and lodging
事项	shìxiàng	n.	item, matter
____	shìnèi		indoor
团	tuán	n.	_____
团体票	tuántǐpiào		group ticket
旺季	wàngjì	n.	peak period
温差	wēnchā	n.	difference in temperature
卧铺	wòpù	n.	berth
____	xiángxì	adj.	detailed
欣赏	xīnshǎng	v.	_____
雪雕	xuědiāo	n.	snow sculpture
____	yángguāng	n.	sunshine
一等	yī děng		first-class
意外	yìwài	n.	accident
硬座	yìngzuò	n.	hard seat
预防	yùfáng	v.	prevent
折扣	zhékòu	n.	_____
至于	zhìyú	prep.	_____
制订	zhìdìng	v.	formulate
转	zhuǎn	v.	transfer
自费	zìfèi	v.	pay one's own expenses
____	zìyóu	adj./n.	free; freedom
龙塔	Lóng Tǎ		Dragon Tower
圣·索菲亚教堂	Shèngsuǒfēiyà Jiàotáng		Saint Sophia Cathedral
松花江	Sōnghuā Jiāng		Songhua River
太阳岛	Tàiyáng Dǎo		Sun Island

UNIT 4

Huānyíng dàjiā de dàolái
欢迎 大家 的 到来!

Welcome, everyone!

LESSON | 1

Vocabulary and listening

1 Work in pairs. Talk about when you can use the expressions below.

祝你在……收获良多！

祝大家在……生活愉快！

我代表……欢迎大家来到……

下面我宣布：……

下面我们请……发言。

2 Work in pairs. Work out the meanings of the idioms.

远道而来	远道：long way 来：come
丰富多彩	丰富： 多彩：
朝夕相处	朝： 夕： 相处：

3 Yeong-min is attending the opening ceremony of the summer camp. Listen to the audio and answer the questions.

1 钱老师请了哪些人发言？
2 除了宣布开营，王主任还介绍了什么？
3 孙小文是谁？

钱老师：各位同学，欢迎来到北京外国语大学国际中学生夏令营！我是你们的领队，我姓钱。今天是我们的开营仪式，首先，我们请国际交流中心的王主任致欢迎辞并宣布开营。

王主任：各位远道而来的同学，我代表北京外国语大学国际交流中心欢迎你们参加国际中学生夏令营。北京外国语大学是中国著名的语言专业类大学，也是最早从事国际中文教学的大学之一。我们的国际中学生夏令营已经成功举办了三届。今年夏令营的主题是"用中国的语言讲中国的故事"。我相信，通过夏令营丰富多彩的语言实践活动，当你们离开夏令营的时候，你们的汉语水平一定会有很大的进步，也一定会对中国有更多的了解，就像前三届夏令营的同学一样。下面我宣布：国际中学生夏令营正式开营！

钱老师：非常感谢王主任的发言。下面，我要给同学们介绍夏令营期间将与你们朝夕相处的两位助理，他们都是来自我们这所大学的学生：孙小文同学和金永民同学。

小文：大家好，我是小文，很高兴能有机会陪你们在中国度过这个夏天！

永民：我是永民，大家好！祝大家在夏令营生活愉快、收获良多！有事儿找我，千万别客气！

4 Match the people with their roles.

1 王主任
2 钱老师
3 金永民
4 孙小文

a 夏令营助理
b 夏令营领队
c 国际交流中心的负责人

5 Check the true statements.

☐ 1 开营仪式上，由钱老师致欢迎辞，王主任宣布开营。
☐ 2 今年的国际中学生夏令营是这个学校举办的第三届。
☐ 3 本届夏令营有丰富多彩的语言实践活动。
☐ 4 两位助理不都是北京外国语大学的学生。

New words

gè wèi 各位	everyone	jiè 届	session, class (for meetings, graduating classes, etc.)	xiàmiàn 下面	following
kāiyíng 开营	open (a camp)	zhǔtí 主题	theme	fāyán 发言	speech; give a speech
yíshì 仪式	ceremony	jiǎng 讲	tell, speak	zhāoxī xiāngchǔ 朝夕 相处	be together day and night
zhǔrèn 主任	director	tōngguò 通过	through	zhùlǐ 助理	assistant
zhìcí 致辞	make a speech	fēngfù-duōcǎi 丰富多彩	rich and colourful	suǒ 所	(for institutions)
xuānbù 宣布	announce	shíjiàn 实践	practise	péi 陪	accompany
yuǎndào'érlái 远道而来	coming from far away	dāng 当	when	liáng duō 良 多	quite a lot
jǔbàn 举办	host, hold				

6 Complete the sentences with the words from the conversation.

1 北京外国语大学是中国最早 _____ 国际中文教学的大学之一。
2 这个国际中学生夏令营是由北京外国语大学的国际交流中心 _____ 的。
3 前三届夏令营的同学汉语水平都有很大的 _____ 。
4 小文和永民将 _____ 夏令营的同学们一起度过这个夏天。

7 You are going to hear a Q&A session at the summer camp. Listen to the audio and match the questions with the students who ask them.

第一个学生	a 去哪儿买手机卡
第二个学生	b 什么时候跟中国家庭见面
第三个学生	c 晚上有没有晚自习
第四个学生	d 不知道室友是谁
	e 能不能上网、看电视
	f 打电话便宜还是上网便宜

8 Listen again and check the true statements.

☐ 1 住宿舍的同学三个人一个房间。
☐ 2 一共有四个同学住中国家庭。
☐ 3 如果想看电视，可以在晚上七点到九点半的时候看。
☐ 4 晚上七点半以后是自由活动时间。
☐ 5 永民会带同学们一起去买手机卡。
☐ 6 小文将带住宿舍的同学去宿舍，永民将带住中国家庭的同学跟中国家人见面。

Now work in pairs and check your answers.

Pronunciation and speaking

1 Listen to the sentences. Pay attention to the expressions often used in a welcome speech.

1 各位远道而来的同学，我代表国际交流中心欢迎你们的到来。
2 我相信你们的汉语水平一定会有很大的进步。
3 祝大家生活愉快、收获良多！

Now repeat the sentences.

2 Work in pairs. Introduce an institution or university to each other using a formal tone. Include:

- 它成立于哪一年
- 它的历史故事
- 它最强的学科或最著名的方面
- 有哪些名人曾在这里学习

3 You are the host of an orientation programme for international students from China. Draft a speech, including:

1 A welcome or greeting for your audience;
2 A brief introduction to your university;
3 Your hopes / wishes / thanks.

Now work in pairs. Take turns to give your speech.

CHINESE TO GO
Ending a welcome speech

Zhù dàjiā zài xiàlìngyíng shēnghuó yúkuài shōuhuò liáng duō
祝大家在夏令营生活愉快、收获良多！

Yǒu shìr zhǎo wǒ
有事儿找我。

I hope you have a productive and enjoyable stay at the summer camp!

Contact me if you need anything.

LESSON | 2

Reading and writing

1 Work in pairs. Choose five items you need to camp in the mountains for two nights from the list. Explain why you need them.

防晒霜　帽子　太阳镜
防蚊药水　常用药品
小刀　伞
洗漱用品
手表　手机　GPS
零用钱
长袖上衣　长裤

- 我需要带长袖上衣、长裤和防晒霜，因为山里气温比较低，太阳比较厉害。
- 我不需要带防晒霜，我穿长袖上衣和长裤、戴太阳镜和帽子就行了。

2 Match the words with their meanings.

1 及时	a each other
2 友好	b before, ahead of time
3 提前	c try one's best
4 单独	d actively
5 尽量	e in time
6 互相	f by oneself
7 积极	g strictly
8 严格	h friendly

Now put the words into the correct categories.

Time

Manner

Degree

3 Use the words in Activity 2 to make phrases with the words below. There can be more than one answer for each blank.

_____ 相处　_____ 通知　_____ 举办
_____ 完成　_____ 支持　_____ 参加
_____ 遵守　_____ 报告

4 Read the inside pages of the summer camp brochure on page 56 and answer the questions.

1 三个部分的主要内容各是什么？
2 需要记好的电话号码是什么？
3 营员每天除了上中文课，还有什么活动？
4 营员需要准备的帽子是做什么用的？

夏令营守则

1. 听从夏令营工作人员的安排，遵守作息时间。

2. 看管好自己的个人物品，贵重物品如丢失应及时向领队或助理报告。

3. 注意饮食卫生和天气变化。身体不舒服应及时通知领队或助理，由助理带去看医生。

4. 按时上课。如因病不能上课，需提前向老师请假。

5. 按时完成作业。晚自习期间有任何功课上的问题，可向值班老师提问。

6. 夏令营期间尽量说中文，少说或不说其他语言。

7. 积极参加各项活动。如有特殊原因不能参加，应提前通知领队或助理。

8. 自由活动期间，不能单独行动。尽量不去不熟悉的地方。记好求助电话号码，有紧急情况时及时拨打。

9. 与其他营员友好相处，互相关心、互相帮助，发扬团队精神。

作息时间

- 08:00—10:00 语言课
- 10:00—12:00 文化课
- 12:00—14:00 午餐，午休
- 14:00—17:30 课外活动，参观游览
- 17:30—19:30 晚餐，自由活动
- 19:30—21:30 晚自习

＊求助号码
紧急求助：110
火　警：119
医疗急救：120

哈尔滨一行　营员需要准备的物品

- 夏季服装
  （另外准备长袖上衣和长裤）
- 防晒用品
  （防晒霜、帽子、太阳镜等）
- 个人常用药品
- 洗漱用品
- 手表、手电筒、水杯、伞、笔记本、笔
- 零用钱（人民币）

New words

shǒuzé 守则	rules	yíngyuán 营员	camper
tīngcóng 听从	obey	yǒuhǎo 友好	friendly
zūnshǒu 遵守	abide by, observe (the rules)	hùxiāng 互相	mutually
zuòxī 作息	work and rest	fāyáng 发扬	carry on
wùpǐn 物品	article	tuánduì jīngshén 团队 精神	team spirit
guìzhòng 贵重	valuable	huǒjǐng 火警	fire alarm
diūshī 丢失	lose	yīliáo 医疗	give medical treatment (to)
bàogào 报告	report	jíjiù 急救	give first aid
yǐnshí 饮食	drink and food	wǔxiū 午休	noon break
wèishēng 卫生	hygiene	kèwài 课外	time outside class
qǐngjià 请假	ask for leave	cháng xiù 长 袖	long sleeve
wánchéng 完成	complete, accomplish	fángshàishuāng 防晒霜	sun cream
zìxí 自习	study by oneself	màozi 帽子	hat
rènhé 任何	any	tàiyángjìng 太阳镜	sunglasses
gōngkè 功课	course	cháng yòng 常 用	commonly used
zhíbān 值班	be on duty	yàopǐn 药品	medicine
jījí 积极	active	xǐshù yòngpǐn 洗漱 用品	toiletries
tèshū 特殊	special	shǒubiǎo 手表	watch
dāndú 单独	alone, by oneself	sǎn 伞	umbrella
shúxī 熟悉	be familiar with	língyòngqián 零用钱	pocket money
jǐnjí 紧急	urgent	rénmínbì 人民币	Renminbi

5 Complete the passage with the words in the box.

> 遵守　听从　参加　看管　通知
> 帮助　报告　相处　完成　行动

　　营员应该 _____ 工作人员的安排，_____ 作息时间，按时上课，按时 _____ 作业。夏令营期间，应该 _____ 好自己的物品，如果发现丢失，要向领队 _____。也要积极 _____ 各种活动，如果有特殊原因不能参加，需要提前 _____ 领队。不要单独 _____，记好求助号码，跟其他营员要友好 _____、互相 _____。

6 Check the appropriate actions according to the rules of the camp.

☐ 1　你发现钱包丢了，马上给父母打电话，两天后才告诉领队。

☐ 2　你上课时觉得身体不舒服，马上告诉了老师和领队。

☐ 3　上课的时候你努力说中文，回宿舍以后你就不说中文了。

☐ 4　星期三下午的安排是去参观历史博物馆。你以前去过，所以你就单独去见朋友了。

☐ 5　你跟同学在外面遇到紧急情况，你马上拨打110。

☐ 6　你下午3点钟的时候在教室里看书。

7 Think of a place to go for the weekend. List five necessities you should bring and explain why.

Now write a short passage based on your list.

Language in use

"Verb + object" as a separable compound

1 Look at the sentences.

	Verb		Object	
我昨天晚上只	睡	了四个小时的	觉。	
王主任将给大家	致	欢迎	辞。	
你给大家	唱	一首英文	歌	吧。
他会	跳	印度	舞。	
我每个星期	跑	两次	步。	

Now check the correct explanations.

☐ 1 "Verb + object" (VO) compounds are verbs which are composed of a verb and an object.

☐ 2 A VO compound is a single word, whose English translation is usually also one word, e.g. 睡觉 = sleep; 唱歌 = sing.

☐ 3 VO compounds can be separated by inserting the aspectual particles 了, 过, 着, but not by duration, frequency, measure words or number.

☐ 4 Because VO compounds already contain an object, they cannot be followed directly by another object. For this reason, *我要见面他 is ungrammatical, and the correct sentence is 我要跟他见面.

2 Underline the separable verbs in the sentences.

1 毕了业，你打算去哪儿工作？
2 上个月我们放了三天假。
3 这门课这个学期一共要考三次试。
4 夏天太热了，我有时候一天洗好几次澡。
5 明天我就不去跟他见面了，我上个星期已经跟他见过面了。

通过 as a preposition

1 Look at the sentences.

	通过	Method	
	通过	各种语言实践活动，	大家的中文水平有了很大的提高。
大家的中文水平	通过	各种语言实践活动，	有了很大的提高。
	通过	研究，	人们发现喝茶对身体很好。
人们	通过	研究	发现喝茶对身体很好。
	通过	他的大学同学，	我们联系到了他。
我们	通过	他的大学同学	联系到了他。

Now check the correct explanations.

☐ 1 通过 as a preposition indicates that a certain method is used to achieve a desired outcome.

☐ 2 The correct structure is "通过 + method + subject + verb phrase" or "Subject + 通过 + method + verb phrase".

☐ 3 The method introduced by 通过 should be expressed in a verb phrase.

2 Complete the sentences.

1 _____ 研究，科学家们发现了治疗这种疾病的方法。
2 现代生活不能没有网络。人们通过网络 _____，也通过网络 _____。
3 通过实习，马克 _____。

3 Work in pairs. Talk about the following topics.

1 如果不上中文课，只通过聊天学习中文，你觉得能学会吗？
2 如果别人想了解你，他们可以通过什么方式？

Introducing the agent or performer of an action using 由

1 Look at the sentences.

Object	由	Agent	Verb
夏令营订票的事情	由	永民	负责。
生病的同学	由	助理	带着去看医生。
明天开会的时间到底	由	谁	通知？
电影《少林寺》	由	李连杰	主演。
参观游览活动全都	由	领队	安排。

Now check the correct explanations.

- ☐ 1 由 as a preposition is used to introduce an agent who performs a certain action.
- ☐ 2 The structure is "由 + agent + object + verb".
- ☐ 3 The agent introduced by 由 should be a noun or a pronoun.

2 Work in pairs. Talk about the following topics.

1 在你的家里，这些事情由谁负责？

收拾屋子　打扫洗手间　扔垃圾
洗衣服　洗碗　买菜　做饭
修理电视　照顾宠物

2 你上次的旅行

上次去_____旅行：
_____票是由_____订的；
_____是由_____决定的；
_____是由_____负责的；
_____是由_____安排的。

Disyllabic words that become monosyllabic in formal style

1 Look at the sentences.

	Disyllabic word	
贵重物品丢失	应（该）	及时向领队报告。
	如（果）	有特殊原因不能上课，要事先请假。
任何问题都	可（以）	向老师询问。
尽量只说中文，少说	或（者）	不说其他语言。
他	已（经）	不再是总统了。

Now check the correct explanations.

- ☐ 1 The monosyllabic forms usually appear in oral Chinese or in an informal style of writing.
- ☐ 2 In written Chinese or formal speech, some disyllabic words may appear in their monosyllabic forms.
- ☐ 3 These words can be modal verbs, conjunctions or adverbs.

2 Find out the meanings of the underlined monosyllabic words and figure out their disyllabic forms.

1 咖啡虽好，多饮伤身。
2 想去哈尔滨的同学，可找钱老师报名。
3 越来越多的外国人到中国工作或居住。
4 你看过《世界因你不同》这本书吗？

▶ Turn to page 186 for grammar reference.

LESSON 3

Communication activity

Work in pairs. Put together a brochure for the Chinese students at your university's summer camp. Include:

- A brief introduction to your university;
- An introduction to the nearby area, including places of interest, local restaurants, things to do in the summer, etc.;
- A daily schedule for the campers;
- Summer camp rules;
- Important contacts;
- A list of things the campers should bring;

Present your brochure to the class and vote for the best one.

> Turn to pages 172 and 178 for more speaking practice.

Cultural corner

Collectivism vs. individualism

While the concept of individualism is deeply rooted in Western societies, collectivism is firmly associated with Chinese and other Asian cultures. In collectivism, the emphasis is placed on people's interdependence, rather than on their independence. Priority is given to the group, the community, or the country rather than to individuals or individual rights. The collective good often triumphs over individual benefit. Children are encouraged to respect rules and obey adults, especially in school, where individual creativity is typically not the focus of education. During the modernization of China, people's awareness of the importance of individuality increased. However, a collectivist approach is still very prevalent.

Review and practice

1 Choose the correct words to complete the sentences.

1 这所大学的留学生 _____ 世界各地。
  a 而来 b 从来 c 来自

2 我们请王校长致欢迎辞 _____ 宣布开营。
  a 并 b 而 c 但

3 我们已经成功地 _____ 了三届中文演讲比赛。
  a 举办 b 办理 c 进行

4 今年世界地球日的 _____ 是"投资我们的星球"。
  a 题目 b 主题 c 话题

5 去年我们在法国南部 _____ 了一个愉快的暑假。
  a 通过 b 经过 c 度过

2 Complete the passage with the words in the box.

> 欢迎　宣布　代表　表示　介绍
> 明显　正式　丰富多彩　远道而来

　　在开营仪式上，王主任首先 _____ 北京外国语大学国际交流中心向 _____ 的各国同学表示 _____。然后，他向同学们 _____ 了北京外国语大学的情况，并 _____，他相信通过 _____ 的语言实践活动，大家的汉语水平一定会取得 _____ 的进步。最后，他 _____ 国际中学生夏令营 _____ 开营。

60　Unit 4　Lesson 3

3 Complete the sentences with the words in the box.

| 一定 | 及时 | 按时 |
| 尽量 | 提前 | 积极 |

1 你们要_____上课，不能迟到。
2 上课的时候，_____要_____参加讨论。
3 不管在哪儿，都应该_____只说中文，不说英文或其他语言。
4 如有贵重物品丢失，应该_____向领队或助理报告。
5 如有特殊情况不能上课，需要_____向老师请假。

4 Read the book club rules below. Match the words with their meanings.

1 交友	a member (of an organization)
2 会员	b member fees
3 非法	c associate with
4 会费	d illegal

书友会守则

一 书友会的目的是"通过阅读交友"。
二 书友会每周举行两次与读书相关的活动。
三 会员应遵守书友会守则，并积极参加书友会组织的活动。
四 参加活动时，会员不可有任何非法行为。
五 如有特殊情况不能参加书友会的活动，要提前通知书友会。
六 书友会每月为会员推荐十本书，会员要尽量读完三到四本。
七 会员之间应友好相处、互相帮助。
八 会员应按时交会费（每月30元）。
九 会员的个人信息如有变化，应及时通知书友会。

活动安排时间表

周三晚上 19:00—21:00　新书推荐，新书讨论，会员聚餐

周六上午 10:00—12:00　书与电影，老书再读，书与音乐

Now check the true statements.

☐ 1 书友会的目的是让会员在读好书的同时也能认识更多的朋友。
☐ 2 书友会会员每个月都得读完十本书。
☐ 3 书友会的会费每年交一次。
☐ 4 会员如果不能参加活动，应该早一点儿通知书友会。
☐ 5 这个星期三的活动可能是听音乐。
☐ 6 星期六的活动可能是看电影，这部电影应该跟一本书有关。

5 Make a list of the activities you would like to organize for the student's club at your university. Write a schedule.

星期	时间	活动
_____俱乐部活动安排时间表		

Now write six rules for the club. Use formal expressions and adverbials expressing restriction or emphasis that you have learnt in Lesson 2.

Vocabulary review

Fill in the blanks.

报告	bàogào	v./n.	_____
长袖	cháng xiù		long sleeve
____	cháng yòng		commonly used
单独	dāndú	adv.	_____
当	dāng	prep.	when
____	diūshī	v.	lose
发言	fāyán	n./v.	speech; give a speech
发扬	fāyáng	v.	carry on
防晒霜	fángshàishuāng		sun cream
丰富多彩	fēngfù-duōcǎi		rich and colourful
各位	gè wèi		everyone
功课	gōngkè	n.	course
贵重	guìzhòng	adj.	_____
____	hùxiāng	adv.	mutually
火警	huǒjǐng	n.	fire alarm
积极	jījí	adj.	active
急救	jíjiù	v.	give first aid
____	jiǎng	v.	tell, speak
届	jiè	measure word	session, class (for meetings, graduating classes, etc.)
紧急	jǐnjí	adj.	urgent
举办	jǔbàn	v.	host, hold
开营	kāiyíng		open (a camp)
课外	kèwài	n.	time outside class
良多	liáng duō		quite a lot
零用钱	língyòngqián		pocket money
	màozi	n.	hat
陪	péi	v.	_____
请假	qǐngjià	v.	ask for leave
人民币	rénmínbì	n.	Renminbi
	rènhé	pron.	any
	sǎn	n.	umbrella
____	shíjiàn	v.	practise
手表	shǒubiǎo	n.	_____
守则	shǒuzé	n.	rules
熟悉	shúxi	v.	be familiar with
所	suǒ	measure word	(for institutions)
太阳镜	tàiyángjìng	n.	sunglasses
特殊	tèshū	adj.	special
听从	tīngcóng	v.	obey
	tōngguò	prep.	through
团队精神	tuánduì jīngshén		team spirit
完成	wánchéng	v.	_____
卫生	wèishēng	n.	hygiene
午休	wǔxiū	v.	noon break
物品	wùpǐn	n.	article
洗漱用品	xǐshù yòngpǐn		toiletries
	xiàmiàn	n.	following
宣布	xuānbù	v.	_____
药品	yàopǐn	n.	medicine
医疗	yīliáo	v.	give medical treatment (to)
仪式	yíshì	n.	ceremony
饮食	yǐnshí	n.	drink and food
营员	yíngyuán	n.	camper
	yǒuhǎo	adj.	friendly
远道而来	yuǎndào'ér lái		coming from far away
朝夕相处	zhāoxī xiāngchǔ		be together day and night
值班	zhíbān	v.	be on duty
致辞	zhìcí	v.	make a speech
主任	zhǔrèn	n.	_____
	zhǔtí	n.	theme
	zhùlǐ	n.	assistant
自习	zìxí	v.	study by oneself
遵守	zūnshǒu	v.	abide by, observe (the rules)
作息	zuòxī	v.	work and rest

Review 1

Vocabulary

1 Match the words to make phrases.

1	制订	a	美食
2	申请	b	要求
3	品尝	c	活动
4	组织	d	工作
5	符合	e	经验
6	积累	f	方案

2 Write two words with each of the characters below.

1 品 _____ _____
2 职 _____ _____
3 守 _____ _____
4 急 _____ _____
5 相 _____ _____
6 历 _____ _____
7 自 _____ _____

3 Circle the odd words out.

1 仔细　开朗　积极　曾经
2 招聘　医疗　面试　求职
3 搜索　住宿　链接　首页
4 组织　策划　整理　差异
5 支持　暂时　鼓励　同情
6 后顾之忧　避暑胜地
　团队精神　丰富多彩

4 Choose the correct words to complete the sentences.

1 贵重物品丢失，应该赶快向警察_____。
　a 报告　　b 发言　　c 请示
2 _____时候你都应该提醒自己注意安全。
　a 任何　　b 全部　　c 所有
3 我们应该_____。
　a 鼓励　　b 鼓励互相　c 互相鼓励
4 感谢你_____时间为我们整理会议记录。
　a 抽　　　b 做　　　c 给
5 这次招聘活动是请专业人士_____的。
　a 策划　　b 制订　　c 讨论
6 因为没有奖学金，所以我得_____去中国留学。
　a 自由　　b 免费　　c 自费
7 本地的小吃很特别，你应该_____一下。
　a 品尝　　b 经历　　c 体会
8 非常_____大家对我的鼓励。
　a 欣赏　　b 感谢　　c 支持

5 Match the words with their opposites.

1	暂时	a	普通
2	特殊	b	长期
3	开朗	c	便宜
4	贵重	d	到达
5	出发	e	过去
6	输入	f	输出
7	团体	g	个人
8	将来	h	内向

Grammar

1 Choose the correct words to complete the sentences.

1 这件衣服我 _____ 在网上买 _____。
   a 是……了   b 是……的
   c 是……

2 李经理让你明天 _____ 给那家公司打个电话。
   a 再   b 又   c 还

3 永民，金老师让你订 _____ 去哈尔滨的火车票。
   a 一点儿   b 一些   c 一下

4 这首歌 _____ 挺好听的。
   a 更   b 又   c 还

5 我和中文兴趣小组的朋友们每个星期 _____。
   a 两次见面   b 见两次面   c 不见面

6 他只来过伦敦三次，却对伦敦熟悉 _____ 不得了。
   a 得   b 的   c 地

7 你怎么又跟妹妹 _____ 了？
   a 吵起架来   b 吵架起来
   c 吵起来架

8 招聘实习生的事情 _____ 销售部负责。
   a 对   b 为   c 由

2 Complete the sentences with the words in the box.

| 回……来 | 回……去 | 进来 |
| 进去 | 上来 | 上去 | 下来 | 下去 |

1 A: 外面太冷了，你要不要 _____？
   B: 没事儿，外面空气好，我一会儿再 _____。

2 A: 毕业以后，你还打算 _____ 上海 _____ 吗？
   B: 上海虽然是我的家乡，不过我更喜欢北京，我打算继续待在北京。

3 A: 你还是别 _____ 了，我站在上面也看不清远处的山。我马上就 _____。
   B: 那你快 _____ 吧，我就不 _____ 了。

4 A: 下个月是你爷爷的生日，你别忘了 _____ 香港 _____ 给爷爷过生日，我们都等着你呢。
   B: 放心，我一定回去，机票都买好了。

3 Complete the conversations with the words given.

1 A: 跟着旅行社旅游价钱贵不贵？行程安排怎么样？
   B: _____（至于）

2 A: 你觉得北京的气候好还是广州的气候好？
   B: _____（不如）

3 A: 李连杰是谁？没听说过。
   B: 你在开玩笑吗？_____
   _____（连……都……）

4 A: 你参加过中文夏令营吗？
   B: 没有，_____
   （一……都没……）

4 Rewrite the sentences by changing the monosyllabic words to disyllabic ones.

1 事虽小，影响大。

2 他已开始行动。

3 如有问题，请与客服部联系。

4 航班因大雨取消。

5 出国旅行应注意些什么？

Integrated skills

1 Listen to the conversation and choose the correct answers to the questions.

1 王宇刚开始打算应聘什么职位？
   a 旅游顾问　　b 市场策划　　c 新闻策划

2 王宇大学的专业是什么？
   a 新闻　　　　b 旅游　　　　c 中文

3 张小姐最有可能在哪个部门工作？
   a 市场部　　　b 人力部　　　c 客服部

4 张小姐认为王宇能不能胜任旅游顾问的职位？
   a 能　　　　　b 不能　　　　c 不清楚

5 张小姐为什么建议王宇申请市场部的职位？
   a 因为王宇有相关的工作经验
   b 因为王宇的专业符合要求
   c 因为王宇对市场策划特别有想法

6 市场部的职位在试用期间一个月多少工资？
   a 两千　　　　b 五千　　　　c 六千

2 Look at the pictures. Choose your favourite city.

a

b

c

d

Now work in pairs. Ask and answer the questions about your favourite cities.

1 什么季节去最好？有什么好玩的活动？

2 可以去哪里逛街？

3 可以去哪里散步？

4 应该品尝哪些美食？

5 可以去什么地方欣赏音乐？

6 最有名的博物馆和广场分别是什么？

3 Complete the passage with the words in the box.

> 遵守　适应　任何　流利　丰富多彩
> 友好　鼓励　相处　互相　吃不惯

　　去年夏天，我去北京参加了一个中文夏令营。去以前我担心自己不能 _____ 北京的生活，特别是怕自己 _____ 中餐。可是没想到，到了北京我一点儿问题都没有。营员们都很 _____，大家都 _____ 营员守则，也会 _____ 帮助，所以我们 _____ 得非常好。夏令营的老师和助理都很热情，我们遇到 _____ 困难都可以找他们帮忙。为了提高我们的中文水平，老师 _____ 我们尽量只用中文交流。虽然开始的时候觉得很难，可是慢慢地我发现我的中文越来越 _____ 了。除了学中文以外，夏令营还有 _____ 的活动，比方说，参观博物馆、游览颐和园。对我来说，参加中文夏令营是一次非常难忘的经历。

4 A Chinese educational organization is going to host an English summer camp in your city. You are recommending activity ideas to help the students improve their English and understand local culture. Write an email to the organization. Include:

- 活动的内容或名字
- 活动对提高英文水平有什么帮助
- 活动对了解当地的文化有什么好处

Enjoy Chinese

艹　艹　艸　艹

草：grass
菜：vegetable, greens
药：medicinal herbs

The radical 艹 originally meant "grass". It then evolved to mean all plants except trees. Therefore, characters that have the 艹 radical are usually related to plants. Can you figure out why the following characters share the 艹 radical?

花：flower
蒜：garlic
茶：tea
荒：waste, barren
苦：bitter
茂：luxuriant, lush

UNIT 5

wǒ yídìng jìnlì'érwéi
我 一定 尽力而为!

I will try my best!

LESSON | 1

Vocabulary and listening

1 Match the words to make phrases.

1	举行	a	机会
2	把握	b	客户
3	接待	c	事情
4	商量	d	玩具
5	制作	e	晚宴

2 Match the questions with the best responses.

1	你一定能做好。	a	谢谢你的关心。
2	听说你病了，我很担心你。	b	谢谢你的信任。
3	有压力才有动力。	c	嗯，有道理。
4	晚会上唱什么歌呢？	d	我再好好想想。

3 Mark's company is about to receive visitors from abroad. His manager, Tang Yu, is talking to him about the arrangements. Listen to the conversation and answer the questions.

1 公司接下来的两周要接待什么客人？
2 唐经理让马克负责什么工作？
3 唐经理问了马克关于哪两件事情的建议？

马克：唐经理，您有事找我？

唐雨：马克，来，沙发这边坐。怎么样，实习的第一个星期还习惯吧？

马克：谢谢您的关心。我很喜欢我的工作，一来就跟同事学到了很多东西。

唐雨：那就好。有问题及时跟同事们交流。接下来的两周我们要接待一个从澳大利亚来的考察团，这次将由你全程陪同，并且主要负责翻译工作。

马克：哦……我一定尽力而为。

唐雨：不过也不用紧张，客服部的同事会全力配合你的工作。我看过你的简历，我对你有信心。

马克：谢谢您的信任。压力的确不小，但对我来说倒是个难得的锻炼机会，我会好好把握。

唐雨：好的。还有两件事想问问你的建议。我们打算为考察团举行一个欢迎晚宴，你认为西餐还是中餐比较合适？

马克：我觉得既然他们来了中国，应该希望尝到地道的中国菜吧？

唐雨：有道理。另外，我们想送他们一些纪念品，你有什么建议吗？

马克：我认为不用送太贵重的礼物。对了，我在公司看到过一只用环保材料制作的玩具熊猫，不但代表我们公司的环保理念，而且具有中国特色，当礼物再合适不过

了。您觉得怎么样？

唐雨：嗯，这个建议也不错。这样吧，关于这个代表团的事情，在周四的例会上我们再具体商量一下。

马克：好的，唐经理。我也再好好想想有没有其他事情需要注意。要是没别的事，我先去忙了。

唐雨：好的。

2 考察团将由马克_____陪同。
3 马克会_____把握这个难得的机会。
4 公司客服部的同事们会_____配合马克的工作。

New words

shāfā 沙发	sofa	jǔxíng 举行	host, hold
péitóng 陪同	accompany	wǎnyàn 晚宴	dinner banquet
fùzé 负责	take charge (of)	jìrán 既然	since
ò 哦	oh (expressing understanding)	cháng 尝	taste
jìnlì' érwéi 尽力而为	try one's best	huánbǎo 环保	environmentally friendly
quánlì 全力	(with) all one's strength	cáiliào 材料	material
pèihé 配合	cooperate	zhìzuò 制作	manufacture, make
xìnrèn 信任	trust	lǐniàn 理念	idea, concept
dào 倒	nevertheless	jùyǒu 具有	have (an abstract quality)
nándé 难得	rare, hard to get	tèsè 特色	characteristic
hǎohǎo 好好	make great efforts	shìqing 事情	matter, affair
bǎwò 把握	grasp, seize	lìhuì 例会	regular meeting

4 Check the true statements.

☐ 1 马克主动找唐经理谈自己的实习。
☐ 2 马克单独负责考察团所有的事情。
☐ 3 马克觉得安排中餐晚宴更合适。
☐ 4 马克觉得礼物一定要非常贵重才行。
☐ 5 马克实习的公司具有环保理念。

5 Complete the sentences with the words in the box.

| 具体 | 全程 | 全力 | 好好 | 及时 |

1 唐经理让马克有问题_____跟同事交流。

Lesson 1 Unit 5 69

6 Choose all the correct answers to the questions.

1 唐经理为什么要马克负责考察团的陪同和翻译？
   a 因为马克对澳大利亚的情况很熟悉。
   b 因为唐经理对马克很有信心。
   c 因为马克的工作经验很丰富。

2 关于这个任务，马克怎么想？
   a 他觉得有压力。
   b 他觉得机会难得。
   c 他会尽自己最大的努力。

3 马克为什么推荐用环保材料做的玩具熊猫作为礼物？
   a 因为它很贵重。
   b 因为它能代表公司的环保理念。
   c 因为它具有中国特色。

7 You are going to hear a conversation about a wedding. Underline the main issues you expect to be discussed.

☐ a 要不要去参加婚礼
☐ b 谁会参加婚礼
☐ c 参加婚礼送什么
☐ d 参加婚礼穿什么

Now listen to the conversation and check the three issues discussed.

8 Listen again and answer the questions.

1 小王为什么建议马克参加婚礼？
2 送红包有什么好处？
3 根据小王的建议，怎么决定送多少钱的红包？

Now work in pairs and check your answers.

Pronunciation and speaking

1 Listen to the sentences asking for advice.

1 我有两件事想问问你的建议。
2 我们打算请朋友吃饭，你觉得四川菜合适还是云南菜合适？
3 我想在北京买一些纪念品送给朋友，你有什么建议吗？
4 我想送他一本中文字典当生日礼物，你觉得怎么样？

Now repeat the sentences.

2 Complete the conversations with the sentences in Activity 1.

1 A: _____
   B: 哪两件事？你说吧，我帮你出主意。

2 A: _____
   B: 如果是我的朋友，我会送一件有中国书法的上衣。

3 A: _____
   B: 既然你的朋友是四川人，就准备四川菜吧。

3 Work in pairs. Ask for and give advice on the following issues.

1 面试穿什么衣服
2 父亲节送什么礼物给爸爸

CHINESE TO GO
Adapting to a new environment

hái xíguàn ma
……还 习惯 吗？ — How are you coping with …?

Wǒ yídìng jìnlì'érwéi
我 一定 尽力而为。 — I will try my best.

Wǒ huì hǎohāor bǎwò
我 会 好好 把握。 — I'll seize the opportunity.

70 Unit 5 Lesson 1

LESSON | 2

Reading and writing

1 Check the words which usually appear in business writing.

☐ 药品 ☐ 材料 ☐ 留言条
☐ 建筑 ☐ 通知 ☐ 会议记录
☐ 行程 ☐ 环保 ☐ 列车

2 Look at the meanings and complete the table.

负责 means _____.	负责人：person who is in charge, director
留言：leave a message	留言条 means _____.
会议：meeting, conference	会议室 means _____.
总结：summary	工作总结 means _____.
邀请：invite	邀请信 means _____.
未：not yet 完成：finish	未完成 means _____.
版本：version	英文版 means _____.

Now work in pairs and check your answers.

3 Match the formal expressions with their informal meanings.

1 需	a 打算
2 并	b 需要
3 未	c 没有
4 拟	d 在
5 于	e 而且

Now work in pairs. Make sentences with the formal expressions.

4 Read the note on page 72 and complete the sentences. 〔1-29〕

谢月给马克的留言条里提到了三件事情：
1 让马克找 _____
2 让马克翻译 _____
3 让马克将翻译好的内容 _____
_____

5 Choose the correct answers to the questions.

1 谢月给马克写留言条的原因是什么？
   a 马克现在不在办公室，她不能当面告诉他这些事情。
   b 马克听不太懂谢月说的话，她觉得写出来会更清楚。
   c 马克最近收不到谢月的电子邮件。

2 马克发给谢月的电子邮件应该是什么内容？
   a 澳大利亚考察团的行程安排
   b 翻译好的英文请柬
   c 公司的中文请柬

3 马克可能什么时候给谢月发电子邮件？
   a 6月27日上午9点15分
   b 6月28日上午10点15分
   c 6月28日下午3点15分

Lesson 2 Unit 5 71

留言条

马克：

唐经理让你回来后去她办公室，主要是布置接待澳大利亚考察团的任务。另外，公司请柬需要制作一个英文版本，麻烦你翻译一下，桌上的中文请柬供你参考。最晚请在明天中午12:00之前发到我邮箱，谢谢！

谢月

6月27日 10:15

会议通知

客户服务部拟于6月30日（周四）召开本月例会，会议安排如下：

时间：上午9:50开始签到，10:00正式开始
地点：总经理办公室旁边的大会议室
参加人员：客服部全体员工
会议内容：

(1) 由各小组负责人汇报本月工作的完成情况和下月的工作计划；需包括对未完成工作的分析，并提出具体的改进建议
(2) 由唐经理作客服部的工作总结
(3) 布置澳大利亚考察团的接待准备工作
(4) 集体讨论客户对新的电子客服系统的反馈

亚深（深圳）客户服务部
6月27日

New words

留言条 liúyán tiáo	leave a message slip, note	之前 zhīqián	before
布置 bùzhì	assign	拟 nǐ	intend
请柬 qǐngjiǎn	invitation card	召开 zhàokāi	call (a meeting)
版本 bǎnběn	version	如下 rúxià	as follows
供 gōng	provide certain support	签到 qiāndào	sign in
参考 cānkǎo	refer to	全体 quántǐ	whole, all
		员工 yuángōng	staff
汇报 huìbào	report	诚意 chéngyì	sincerity
未 wèi	not yet	兹定于 zī dìng yú	scheduled for
分析 fēnxī	analyse	恭请 gōngqǐng	invite respectfully
改进 gǎijìn	improve	届时 jièshí	at the appointed time
总结 zǒngjié	summary; summarize		
系统 xìtǒng	system		
反馈 fǎnkuì	feed back		

请柬

亚深国际贸易有限公司深圳分公司

诚意邀请

尊敬的 _____（先生/女士）

兹定于 ___ 年 ___ 月 ___ 日（周 ___）___ 时

举行 _____

恭请届时光临！

地址：_____

电话：_____

总经理：李树青

___ 年 ___ 月 ___ 日

6 Read the notice about the meeting on page 72 and check the true statements.

1 9点55分去签到也来得及。
2 开会地点是总经理办公室。
3 每个员工都要汇报本月工作的完成情况。
4 考察团的接待准备工作是这次例会的内容之一。
5 新的电子客服系统很受客户欢迎。

7 Read the note below and complete the table.

> 小文：
> 　　7月8号（周五）中午12点我们要举办一个欢迎宴会，欢迎国际夏令营的学生和相关客人，地点在第二餐厅。请你以国际交流中心王云青主任的名义制作一份请柬，并在明天下午4点以前发到我的邮箱。
> 　　　　　　　　　　钱老师
> 　　　　　　　　7月3号 11:18

欢迎宴会

时间	
地点	
举办单位	
邀请的人员	
请柬签名人	

Now write a formal invitation card based on the information and the invitation card on this page.

Language in use

Concessive clauses with 倒

1 Look at the sentences.

Clause 1（negative）	Clause 2（倒 positive）
这次任务的确不轻，	但对我来说倒真是个难得的锻炼机会。
他说中文，发音虽然不太准确，	说得倒很流利。
这间屋子真够小的，	不过倒挺干净。

Clause 1（倒 positive）	Clause 2（negative）
这次机会倒真是难得，	不过我觉得压力太大了。
他说中文，说得倒还流利，	可发音不太准确。
这间屋子倒是干净，	不过实在是太小了。

Now check the correct explanations.

- [ ] 1 倒 serves as an adverb marking a turning point or concession in the sentence.
- [ ] 2 If clause 1 expresses a negative comment, clause 2 uses 倒 to introduce a positive comment.
- [ ] 3 If clause 1 uses 倒 to show a concession to introduce a positive comment, clause 2 should also express a positive comment.
- [ ] 4 Clause 2 often contains 不过/但是/可是.
- [ ] 5 The comments in clause 2 are what the speaker wants to emphasize or highlight.

2 Work in pairs. Talk about the following topics using 倒.

1 你去过的饭店中，有哪个你不太喜欢？为什么？
2 有没有一部电影，你对它的看法跟周围的人不一样？哪里不一样？

Expressing "doing well" with 好好

1 Look at the sentences.

	好好 + verb phrase
这是一次难得的锻炼机会，	我会好好把握的。
嗯，这个建议不错，	我再好好想想。
身体不舒服，你就别工作了，	还是好好休息吧。
他唱得也太难听了，	应该再好好练练。
	我们要好好利用这次机会展示公司的形象。

Now check the correct explanations.

- [ ] 1 好好 as an adverbial modifies the verb phrase which follows it, meaning "doing something thoroughly" or "doing something as well as possible".
- [ ] 2 Sometimes modal verbs like 想/会/应该/得/要 are used after 好好 to emphasize the tone or the attitude of the speaker.
- [ ] 3 In colloquial expressions, the second 好 changes to "hāor", "好好" pronounced as "hǎohāor".

2 Complete the conversations using 好好.

1 A: 马上就要考完试了。你有什么打算？
   B: 我已经想好了，等考完试了，我要先 _____，再 _____，最后还要 _____。

2 A: 大夫，我最近老觉得没什么精神，每天都累得不得了。
   B: 你觉得累就是因为你不 _____，不 _____，也不 _____。你需要改变你的生活习惯。

Making deductions with 既然

1 Look at the sentences.

Clause 1（既然）	Clause 2
我觉得既然他们到中国来，	应该希望尝到地道的中国菜吧。
既然那所大学已经接受他了，	他就不会去别的大学了。
既然他们都这么忙，	我们就别打扰他们了。

	Clause 1（既然）	Clause 2
A: 我不进去了，我走了。	B: 既然都来了，	为什么不进来坐一会儿呢？
A: 你穿这件衣服真好看。	B: 既然你也觉得好看，	那我就买啦。

Now check the correct explanations.

☐ 1 The conjunction 既然 is used in clause 1 to restate a known fact, reason or premise.

☐ 2 Clause 2, as the main clause, presents a logical inference or suggestion deduced from the fact, reason or premise in clause 1.

☐ 3 Clause 2 often has 那 or 就, meaning "then" to show the inference or suggestion is natural and logical.

☐ 4 If there is a subject in clause 2, the subject goes after 那 or 就.

☐ 5 Clause 2 sometimes contains a rhetorical question indicated by 为什么 to show a strong tone.

2 Complete the sentences.

1 A: 火车票已经卖光了，怎么办啊？
   B: 既然_____，那_____。

2 A: 我劝过他很多次了，他不听。
   B: 既然_____，_____。

3 既然吸烟对健康特别不好，那_____？

Stressing an extreme degree with 再……不过了

1 Look at the sentences.

	再……不过了
把玩具熊猫送给客户	再合适不过了。
他对她有意思，这	再明显不过了。
这种巧克力	再受欢迎不过了。
如果能打到车，就	再好不过了。
把工作交给马克，经理	再放心不过了。

Now check the correct explanations.

☐ 1 再……不过了 is used to stress an extreme degree, and means "nothing is more ... than".

☐ 2 The words inserted between 再 and 不过了 can be either adjectives or emotional verbs.

☐ 3 The adjectives or emotional verbs usually have negative meanings.

2 Work in pairs. Talk about the following topics using 再……不过了.

1 怎么过夏天最舒服？
2 你看过电影《哈利·波特》（*Harry Potter*）吗？你觉得哪个演员演得最好？
3 你为家人做什么事情会让他们很高兴？
4 很多人说做饭很难，你觉得呢？

▶ Turn to page 187 for grammar reference.

LESSON 3

Communication activity

You are helping a group of Chinese teachers who are attending a conference in your city.

1 Leave a note for your partner and ask him/her to get back to you to discuss your responsibilities.

2 Work in pairs. Discuss the following with your partner:

- where you should take the teachers to have dinner on the first and the last nights;
- the places where you should take them for a half-day tour, include details about what they will see and what activities they can do;
- what souvenirs to buy for the teachers;

> Turn to pages 173 and 179 for more speaking practice.

Review and practice

1 Choose the correct words to complete the sentences.

1 我们马上要 _____ 一个从加拿大来的考察团。
   a 接受   b 接待   c 收到

2 A: 小唐，这次美国客户的接待工作主要由你负责。
   B: 经理，您放心，我 _____ 尽力而为。
   a 好好   b 的确   c 一定

3 我知道你能力很强，我对你有 _____ 。
   a 信心   b 信任   c 相信

4 这家国际公司的发展 _____ 是"服务与创新"。
   a 意见   b 想法   c 理念

5 你的建议很有 _____ ，我会再跟其他同事商量商量。
   a 理由   b 优点   c 道理

Cultural corner

Nature reserves and wildlife protection in China

By now, China had established around 2750 nature reserves nationwide. The most famous include Wolong in Sichuan Province (for pandas), Shennongjia in Hubei Province (for golden monkeys), and Changbai Mountain in Northeast China (for Siberian tigers). The biggest challenge faced by wildlife conservation in China is the conflict between environmental protection and economic growth. Experts agree that to maintain nature reserves successfully, committed financial support from national and local governments is required as well as extensive wildlife protection laws, successful implementation of such laws, and cooperation between the government and other domestic or international organizations. In recent years, the Chinese government nevertheless has made ambitious plans to revive nature reserves and strengthen wildlife protection, and there has been substantial progress.

2 Complete the passage with the words in the box.

把握　纪念品　难得　任务　制作　配合
建议　关心　接下来　举办　负责

今天唐经理找我谈了一些工作上的事情。她首先很 _____ 地问了我实习第一周的情况，然后她告诉我 _____ 的两周我们要接待一个澳大利亚考察团，由我 _____ 陪同工作和主要的翻译工作。尽管会有客服部的同事们 _____ 我的工作，我还是觉得 _____ 非常重。不过，这是一次 _____ 的锻炼机会，我一定会好好 _____。另外，我还 _____ 公司在 _____ 欢迎宴会时选用中餐，把用环保材料 _____ 的玩具熊猫作为 _____ 送给考察团的客人。

3 Complete the sentences with the words in the box.

交代　制作　召开　总结　分析
参考　提出　完成　布置

1 请你 _____ 这份请柬 _____ 一份新的请柬。
2 经济系拟于本周四下午三点 _____ 全系大会，请全系师生准时参加。
3 天亮，你休假之前别忘了跟马克 _____ 一下电子客服系统的事情。
4 昨天的公司大会上，人事部的同事们 _____ 了一些很有用的建议。
5 上个星期刘经理 _____ 给你的任务，你 _____ 得怎么样了？
6 这两天真忙，不但要 _____ 上个月的工作情况，还要 _____ 客户的反馈意见。

4 Read the notice and check the true statements.

会议通知

国际交流中心拟于5月30日（周三）召开本月例会，会议安排如下：

1 时间：下午4:00 — 5:30
2 地点：国际交流中心大会议室
3 参加人员：国际交流中心全体老师和各项目学生助理
4 会议内容：
（1）由各项目的负责老师汇报各项目的进展情况
（2）由王主任布置暑期三个项目的具体准备工作，包括国际中学生夏令营项目、大学生社会实践项目、短期语言培训项目
（3）讨论项目助理的培训办法

请大家提前做好准备并准时参加。

国际交流中心主任办公室
5月25日

☐ 1 会议时长是2个小时。
☐ 2 只有交流中心的老师们需要参加这个会议。
☐ 3 会上，王主任会布置暑期三个项目的准备工作。
☐ 4 助理被聘用以后需要参加培训。

Now work in pairs. Write down the meanings of the words.

短期：_____　暑期：_____
进展：_____　培训：_____

5 Write an email to Yeong-min and Xiaowen on behalf of Mr Qian, notifying them of the meeting in Activity 4.

Lesson 3　Unit 5　77

Vocabulary review

Fill in the blanks.

把握	bǎwò	v.	grasp, seize
版本	bǎnběn	n.	version
布置	bùzhì	v.	assign
材料	cáiliào	n.	_____
_____	cānkǎo	v.	refer to
尝	cháng	v.	_____
诚意	chéngyì	n.	sincerity
倒	dào	adv.	nevertheless
反馈	fǎnkuì	v.	feed back
	fēnxī	v.	analyse
负责	fùzé	v.	take charge (of)
改进	gǎijìn	v.	_____
供	gōng	v.	provide certain support
恭请	gōngqǐng	v.	invite respectfully
好好	hǎohǎo	adv.	make great efforts
环保	huánbǎo	adj.	environmentally friendly
汇报	huìbào	v.	report
	jìrán	conj.	since
	jièshí	adv.	at the appointed time
届时			
尽力而为	jìnlì' érwéi		try one's best
举行	jǔxíng	v.	host, hold
具有	jùyǒu	v.	_____
理念	lǐniàn	n.	idea, concept
例会	lìhuì	n.	regular meeting
留言	liúyán	v.	leave a message

难得	nándé	adj.	rare, hard to get
拟	nǐ	v.	intend
	ò	interj.	oh (expressing understanding)
陪同	péitóng	v.	accompany
配合	pèihé	v.	cooperate
签到	qiāndào	v.	sign in
请柬	qǐngjiǎn	n.	invitation card
全力	quánlì	adv./n.	(with) all one's strength
	quántǐ	n.	whole, all
如下	rúxià	v.	as follows
沙发	shāfā	n.	_____
	shìqing	n.	matter, affair
特色	tèsè	n.	_____
条	tiáo	n.	slip, note
晚宴	wǎnyàn	n.	dinner banquet
未	wèi	adv.	_____
	xìtǒng	n.	system
信任	xìnrèn	v.	_____
员工	yuángōng	n.	staff
召开	zhàokāi	v.	call (a meeting)
之前	zhīqián	n.	before
制作	zhìzuò	v.	manufacture, make
兹定于	zī dìng yú		scheduled for
总结	zǒngjié	n./v.	summary; summarize

78 Unit 5 Vocabulary

UNIT 6

Nǐmen liǎng gè pèihé de hěn hǎo
你们两个配合得很好!

You two make a good team!

LESSON | 1

Vocabulary and listening

1 Work in pairs. Check the topics which you think are appropriate for small talk between two colleagues.

- ☐ 1 天气
- ☐ 2 收入
- ☐ 3 专业
- ☐ 4 工作经历
- ☐ 5 最喜欢的电视节目
- ☐ 6 兴趣爱好
- ☐ 7 家庭
- ☐ 8 老家

Now give one or two examples for each topic.

你是哪个地方的人？
听说你是中文专业高材生。

2 After the welcome dinner, Mark is talking with his colleagues. Listen to the conversation and answer the questions.

1 马克在欢迎晚宴上的表现怎么样？
2 周详是学什么专业的？
3 谢月在公司的哪两个部门工作过？
4 他们打算晚上去做什么？

谢月：马克，你今天表现不错啊！
马克：谢谢，其实我当时都紧张死了，就怕没听清楚或者翻译得不准确，漏掉了重要的信息。
谢月：是吗？没看出来啊。
马克：那就好。多亏周详事先帮我准备资料，要不然我今天的表现肯定很糟糕。
周详：你太谦虚了，马克。同事之间互相帮忙是应该的。
谢月：是啊，你们两个配合得很好！
周详：谢谢夸奖。马克，我真佩服你，中文学得这么好！要是我的英文能说得跟你的中文一样就好了。
马克：你的英文已经很好了啊！我还想跟你学习外贸知识呢！
谢月：是啊，周详是外贸专业的高材生。你们俩正好可以取长补短，共同进步。
马克：我们更应该向你和公司的其他前辈学习。实践经验可比书本知识重要多了。
周详：马克说的一点儿没错。对了，谢月，你一来公司就是在客服部吗？
谢月：不是，我刚来的时候是在销售部，但是后来发现自己更适合做客服，于是不周详：……到一年就转到这边来了。

周详：是这样啊。如果有机会，我也想去销售部学习学习。

谢月：是吗？那过一段时间我推荐你过去实习吧。

周详：那太好了！

谢月：怎么样，你们俩累不累？还有兴致去唱卡拉OK吗？

马克：现在吗？周详，看你的，你去我就去。

周详：反正明天是周末，也不着急睡觉。走吧，唱完歌我请大家吃夜宵。

3 Check the true statements.

☐ 1 马克做翻译的时候不太紧张。
☐ 2 周详事先帮马克准备了翻译资料。
☐ 3 马克想跟谢月学习外贸知识。
☐ 4 谢月以前在销售部工作了一年多。
☐ 5 谢月请马克和周详先去唱歌再去吃夜宵。

4 Complete the sentences.

1 马克翻译的时候怕自己翻译得 _____。
2 谢月夸奖马克和周详配合得 _____。
3 周详佩服马克中文说得 _____。
4 周详希望自己说英文能说得 _____。

New words

sǐ 死	extreme	gāocáishēng 高材生	top student
zhǔnquè 准确	accurate, precise	qǔcháng-bǔduǎn 取长补短	complement each other
lòudiào 漏掉	miss	gòngtóng 共同	jointly
kàn chulai 看出来	discern, make out	qiánbèi 前辈	senior
duōkuī 多亏	owe sth to sb	yúshì 于是	thereupon
zāogāo 糟糕	terrible	guò 过	pass time, over
qiānxū 谦虚	modest, humble	xìngzhì 兴致	mood to enjoy
kuājiǎng 夸奖	praise, compliment	fǎnzhèng 反正	since, as
pèifú 佩服	admire	yèxiāo 夜宵	nighttime snack
wàimào 外贸	foreign trade		

Lesson 1　Unit 6　81

5 Choose the best answer.

1 谢月说她没看出来马克紧张是因为 _____。
  a 她没在现场
  b 马克的表现很不错
  c 马克事先做了很多准备

2 谢月说自己后来"转到这边来了"，指的是转到 _____；她说要推荐周详"过去实习"，是指去 _____ 实习。
  a 客服部 b 销售部 c 总经理办公室

3 谢月离开销售部是因为 _____。
  a 她不喜欢销售部的同事
  b 公司安排她去客服部
  c 自己不太适合做销售

6 You are going to hear a conversation between Mark and his colleagues. Listen to the conversation and put the topics in the order you hear them.

> 问好　介绍　专业
> 女朋友　为什么转行

1 ☐　　4 ☐
2 ☐　　5 ☐
3 ☐

7 Listen again and check the true statements.

☐ 1 周乐杰不喜欢跟人打交道。
☐ 2 周乐杰比小王进公司晚。
☐ 3 马克并没有因为周乐杰的问题生气。

Now answer the questions.

4 马克是什么时候认识周乐杰的？
5 周乐杰和女朋友是怎样认识的？
6 周乐杰为什么不帮小王介绍男朋友？
7 小王为什么不让周乐杰问马克的工资？

Pronunciation and speaking

1 Listen to the sentences with 就.

1 其实我当时紧张得要死，就怕没听清楚。
2 A: 我没看出来你紧张啊。
   B: 那就好。
3 她一来公司就在客服部了。
4 她不到一年就转到这边来了。
5 看你的，你去我就去。
6 要是我的英文能说得跟你的中文一样就好了。
7 我寒假哪儿也没去，就在学校学中文。
8 你这么早就开始为找工作做准备了？
9 面试上个星期三就结束了。
10 至于火车票，选择就比较多了。
11 我一来公司就跟同事学到了很多东西。

Now match them to the explanations by writing the numbers in the table.

a 就 means "only" or "just", with an emphatic tone.	
b 就 means "then", indicating a logical connection.	
c 就 indicates earliness.	
d ……就…… means "as soon as", showing two events in quick succession.	

Now repeat the sentences.

2 Work in pairs. Talk about the most pleasant topics for small talk and make a list.

Now act out a conversation between two people meeting for the first time.

CHINESE TO GO
Reassurances

Méi kàn chulai a
没看出来啊。 — No one could tell.

Shuō de yìdiǎnr méi cuò
说的一点儿没错。 — That's absolutely right.

Kàn nǐ de
看你的。 — It's up to you.

LESSON 2

Reading and writing

1 Match the words with their meanings.

1	附件	a	forward
2	查看	b	download
3	下载	c	document
4	文件	d	attachment
5	另存为	e	save as
6	打印	f	print
7	收件箱	g	sent mails
8	已发邮件	h	inbox
9	回复	i	view
10	转发	j	reply

2 Look at the meanings of the characters and write down the meanings of the words.

邀请：invite	邀：invite
	请：invite, ask politely
寻求：_____	寻：search
	求：seek, find
祝愿：_____	祝：wish
	愿：hope, wish
查看：_____	查：review, check
	看：look, see
引导：_____	引：lead
	导：guide

Now work in pairs. Talk about the features of these words and think of similar two-character words.

3 Match the words to make phrases.

1	主持	a	合作
2	接待	b	会议
3	寻求	c	来宾
4	回顾	d	历史
5	欣赏	e	音乐

Now make three sentences using any of the above phrases.

4 Read the email Zhou Xiang sent to Mark on page 84 before the welcome dinner and complete the sentences.

周详在给马克的电子邮件里，一共告诉马克三件事情：

1 晚宴的 _____ 和 _____ 在附件里。
2 总经理致辞 _____。
3 如果需要帮助 _____。

邮箱

邮箱首页 | 设置

《返回 回复 转发 删除 举报 拒收 标记为... ▼ 移动到... ▼

晚宴文件
发件人：周详
时　间：7月10日
收件人：马克
附　件：附件1：晚宴分工及流程
　　　　附件2：总经理致辞（提纲）

马克：

　　附件是后天晚宴要用到的两份文件，一份是晚宴的分工和流程，一份是总经理致辞的提纲。总经理这次发言的时间不长，也不准备用讲稿，所以只有一个大概的内容。你还需要什么资料，马上告诉我，我来帮你找。

附件（2个）

📄 晚宴分工及流程　查看　下载　　📄 总经理致辞（提纲）　查看　下载

晚宴分工及流程

文件　编辑　格式　查看　帮助

澳大利亚考察团欢迎晚宴分工及流程

时间：2023年7月12日18:30—22:00

地点：深圳酒店一楼宴会厅

接待：客服部接待组

翻译：马克

主持：唐雨

18:30　参加晚宴的来宾开始入场，由接待组引导就座

18:45　澳大利亚代表团成员和公司主要领导就座

19:00　主持人介绍公司领导及重要来宾

19:10　总经理致欢迎辞

19:20　澳大利亚代表团致答谢辞

19:30　晚宴正式开始，中间穿插民乐演奏

22:00　晚宴结束

总经理致辞（提纲）

文件　编辑　格式　查看　帮助

晚宴欢迎辞（提纲）

一、开场白

　　"从澳大利亚远道而来的各位代表、来自深圳的业界同仁，女士们、先生们，大家晚上好！我代表亚深公司深圳分公司的全体员工，向前来我公司考察的澳大利亚代表团表示最热烈的欢迎！"

二、简单回顾亚深公司的发展历史；着重介绍深圳分公司现阶段的主要业务和国际合作伙伴。

三、介绍公司今后两年在澳大利亚发展业务、寻求合作伙伴的计划。祝愿考察团在中国的考察大有收获。

四、结束语

　　"最后，我提议：为我们的友谊和将来的合作，为在座的各位先生、女士干杯！"

New words

fùjiàn 附件	attachment	láibīn 来宾	guest	rèliè 热烈	warm, enthusiastic	zhùyuàn 祝愿	wish
wénjiàn 文件	document, file	rùchǎng 入场	enter	huígù 回顾	review, retrospect	tíyì 提议	propose
fēngōng 分工	divide the jobs	yǐndǎo 引导	guide	jiēduàn 阶段	phase	yǒuyì 友谊	friendship
liúchéng 流程	programme	jiùzuò 就座	take one's seat	yèwù 业务	business	zàizuò 在座	be present
tígāng 提纲	outline	dáxiè 答谢	express appreciation	hézuò 合作	cooperate	gānbēi 干杯	drink a toast
jiǎnggǎo 讲稿	speech notes, script	mínyuè 民乐	folk music	huǒbàn 伙伴	partner		
xiàzài 下载	download	kāichǎngbái 开场白	opening words	jīnhòu 今后	from now on		
zhǔchí 主持	host	yèjiè tóngrén 业界 同仁	colleagues	xúnqiú 寻求	seek		

5 Choose all the correct answers to the questions.

1 哪些情况需要马克做翻译？
  a 主持人介绍公司领导及重要来宾
  b 总经理致欢迎辞
  c 澳大利亚代表团致答谢辞

2 马克可能还需要什么资料？
  a 代表团成员、公司领导、重要来宾的名单
  b 公司的发展史
  c 深圳分公司现阶段的主要业务和合作伙伴

3 举办欢迎晚宴的目的是什么？
  a 祝愿考察团在中国考察顺利
  b 让来宾欣赏民乐
  c 介绍公司业务、寻求合作伙伴

6 Read the email and complete the schedule.

7 Write an outline for Ms Wang's speech for the competition. Use the speech on page 84 to help you.

《返回　回复　转发　删除　举报　拒收　移动到...▼

发件人：钱老师
时　间：7月7日
收件人：永民

永民：

　　演讲比赛定在本月最后一个星期五下午1至4点。由你负责全程带领参赛的学生，小文负责安排评委和观看比赛的师生就座，我主持比赛。比赛开始的时候王主任会简短致辞，比赛结束后也由王主任为学生发奖，最后全体拍照留念。请你做一份演讲比赛的分工及流程说明，做好以后用电子邮件发给我。有不清楚的地方可以随时给我打电话。

　　祝好！

钱老师

夏令营中文演讲比赛分工及流程

带领参赛学生	
	小文
主持	
致辞及发奖	
1:00	参赛学生、评委、观众入场
1:20	
1:30	比赛开始
3:30	
3:45	集体照
4:00	结束

Language in use

Indicating an extreme degree with ……死了

1 Look at the sentences.

	Adj. + 死了
我翻译的时候都要	紧张死了。
这两天	热死了。
我们宿舍的网速	慢死了。
坐地铁	挤死了。
到现在还没吃饭呢，	饿死我了。
搬家	累死我了。
找到这么好的工作，他一定	高兴死了。
见到她最喜欢的明星让她	兴奋死了。

Now check the correct explanations.

☐ 1 死了 is used as a degree complement to intensify the adjectives preceding it, indicating an extreme degree of the adjective in question.

☐ 2 死了 is similar to "deadly …" or "…to death" in English. For example, 冷死了 means "deadly cold".

☐ 3 Usually the adjectives preceding 死了 have negative meanings, but 死了 can also be used to show positive emotions, e.g. 高兴, 开心, 兴奋.

☐ 4 If the speaker uses 死了 to express that they personally are affected to an extreme degree, 我 can be inserted between 死 and 了.

2 Work in pairs. Talk about the following topics using 死了.

1 你喜欢冬天还是夏天？为什么？
2 你最喜欢/不喜欢的电影或小说是哪一部，为什么？
3 你在学中文的时候，觉得最困难的地方是什么？
4 最近一个月，你最开心的事情是什么？

Expressing wishes and hopes with 要是/如果……就好了

1 Look at the sentences.

（要是/如果）clause	就好了
要是我的英文能说得像你这样	就好了。
如果在伦敦也能吃到地道的西安小吃	就好了
我会游泳	就好了。
要是你没回去	就好了。
这套房子要是有三个卧室	就好了。

Now check the correct explanations.

☐ 1 要是/如果……就好了 is a structure in the subjunctive mood which expresses a wish or hope.

☐ 2 要是/如果……就好了 means "It would be great, if only …".

☐ 3 要是/如果 cannot be omitted.

2 Complete the conversations.

1 A：没想到今天会堵车堵得这么厉害。我们真不应该打车。
   B：是啊，要是 _____ 就好了。

2 A：这张沙发很舒服，就是太贵了！
   B：嗯，如果 _____ 就好了。

3 A：你的脚怎么了？
   B：我昨天边走路边看手机扭了脚，要是 _____ 就好了。

3 Work in pairs. Talk about something you want to invent using the following expression.

要是能发明一种 _____ 就好了，这样就可以 _____。

86　Unit 6　Lesson 2

Expressing emphasis using 可

1 Look at the sentences.

Subject	可	Verb phrase
实践经验	可	比书本上的知识重要多了。
你	可	别忘了买牛奶回来。
我家	可	没有钱换新车。
她	可	不是你以前认识的李安安了。
我	可	知道上下班时间挤地铁是什么感觉了。

Subject	可	Adj. + 了
他的狗	可	聪明了。
香港	可	好玩儿了。

Now check the correct explanations.

☐ 1 可 is used to emphasize a statement. Without 可, the meaning of the statement does not change, but the tone of the statement is weakened.

☐ 2 The emphatic 可 is a conjunction.

☐ 3 The emphatic 可 is mainly used in a colloquial context.

☐ 4 可……了 can also be employed to intensify an adjective. It is similar to 很, but its tone is slightly stronger.

2 Complete the conversations using 可.

1 A: 你有空吗，下午陪我去趟邮局吧？
  B: 不行啊，我今天 _____。

2 A: 昨天我见到小李了，他好像变了。
  B: 现在的小李 _____。

3 A: 他把房子和车都卖了，把工作也辞了，就是为了体验一次环球（around the world）旅行。
  B: _____。

Justifying an opinion or decision using 反正

1 Look at the sentences.

	反正 + justification
A: 这么晚了还去唱歌吗？	B: 去，反正明天是周末，也不着急睡觉。
A: 明天的聚会，我不太想去。	B: 那你就别去了，反正聚会也不一定有意思。
A: 要不咱们去吃披萨？	B: 行啊，反正对我来说吃什么都一样。
A: 我明天就去上海了，可能没有时间跟你见面了。	B: 没关系，反正以后还有机会呢。

Now check the correct explanations.

☐ 1 反正 as a modal adverb means "anyway" or "anyhow".

☐ 2 The clause involving 反正 indicates a reason to support the speaker's subjective attitude or judgment of a situation which usually involves options or choices.

☐ 3 反正 can only appear at the very beginning of a clause.

2 Complete the conversations with different answers.

1 A: 这件衣服很好看，不过挺贵的，你说我买不买？
  B: _____，反正你赚钱多。
  A: _____，反正我有几件类似的衣服了。

2 A: 我星期五晚上要不要做作业呢？
  B: 星期五晚上休息休息吧，反正 _____。
  A: 反正 _____，早点儿做完，就轻松啦。

▶ Turn to page 188 for grammar reference.

Lesson 2　Unit 6　87

LESSON 3

Communication activity

1. Work in groups of three. Plan an event for a group of high school principals from China visiting your university next week.

   • **Student A:** You are the vice principal who will host the event. Write an outline of a welcome speech.

   • **Student B:** You are the assistant to the vice principal. Write an email calling for a meeting to discuss the event.

   • **Student C:** You are a teacher who used to live in China. Prepare the itinerary for the visitors.

   Now discuss and polish your works.

2. Present the email, the itinerary and the speech outline to the class and vote for the best one.

> Turn to pages 173 and 179 for more speaking practice.

Review and practice

1. Choose the correct words to complete the sentences.

   1 开会的时候我紧张死了,就 _____ 总经理对我的报告不满意。
   a 不怕 b 怕

   2 不是所有的人都 _____ 做销售工作。
   a 适合 b 合适

   3 你太 _____ 了,就算没有我的帮助,你也一定能做得很好。
   a 骄傲 b 谦虚

   4 你是学销售的,他是学外贸的,你们俩 _____ 可以互相学习学习。
   a 正好 b 幸好

   5 我爸 _____ 好的时候就会给我们表演几段京剧。
   a 兴趣 b 兴致

Cultural corner

Humility

The Chinese have always placed great importance on humility, or being humble, and it has been considered to be a characteristic of the Chinese for many centuries. Confucius says, "where there are three men walking together, one of them must be qualified to be my teacher". Laozi also attaches great importance to humility, the common metaphor he uses is that of water, which runs deep and low but gives strength to others in the way it conforms to the laws of nature.

Even today it's considered impolite to boast, so it's still common to respond to a compliment or praise with a self-deprecating response. If you commend your host on the wonderful dinner you've been served, the reply might be "No, it's nothing". Even someone who has all the trappings of wealth and power would claim their business isn't doing very well, in order to show humility.

2 Complete the passage with the words in the box.

> 当时　现在　刚来　后来　未来
> 两年后　第一年　过段时间

我 _____ 的时候也是什么都不懂，于是就一边向公司的前辈学习，一边努力工作。_____ 想一想，自己在公司的 _____ 真是特别辛苦，_____ 几乎每个周末都在加班，好像有做不完的工作。_____ 自己通过实践慢慢地熟悉了业务，经验也多了，_____ 我当上了客服部的经理。我打算 _____ 去读MBA，我相信多学点儿东西一定会对我 _____ 的发展有很大的帮助。

3 Read the thank-you speech and put the parts into the correct order.

____ a 在开场白中向对方表示感谢
____ b 再次感谢并祝愿对方
____ c 提及对方的致辞
____ d 向大家问好
____ e 介绍自己方面的情况并表达对对方的回应

Now check the true statements.

☐ 1 考察团还不清楚亚深公司的情况。
☐ 2 考察团里的代表都是从事玩具制造业的。
☐ 3 考察团认为中国经济发展很快、市场潜力很大。
☐ 4 考察团对他们这次在中国的考察很有信心。

澳大利亚代表团的答谢辞

由马克翻译整理

尊敬的李总经理、尊敬的各位来宾：

非常感谢亚深公司深圳分公司为我们举办这一欢迎宴会，我代表我们澳大利亚考察团的全体同仁对贵公司热情的款待和周到的安排表示衷心的感谢。

通过李总经理的介绍，我们了解到了贵公司的发展历史、现阶段的主要业务以及国际合作伙伴的情况，特别是贵公司希望在澳大利亚寻求合作伙伴的强烈愿望。

我们这个考察团的代表来自跟外贸相关的多个行业，包括从玩具制造到进出口运输的30多家公司。随着中国经济的快速发展，我们越来越感觉到中国市场的巨大潜力以及与中国公司合作的重要性。我们都希望能借此次考察之机探讨与中国公司——特别是像亚深公司这样的大公司——合作的可能性。虽然我们的中国之行才刚刚开始，但是我们相信这次考察一定会有巨大的收获。

最后，我想再次感谢李总经理为我们安排的晚宴，也祝愿亚深公司今后有更大的发展。

谢谢！

代表团团长　埃里克

4 Write a complete welcome speech for the communication activity based on the outline your group has worked out or the following outline.

- 开场白
- 你们学校的历史
- 学校以前跟中国的合作情况以及将来的计划
- 结束语

Vocabulary review

Fill in the blanks.

答谢	dáxiè	v.	express appreciation		谦虚	qiānxū	adj.	modest, humble
多亏	duōkuī	v.	owe sth to sb		前辈	qiánbèi	n.	senior
___	fǎnzhèng	adv.	since, as		取长补短	qǔcháng-bǔduǎn		complement each other
分工	fēngōng	v.	divide the jobs		热烈	rèliè	adj.	warm, enthusiastic
附件	fùjiàn	n.	attachment		入场	rùchǎng	v.	enter
___	gānbēi	v.	drink a toast			sǐ	adj.	extreme
高材生	gāocáishēng	n.	top student		提纲	tígāng	n.	outline
共同	gòngtóng	adv.	___		提议	tíyì	v.	___
过	guò	v.	___		外贸	wàimào	n.	foreign trade
合作	hézuò	v.	cooperate			wénjiàn	n.	document, file
回顾	huígù	v.	review, retrospect		下载	xiàzài	v.	___
伙伴	huǒbàn	n.	___		兴致	xìngzhì	n.	mood to enjoy
讲稿	jiǎnggǎo	n.	speech notes, script		寻求	xúnqiú	v.	seek
阶段	jiēduàn	n.	phase		业界同仁	yèjiè tóngrén		colleagues
今后	jīnhòu	n.	___		业务	yèwù	n.	business
就座	jiùzuò	v.	take one's seat		夜宵	yèxiāo	n.	nighttime snack
开场白	kāichǎngbái	n.	opening words		引导	yǐndǎo	v.	guide
看出来	kàn chulai		discern, make out			yǒuyì	n.	friendship
夸奖	kuājiǎng	v.	___		于是	yúshì	conj.	___
来宾	láibīn	n.	guest		在座	zàizuò	v.	be present
流程	liúchéng	n.	programme		糟糕	zāogāo	adj.	terrible
漏掉	lòudiào		miss		主持	zhǔchí	v.	host
民乐	mínyuè	n.	folk music		祝愿	zhùyuàn	v.	wish
佩服	pèifú	v.	admire		___	zhǔnquè	adj.	accurate, precise

UNIT 7

Gùkè yǒngyuǎn shì duì de
顾客 永远 是 对 的!

The customer is always right!

LESSON 1

Vocabulary and listening

1 Look at the words to describe the service in a shop. Which are the most important to you?

> 态度　诚恳　热情　折扣
> 送货时间　讲信用　道歉

2 Match the words to make phrases.

1 取得	a 上司
2 处理	b 问题
3 请示	c 谅解

4 找	d 信用
5 接	e 电话
6 讲	f 借口

3 Mark has got some problems at work. Listen to the conversation and answer the questions.

1 马克碰到了什么问题？
2 谢月给了马克什么建议？
3 马克下一步应该怎么办？

4 Check the true statements.

☐ 1 马克的公司不讲信用，要取消客户的订单。
☐ 2 工厂不能按时完成订单是因为工人不够。
☐ 3 马克向客户提出了解决办法。
☐ 4 谢月认为这全是马克的责任。
☐ 5 谢月认为只要态度诚恳地向客户道歉，问题就一定能解决。

谢月：马克，办公室就剩你了。你怎么还不走，打算加班吗？

马克：唉，加班也不一定能解决问题啊。

谢月：愿意和我说说吗？

马克：是这样的，昨天我接到工厂的电话，说有个订单无法按时完成。我直接给客户发邮件说了这个情况，没想到他们非常生气，批评我们不讲信用，还说要取消订单。我是不是闯祸了？

谢月：别着急，先冷静一下。究竟是什么原因导致工厂不能按时完成订单？

马克：据说是因为最近在劳务市场上请不到合格的工人。

谢月：这倒是有可能。那你在邮件中有没有提出什么解决办法？

马克：没有，我只是解释了一下情况。

谢月：这也不能全怪你，处理这种问题的确需要经验。如果我是客户，我会认为你不过是在找借口罢了。

马克：那我现在该怎么办呢？

谢月："顾客永远是对的"，你不仅要态度诚恳地向客户道歉，还要提出解决办法，比如缩短送货时间或者给客户一些折扣等等。但是，具体怎么处理你应该请示唐经理。记住，以后遇到类似的问题，一定要马上请示你的上司。

马克：太谢谢你了……你觉得唐经理会原谅我吗？

谢月：别担心了，先下班吧。

New words

Pinyin	Hanzi	English
shèng	剩	remain, be left over
jiābān	加班	work overtime
jiějué	解决	solve
gōngchǎng	工厂	factory
dìngdān	订单	order
wúfǎ	无法	be unable
pīpíng	批评	criticize
jiǎng xìnyòng	讲信用	keep one's word
chuǎnghuò	闯祸	get into trouble
lěngjìng	冷静	calm
jiūjìng	究竟	on earth, exactly
dǎozhì	导致	cause
láowù	劳务	(labour) services
shìchǎng	市场	market
qǐng	请	hire
hégé	合格	qualified
gōngrén	工人	worker
guài	怪	blame
búguò	不过……	just, only
bàle	罢了	
jièkǒu	借口	excuse
gùkè	顾客	customer
yǒngyuǎn	永远	forever
chéngkěn	诚恳	sincere
dàoqiàn	道歉	apologize
suōduǎn	缩短	shorten
sòng huò	送货	deliver goods
qǐngshì	请示	ask for instructions
lèisì	类似	similar (to)
shàngsi	上司	superior
yuánliàng	原谅	forgive

Lesson 1 Unit 7 93

5 Put the events in the order they took place.

___ a 客户非常生气
___ b 马克接到工厂的电话
___ c 劳务市场工人不足
___ d 马克向谢月请教
___ e 马克给客户发邮件
___ f 工厂发现无法按时完成订单

6 You are going to hear a conversation between Mark and Zhou Xiang about their internship. Predict what their dislikes are in the work.

☐ 1 常常加班　　☐ 6 成就感很小
☐ 2 常常出差　　☐ 7 老板难相处
☐ 3 没有意思　　☐ 8 同事难相处
☐ 4 压力很大　　☐ 9 客户难沟通
☐ 5 麻烦很多　　☐ 10 实习工资低

Now listen to the conversation and check your answers.

7 Listen again and check the true statements.

☐ 1 马克需要继续处理上次订单的事情。
☐ 2 马克在帮加拿大客户订机票和酒店。
☐ 3 如果客户早一点儿跟马克的公司联系，机票就不会这么难订了。
☐ 4 马克今天下午花了三四个小时忙订机票的事情。
☐ 5 下班的时候，马克还没订好客户的机票。

Pronunciation and speaking

1 Listen to the sentences showing care or expressing reassurance.

1 出什么事了？愿意跟我说说吗？
2 别着急，先冷静一下。
3 如果我是你的话，可能也会这么处理的。
4 这件事也不能都怪你。
5 别担心，问题肯定会解决的。

Now repeat the sentences.

2 Choose the correct sentences to complete the conversations.

1 A: 怎么办，订单出了问题，可是客户那边的电话总是打不通！
　 B: _____ 我们一起想想还有没有别的办法。
2 A: _____
　 B: 我不小心把应该发给经理的信发给客户了。
3 A: 我想先请示经理再给客户答复，可是经理突然出差了，这两天联系不到他。现在客户那边非常着急。
　 B: _____

3 Work in pairs. Talk about something that has been bothering you recently. Reassure each other and offer some suggestions.

我同屋总是听很吵的音乐，……

CHINESE TO GO

Consolations

| Yuànyì gēn wǒ shuōshuo ma | Do you want to talk |
| 愿意 跟 我 说说 吗？ | about it with me? |

| Zhè dàoshì yǒu kěnéng | |
| 这 倒是 有 可能。 | That's quite possible. |

| Bié zháojí　xiān lěngjìng yíxià | Relax and calm |
| 别 着急，先 冷静 一下。 | down first. |

LESSON | 2

Reading and writing

1 Work in pairs. Compare handwritten letters with emails and complete the table.

	手写的信	电子邮件
好处		
坏处		

2 Match the words to make phrases.

1 回不完的　　a 功课
2 做不完的　　b 资料
3 打不完的　　c 邮件
4 查不完的　　d 电话

3 Look at the meanings of the words and complete the sentences.

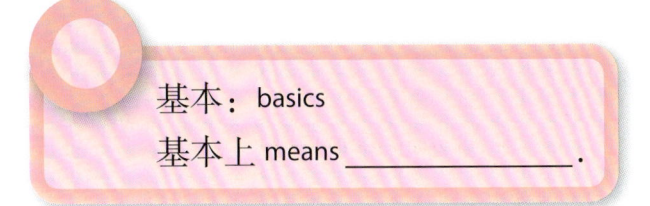

基本：basics
基本上 means _____.

随便：random; with no limit on scope or amount
随时 means _____.

活动：exercise
活力 means _____.

4 Read the letter on page 96 and complete the sentences.

马克在信中说到哪些事情？

1 为什么要 _____。
2 _____ 很忙碌。
3 每天都在 _____。
4 公司的领导和同事 _____。
5 业余时间 _____。
6 _____ 照片。
7 问一问 _____。

Lesson 2　Unit 7　95

王玉：

　　你好！

　　现在大家都习惯发邮件和上网聊天，基本上不写信了，可我还是觉得手写信有意思，还可以练练字。

　　我在深圳的公司已经实习一个多月了。上班跟上学的感觉很不一样。我每天早出晚归，有查不完的资料、回不完的邮件、打不完的电话，同事们还经常来问我跟英语和文化差异有关的问题。下班后脑子也停不下来，总是很兴奋！可我觉得自己变聪明了，因为每天的忙碌给了我很多学习新东西的机会。

　　比如，上周我第一次出差，陪客户参观工厂。从订酒店、订机票、安排行程到翻译，一切都要自己来。尽管有点儿手忙脚乱，可是做这些事情很锻炼我的能力。

　　我觉得自己非常幸运，公司里的领导和同事都对我特别好，我有什么问题都可以随时请教他们。就在昨天，因为经验不足，我在工作中犯了一个不小的错误，而领导不但没有批评我，还给了我很好的建议，这让我特别感动。我真希望毕业以后能继续在这家公司工作。

　　业余时间我经常跟同事去KTV，我现在已经会唱好几首中文歌了！等你回来，我们一起去唱歌吧！

　　随信寄去一张我自己拍的照片，是深圳的街景。我非常喜欢这个城市，因为它充满了活力。

　　你在美国怎么样？是不是交了很多新朋友？有空的时候也给我写写信吧。

　　祝一切顺利，心想事成！

　　　　　　　　　　　你的朋友：马克

　　　　　　　　　　　7月24日于深圳

New words

xìn 信	letter	
shǒuxiě 手写	write by hand	
nǎozi 脑子	brain	
xīngfèn 兴奋	excited	
cōngmíng 聪明	smart	
mánglù 忙碌	busy	
yíqiè 一切	everything	
zìjǐ lái 自己 来	do by oneself	
shǒumáng-jiǎoluàn 手忙脚乱	be in a rush	
xìngyùn 幸运	lucky	
suíshí 随时	at any time	
qǐngjiào 请教	ask for advice	
bùzú 不足	insufficient	
fàn 犯	commit (error, crime)	
cuòwù 错误	mistake, error	
gǎndòng 感动	be touched	
jì 寄	mail	
chōngmǎn 充满	be filled with	
huólì 活力	energy	
xīnxiǎng-shìchéng 心想事成	all wishes come true	

96　Unit 7　Lesson 2

5 Choose all the correct answers to the questions.

1 马克为什么要手写这封信？
  a 他手机坏了。
  b 他觉得挺有意思的。
  c 他想练练写字。

2 马克为什么说"下班后脑子也停不下来"？
  a 一下班马克就很兴奋。
  b 下班后他可能还在想工作上的事情。
  c 下班以后他还要学中文。

3 上周马克做了什么事情？
  a 出差
  b 订酒店、订机票、安排行程
  c 翻译

4 马克出了错，他的上司是怎样处理的？
  a 给他建议
  b 批评他
  c 不让他继续工作

6 Choose four words from the box to describe Mark's feelings.

忙碌　做不完　停不下来　兴奋
充实　手忙脚乱　很锻炼人
幸运　感动　充满　活力

马克已经实习一个多月了，他的感受特别多。……

7 Read Mark's journal and check the true statements.

问题解决了

……

昨天跟谢月谈了以后，虽然还是非常担心，但是知道应该怎么做了，所以今天一到公司就马上向唐经理请示具体的处理办法。我很诚恳地告诉唐经理这件事情是由于我经验不足导致了客户的不满。唐经理听了以后，建议我马上给客户打电话，告诉他们我们公司会尽量缩短送货时间，争取在十月底以前将货品送到。我向客户道了歉，并提出这个解决办法。他们听了以后很满意。这让我既高兴又感动，我没想到唐经理和客户最后都原谅了我。

☐ 1 跟谢月的谈话让马克明白了自己应该怎么做。
☐ 2 向经理汇报时，马克承认了自己的错误。
☐ 3 客户并不接受缩短送货时间的解决办法。
☐ 4 唐经理原谅了马克，但客户不愿意原谅他。

8 Write a letter to your best friend about a difficulty you have encountered. Include:

• 问题是什么
• 你向谁求助了
• 问题是否解决了
• 你的感受如何

Lesson 2　Unit 7　97

Language in use

Expressing "how come" with 怎么

1 Look at the sentences.

你怎么还没走？打算加班吗？
他的女朋友怎么没来？
那个订单不是已经确认过了吗？怎么还有问题？
今年夏天的天气怎么这么奇怪？
他怎么那么容易忘事儿？

Now check the correct explanations.

☐ 1 怎么 is a question word used to ask for a reason or explanation.

☐ 2 怎么 has a similar tone and connotation to "how come" in English. It not only asks "why", but also expresses a tone of surprise.

☐ 3 怎么 always appears at the beginning of a sentence.

2 Ask questions about the following scenarios using 怎么.

1 在去北京的飞机上你突然看见了你小时候的朋友。
2 下午三点了，你发现你的室友还没吃午饭。
3 上课已经十分钟了，可是班里一半的同学还没到。
4 在你最喜欢的咖啡店里，你点了你每天都喝的咖啡，可是店员告诉你咖啡涨价了。

Emphasizing an inquiry with 到底/究竟

1 Look at the sentences.

Subject	到底/究竟 + question forms
	究竟是什么原因导致工厂不能按时完成订单？
那我现在	到底应该怎么办呢？
你	到底能不能来开会？
老板，你	到底卖不卖？
我们	到底要请张教授还是请王教授？
这种病毒（virus）	究竟是从猴子身上来的还是从人身上来的？

Now check the correct explanations.

☐ 1 到底 and 究竟 express an incredulity or intensity similar to the phrase "on earth". They are adverbs used to emphasize the question or to press the other speaker to give an answer or tell the truth.

☐ 2 到底 and 究竟 emphasize three question forms: questions beginning with wh-words; questions posed by a verb; and questions which offer an "either ... or ..." alternative.

☐ 3 到底 and 究竟 cannot be used in an embedded question.

☐ 4 究竟 is more formal than 到底.

2 Work in pairs. Talk about the discrepancies between the two messages about the same event using 到底.

大家好：
　　这个星期五我们公司要在明珠酒店为美国纽约来的客户举办一个欢迎宴会。欢迎大家都来参加。有问题请跟客服部的王风联系。
　　　　　　　　　　　赵成功（经理）

大家好：
　　这个星期六我们公司要在东方酒店为美国纽约来的客户举办一个欢迎宴会。欢迎大家都来参加。如果有问题，请联系客服部的王风。
　　　　　　　　　　　张光希（总经理）

98　Unit 7　Lesson 2

Minimizing a situation with 不过/只不过/只+是……（罢了）

1 Look at the sentences.

	不过/只不过/只+是		（罢了）	
你的这些解释	不过是	在找借口	罢了。	
她	只不过是	个孩子，		当然会犯错误。
他	只不过（是）	开个玩笑	罢了，	你怎么那么生气？
你快来吧，	只是	一顿饭	罢了，	花不了你太多时间。

Now check the correct explanations.

☐ 1 不过/只不过/只+是……（罢了）is a structure used to minimize or downplay the thing, the situation, or the number it modifies.

☐ 2 不过/只不过/只 means "merely".

☐ 3 罢了 is a modal particle expressing a minimizing tone.

☐ 4 罢了 should always appear at the end of the clause; it cannot be omitted.

2 Complete the conversation using 不过/只不过/只+是……（罢了）and the given words.

A: 你 _____，怎么这么多天不去上课呢？（跟……分手）

B: 你又没有女朋友，你懂什么。

A: 可是我能明白你的感受。其实我早就知道她不喜欢你了，我没告诉你，_____。（难过）

B: 我总是想着我们在一起时的那些快乐的事情。

A: 你会把她忘了的，_____。（需要）

Indicating "not only ..., but also ..." with 不但/不只/不仅/不光……而且/还/也……

1 Look at the sentences.

Subject	不但/不只/不仅/不光	而且/还/也
老板	不但没有批评我，	还给了我很好的建议。
他	不但听了我的烦恼，	而且给我出了很多主意。
你	不光要态度诚恳地跟客户道歉，	还要商量解决办法。
他的中文	不但很流利，	而且很地道。
那家公司	不仅工作环境很好，	而且为员工提供了非常好的待遇。

Now check the correct explanations.

☐ 1 不但……而且…… is the most commonly used structure to express "not only …, but also …".

☐ 2 There are some other structures which can be used to express the same meaning. 不但 can be replaced with 不仅/不只/不光; 而且 can be replaced with 还/也.

☐ 3 Besides adjectives and verb phrases, noun phrases can also follow 不但/不只/不仅/不光 and 而且/还/也. Therefore, a sentence like 他会说不但法文，而且中文 is acceptable.

2 Work in pairs. Talk about the following topics using 不但/不只/不仅/不光……而且/还/也……。

1 如果你是公司经理，你想招什么样的职员？
2 如果你是公司的员工，你想要什么样的上司？

▶ Turn to page 189 for grammar reference.

LESSON 3

Communication activity

1 Write a letter to a customer service representative about a recent purchase. Complain about one or more of the following:

- quality of the product;
- problems with delivery;
- poor after-sales services.

2 Work in pairs. In turns, act out a telephone conversation between the salesperson and the customer about how to solve the problem.

> Turn to pages 174 and 180 for more speaking practice.

Review and practice

1 Choose the correct words to complete the sentences.

1 他对咖啡太有研究了，一说到咖啡他就_____。
   a 不停下来   b 停不下来   c 不能停

2 这份实习工作虽然非常辛苦，每天都从早忙到晚，但是让我感到特别_____。
   a 充满   b 丰富   c 充实

3 听到他唱那首歌，我一下子就被_____了。
   a 感动   b 感觉   c 感受

4 从看房子、刷墙、买家具到搬家，_____都要自己来。
   a 全体   b 任何   c 一切

5 这样做_____不能解决问题，_____会带来更多麻烦。
   a 不是……而是……
   b 不但……而且……
   c 不只……连……

Cultural corner

The square and the circle

Of all geometric shapes, the square (方) and the circle (圆) are especially prominent in Chinese culture. Ancient Chinese people believed that the sky was round, and the earth was square, so the word 方圆 can refer to "neighbourhood" or "vicinity". The figurative meaning of the square is often associated with rule, principle and appropriateness, as the word 方正 (upright and righteous) indicates. The round shape is related to perfection or fulfilment. For example, 圆满 indicates that something is satisfactory, 圆梦 means a dream has been fulfilled, and 团圆 refers to a reunion of family or friends. The two shapes illustrate the complexity of Chinese social life: on the one hand, Chinese culture stresses integrity and proper behaviour, but on the other hand, it also emphasizes the importance of flexibility and avoiding conflict in social interaction (see the meaning of 圆通).

2 Complete the sentences with the words in the box.

批评　道歉　棘手　谅解　市场
合格　无法　导致　讲信用

1 家庭生活中最_____的问题可能就是孩子的教育。
2 那家旅行社也太不_____了，已经定好的行程，怎么能随便改变呢？
3 他说他永远_____原谅出卖朋友的人。
4 他的新书受到了来自周围人的各种各样的_____。
5 不管她怎么努力，都无法取得女儿的_____。
6 他最喜欢说："如果_____有用，还要警察做什么？"
7 这些不_____的产品，一件都不能进入_____。
8 过度开发和过度放牧_____草原沙化越来越严重。

3 Complete the passage with the words in the box.

不足　充实　分享　实在
手忙脚乱　错误　继续　随时
感动　很锻炼人　忙碌

马克在写给王玉的信中_____了很多他实习以后的感受。他觉得上班和上学的感觉_____是不一样。工作让他既_____又_____：一方面每天都有做不完的事情，一方面每天都在学习新东西。虽然有的时候他会_____，可是他觉得这些工作_____。不管是老板还是同事都对马克很好，他可以_____向他们请教。尽管他由于工作经验_____犯了_____，可是上司并没有批评他，这让他非常_____。他希望毕业以后还能_____在这家公司工作。

4 Read the email and check the true statements.

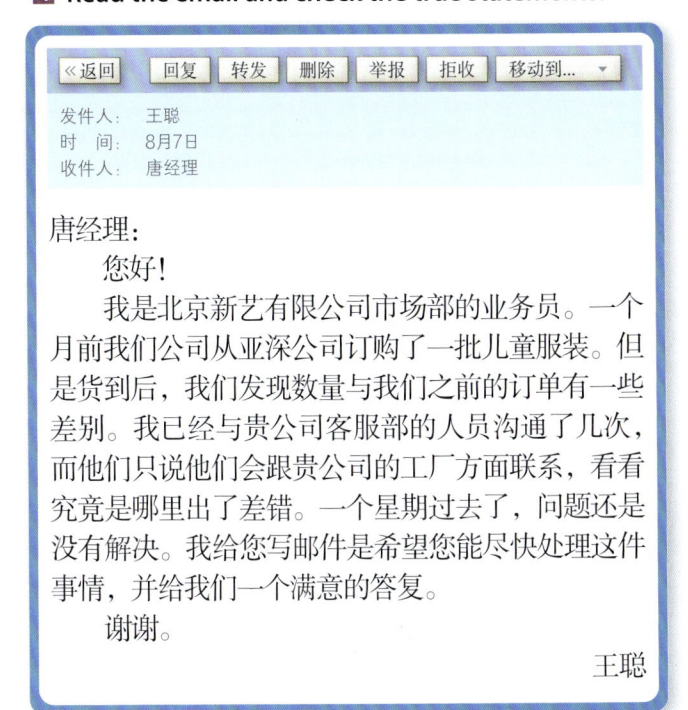

发件人：王聪
时间：8月7日
收件人：唐经理

唐经理：
　　您好！
　　我是北京新艺有限公司市场部的业务员。一个月前我们公司从亚深公司订购了一批儿童服装。但是货到后，我们发现数量与我们之前的订单有一些差别。我已经与贵公司客服部的人员沟通了几次，而他们只说他们会跟贵公司的工厂方面联系，看看究竟是哪里出了差错。一个星期过去了，问题还是没有解决。我给您写邮件是希望您能尽快处理这件事情，并给我们一个满意的答复。
　　谢谢。
　　　　　　　　　　　　　　王聪

☐ 1 新艺公司从亚深公司订购的货物是儿童玩具。
☐ 2 亚深公司发给新艺公司的货物数量不对。
☐ 3 亚深公司的客服部还没找到出问题的原因。
☐ 4 王聪给唐经理写信是因为他觉得亚深公司客服部处理问题的速度太慢了。

Now match the words with their meanings.

1 业务员	a batch
2 批	b mistake
3 数量	c reply
4 差错	d salesman
5 答复	e amount

5 Write an email to your friend. Include:

• 一件很有趣的事情
• 一段不开心的经历
• 问候这位朋友最近的情况

Vocabulary review
Fill in the blanks.

汉字	拼音	词性	英文
不过……罢了	búguò…bàle		just, only
不足	bùzú	adj.	insufficient
诚恳	chéngkěn	adj.	sincere
充满	chōngmǎn	v.	_____
闯祸	chuǎnghuò	v.	get into trouble
____	cōngmíng	adj.	smart
错误	cuòwù	n.	mistake, error
导致	dǎozhì	v.	cause
道歉	dàoqiàn	v.	_____
订单	dìngdān	n.	order
犯	fàn	v.	commit (error, crime)
感动	gǎndòng	adj.	be touched
工厂	gōngchǎng	n.	_____
____	gōngrén	n.	worker
顾客	gùkè	n.	customer
____	guài	v.	blame
合格	hégé	adj.	_____
活力	huólì	n.	energy
____	jì	v.	mail
加班	jiābān	v.	_____
讲信用	jiǎng xìnyòng		keep one's word
解决	jiějué	v.	solve
借口	jièkǒu	n.	excuse
究竟	jiūjìng	adv.	on earth, exactly
劳务	láowù	n.	(labour) services

汉字	拼音	词性	英文
类似	lèisì	v.	similar (to)
冷静	lěngjìng	adj.	calm
忙碌	mánglù	adj.	busy
脑子	nǎozi	n.	brain
批评	pīpíng	v.	criticize
____	qǐng	v.	hire
请教	qǐngjiào	v.	ask for advice
请示	qǐngshì	v.	ask for instructions
上司	shàngsi	n.	superior
剩	shèng	v.	_____
市场	shìchǎng	n.	market
手忙脚乱	shǒumáng-jiǎoluàn		be in a rush
手写	shǒuxiě	v.	_____
送货	sòng huò		deliver goods
____	suíshí	adv.	at any time
缩短	suōduǎn	v.	shorten
无法	wúfǎ	v.	be unable
心想事成	xīnxiǎng-shìchéng		all wishes come true
信	xìn	n.	letter
兴奋	xīngfèn	adj.	_____
幸运	xìngyùn	adj.	lucky
一切	yíqiè	pron.	everything
永远	yǒngyuǎn	adv.	_____
原谅	yuánliàng	v.	forgive
自己来	zìjǐ lái		do by oneself

102　Unit 7　Vocabulary

UNIT 8

Yúnnán zhēn shì gè hǎo difang
云南真是个好地方!

Yunnan is an amazing place!

LESSON 1

Vocabulary and listening

1 Work in pairs. Talk about what a typical office job is like.

> 白领　典型　收入
> 享受　体面　压力

Now ask and answer the questions.

1 在现代社会中，为什么人们都觉得压力很大？
2 只有在度假或旅游时才能"享受生活"吗？

2 Work out the meanings of the idioms.

> 如：like, as
> 画：painting, picture
>
> 风景如画：＿＿＿＿＿＿

> 名：fame,
> 虚：vain, fake
> 传：spread
>
> 名不虚传：＿＿＿＿＿＿

3 Steve meets Da Liu during his holiday in Yunnan. Listen to the conversation and answer the questions.

1 大刘是本地人吗？他以前是做什么的？
2 史蒂夫喜欢不喜欢云南？
3 史蒂夫和大刘接下来会做什么？

史蒂夫：你好，我叫史蒂夫，你怎么称呼？

大刘：叫我大刘吧。你的中文真棒！是第一次来丽江吗？

史蒂夫：谢谢，大刘，我是第一次来云南，昨天刚从昆明到了丽江。云南真是个好地方！你是本地人吗？能住在这里真是再幸福不过了！

大刘：我不是本地人。七年前我来旅游，来了就不想走了。后来就辞了职，搬到丽江来了。

史蒂夫：那你过去是做什么的？

大刘：我以前在上海工作，是个典型的白领。工作看着体面，其实压力大得不得了，常常失眠。我那时总怀疑这是不是自己想要的生活。来丽江旅游的时候，忽然体会到了享受生活的感觉……我问自己，为什么不能换一种生活方式呢？我实在是太讨厌原来的生活了。

史蒂夫：嗯，我采访过一个老师，她也是放弃了北京的生活，去内蒙古教书。

大刘：原来你是记者啊，是来采访的吗？

史蒂夫：我是来度假的。早就听说云南风景如画，是摄影爱好者

…的天堂,果然名不虚传。

大刘：你觉得丽江怎么样？

史蒂夫：丽江是个很美的小城,不过商业化的程度比我想象中的高。下一步去哪儿我还没想好,你有什么建议吗？

大刘：你算是问对人啦！你等着,我去拿张地图,然后跟你说说云南你必须去、不去会后悔的地方。

史蒂夫：太好了,一会儿请你喝啤酒！

4 Check the true statements.

☐ 1 史蒂夫以前没来过云南。
☐ 2 大刘在丽江已经住了七年了。
☐ 3 史蒂夫曾经采访过一个老师。
☐ 4 史蒂夫是来丽江采访的。
☐ 5 史蒂夫为云南之行做了很全面的计划。

5 Choose all the correct answers to the questions.

1 大刘对以前的工作有什么不满意？
  a 不体面   b 薪水不高   c 压力大
2 史蒂夫对丽江的印象怎么样？
  a 他觉得丽江很美。
  b 他没想到丽江的商业化程度这么高。
  c 他想立刻离开丽江。

New words

Lìjiāng 丽江	Lijiang	shīmián 失眠	suffer from insomnia	yuánlái 原来	former; as it turns out
Yúnnán 云南	Yunnan Province	huáiyí 怀疑	doubt, suspect	fàngqì 放弃	give up
Kūnmíng 昆明	Kunming	hūrán 忽然	all of a sudden	fēngjǐng rú huà 风景如画	picturesque landscape
cízhí 辞职	resign	tǐhuì 体会	experience	shèyǐng 摄影	take a photograph
diǎnxíng 典型	typical	xiǎngshòu 享受	enjoy	àihàozhě 爱好者	buff, enthusiast
báilǐng 白领	white-collar worker	shízài 实在	indeed, really	tiāntáng 天堂	heaven
tǐmiàn 体面	decent, respectable	tǎoyàn 讨厌	dislike, loathe	guǒrán 果然	sure enough
míngbùxūchuán 名不虚传	live up to one's name	chéngdù 程度	degree	xiǎngxiàng 想象	imagine
bìxū 必须	must	hòuhuǐ 后悔	regret	píjiǔ 啤酒	beer

6 Draw a timeline of Da Liu's life noting the key events that have changed it.

过去 → 七年前 → 现在

7 Steve is talking to another tourist in Lijiang. Predict what questions Steve will ask.

Now listen to the conversation, write down the three questions and check the reasons why they are asked.

1 _____
2 _____
3 _____

☐ a 这是游客之间常问的一个问题。
☐ b 史蒂夫想知道这个游客有多长时间的假期。
☐ c 史蒂夫觉得丽江并不清静。
☐ d 史蒂夫觉得这个游客只是路过这里。
☐ e 史蒂夫想知道这个游客对商业化和传统文化的关系的看法。
☐ f 史蒂夫对商业化影响的态度不太乐观。

8 Listen again and check the true statements.

☐ 1 这里的吵闹跟大城市一样。
☐ 2 这是一个令人放松的地方。
☐ 3 这座城市有超过五百年的历史。
☐ 4 这里有重视商业发展的传统。
☐ 5 由于商业化程度太高，这里的传统和文化已经被严重破坏了。
☐ 6 这里的自然环境将来一定会受到破坏。

Pronunciation and speaking

1 Listen to the sentences. Notice how the tone of each sentence is changed by the underlined word.

1 工作看着体面，<u>其实</u>压力大得不得了。
2 我<u>忽然</u>体会到了享受生活的感觉。
3 我<u>实在</u>是太讨厌原来的生活了。
4 <u>原来</u>你是记者啊，是来采访的吗？
5 听说这里风景如画，<u>果然</u>名不虚传。

Now repeat the sentences.

2 Choose the correct underlined words from Activity 1 and put them in the right places to complete the sentences.

1 a 他看起来 b 像大学刚毕业，c 已经 d 工作五年了。
2 a 他们说你 b 没去上课，c 你 d 在宿舍里啊。
3 a 早上 b 出门天气还好好的，c 就 d 开始下雨了。
4 a 这些衣服我 b 能明天再洗吗？c 我现在 d 累了。
5 a 到了香港 b 我 c 才明白，d "的士"就是出租车啊。

3 Work in pairs. Act out a conversation between two tourists meeting at a scenic spot that you are familiar with. Include the following topics:

假期　风景　游客对环境的影响

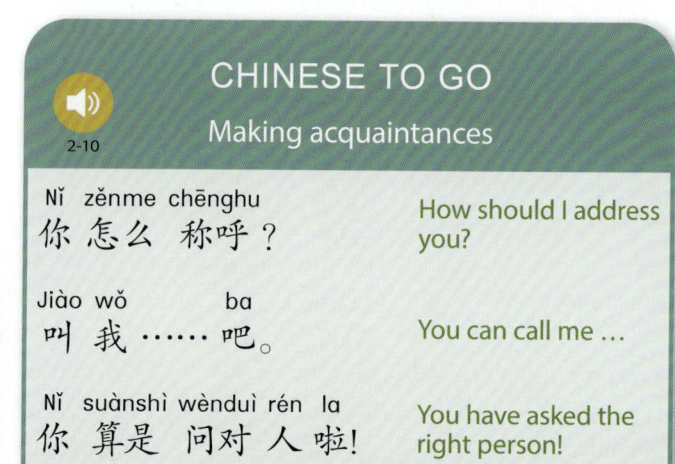

CHINESE TO GO
Making acquaintances

Nǐ zěnme chēnghu	How should I address you?
你 怎么 称呼？	
Jiào wǒ ...... ba	You can call me ...
叫 我 …… 吧。	
Nǐ suànshì wènduì rén la	You have asked the right person!
你 算是 问对 人 啦！	

106　Unit 8　Lesson 1

LESSON | 2

Reading and writing

1 Number the words according to the strength of the tone (1 is the weakest, 4 is the strongest).

__十分   __挺   __最   __有点儿

Now complete the sentences.

a _____ 挺危险。
b _____ 十分危险。
c _____ 最危险。
d _____ 有点儿危险。

2 Work in pairs. Talk about your favourite holiday destinations for different seasons.

You can use the words in the box to help you.

| 阳光 | 懒 | 最爱 |
| 季节 | 停止 | 散步 |

3 Look at the meanings of the words and complete the sentences.

傣族：Dai ethnic group   傣家菜 means _____.

孔雀：peacock
舞蹈：dance   孔雀舞 means _____.

神：god, deity, divine   神山 means _____.

4 Read the postcards on page 108 and complete the table.

史蒂夫的明信片

从哪里	寄给谁	信息
	永民	春城，石林，_____
丽江		发呆，慢生活
	阿曼达	藏族，_____
		骑马，雨崩村，_____

Lesson 2   Unit 8   107

永民：
　　我现在在云南昆明。昆明无论什么季节都温暖如春，所以也叫"春城"。图片上就是著名的"石林"。这里好吃的东西特别多，我的最爱是傣家菜。傣族是云南的一个民族，他们的孔雀舞非常美。傣族还有一种乐器叫"葫芦丝"，声音很有特点，你一定会喜欢！

史蒂夫
于云南昆明

王玉：
　　你在美国一切都好吗？我现在在云南丽江，一个十分古老的小城。在这里，生活可以很懒、很慢，时间似乎停止了。要是你也在这儿就好了，我们可以一起享受阳光，一起发呆……
　　在丽江我碰到了一群又一群来自大城市的年轻人，他们常常提到的一个词是"慢生活"，你听说过吗？

史蒂夫
于云南丽江

阿曼达：
　　很久没有你的消息了，希望你回巴西后一切顺利！我现在在云南香格里拉。这里的一切都带着藏族的文化色彩，跟外面的世界很不一样。明天我就要出发去梅里雪山了，心里非常激动。希望这座"神山"能给我带来好运气！

史蒂夫
于云南香格里拉

马克：
　　我来云南已经两个星期了，很多地方还来不及去，可惜今天就要离开了。这一趟印象最深的是骑马去梅里雪山背后的雨崩村。虽然有的地方路很窄，有点儿危险，我的高原反应也挺厉害，但是到雨崩村之后，我觉得实在太值得了！竟然真的有这么一个世外桃源！

史蒂夫
于云南昆明机场

New words

jìjié 季节 season	shífēn 十分 very	xiāoxi 消息 news	qí 骑 ride (an animal / a bike)
wēnnuǎn rú chūn 温暖如春 as warm as springtime	lǎn 懒 lazy, sluggish	Xiānggélǐlā 香格里拉 Shangri-La	Yǔbēng Cūn 雨崩村 Yubeng Village
Shílín 石林 the Stone Forest	sìhū 似乎 seemingly; as if	Zàngzú 藏族 Tibetan ethnic group	zhǎi 窄 narrow
zuì ài 最爱 favourite	tíngzhǐ 停止 stop	sècǎi 色彩 certain sentiment; colour	wēixiǎn 危险 dangerous; danger
Dǎizú 傣族 Dai ethnic group	fādāi 发呆 stare blankly	jīdòng 激动 excited	gāoyuán fǎnyìng 高原反应 altitude sickness
húlúsī 葫芦丝 cucurbit flute	qún 群 group, flock	láibují 来不及 have no time to do sth	jìngrán 竟然 to one's surprise
shēngyīn 声音 sound, voice	niánqīng rén 年轻人 young people	tàng 趟 measure word (used for a round trip)	shìwài-táoyuán 世外桃源 fictitious land of peace
tèdiǎn 特点 feature	tídào 提到 mention		

5 Check the true statements.

☐ 1 昆明的冬天非常冷。

☐ 2 史蒂夫在丽江碰到了很多老年人。

☐ 3 香格里拉和传说中的很不一样，这让史蒂夫觉得很激动。

☐ 4 去雨崩村的路有点儿危险。

☐ 5 云南值得去的地方太多了，史蒂夫觉得两个星期时间是不够的。

6 Complete the sentences.

"神山"指的是云南的梅里雪山，据说看见"神山"的人会有好运气。

1 "春城"指的是＿＿＿＿＿＿＿，因为这里＿＿＿＿＿＿＿＿＿＿。

2 "慢生活"是说在＿＿＿＿＿＿那样的生活，可以＿＿＿＿＿＿＿。

3 "世外桃源"是指像＿＿＿＿＿＿那样的地方，也许很难找到，但很值得去。

7 Write a travel journal for Steve's social platform. Include the three places Steve mentions in his postcards that impress you most.

《云南游记》

- 到了哪些地方
- 遇到了什么人
- 有什么难忘的经历
- 心情怎么样
- 有什么感受

Language in use

Comparing 后来 and 然后

1 Look at the sentences.

Past event 1	后来 + past event 2
七年前，我来云南旅游，来了就不想走了。	所以后来就辞职，搬到丽江来了。
我刚来的时候是在销售部，	但是后来发现自己更适合做客服。
大概三年前我在一次聚会上见过他，	后来就再也没见过他了。

Action 1	然后 + action 2
你等着，我去拿张地图，	然后跟你说说你必须去的地方。
我们还是先去吃饭，	然后再去看电影吧。
她先抱了抱那个孩子，	然后又亲了亲他的小脸。

Now check the correct explanations.

☐ 1 后来 refers to a certain period of time long ago in the past.

☐ 2 后来 can be used to give the sequence of past events. It is similar to "afterwards" or "later on" in English.

☐ 3 然后 is used together with 先 and 最后 to indicate the sequence of actions.

☐ 4 Both 后来 and 然后 can be used to indicate the sequence of actions in the future.

2 Work in pairs. Talk about the schools you went to using ……年以前……后来……再后来……现在…….

3 Work in pairs. Tell each other a simple recipe using 先……然后……最后…….

Expressing "no matter what / how / whether" with 无论/不论/不管……都……

1 Look at the sentences.

无论/不论/不管 + circumstances	都 + result
昆明无论什么季节	都温暖如春。
这一时期的艺术，无论是音乐还是绘画，	都达到了前所未有的高度。
不论在哪个行业工作，	都应该认真负责。
不管是冬天还是夏天，	这里的游客都多得不得了。
不管你讨厌不讨厌她，	你都得去采访她。

Now check the correct explanations.

☐ 1 无论, 不论 and 不管 mean "no matter what / how / whether", and appear in the first part of the sentence to introduce the circumstances.

☐ 2 都 appears in the second part of the sentence to emphasize that the result will not change.

☐ 3 无论, 不论 and 不管 are always used with wh-questions, questions which offer "either … or …" alternatives (是 A 还是 B), or questions in the "V不V" form.

☐ 4 The progression of the three in terms of formality is 无论, 不论 and 不管. 无论 can only be used in colloquial speech, and 不管 only in formal writing.

2 Complete the sentences using 无论/不论/不管……都…….

1 _____，都辛苦得不得了。

2 _____，都得参加新生欢迎会。

3 无论是太阳能还是风能，_____。

4 无论是哪一门外语，_____。

110 ★ Unit 8 Lesson 2

| **Expressing tones with adverbs** | 原来、果然、竟然 |

1 Look at the sentences.

	原来
教室里这么热，	原来是空调坏了。
我以为你会说法语，	原来你不会啊。

	果然
听你的口音，我就觉得你是上海人，	我果然猜对了。
吃了医生开的药后，	他的病果然很快就好了。

	竟然
什么？	你竟然没见过熊猫？
只不过两年没见，	他竟然不记得我是谁了。

Now check the correct explanations.

☐ 1 原来 is used for recently discovered information. The tone is that of sudden realization.

☐ 2 果然 is used to indicate that the fact or the situation is unexpected from the speaker's point of view, or is an unusual situation.

☐ 3 竟然 is used to confirm that the fact indeed corresponds to the previous statement, assumption or expectation.

☐ 4 All three adverbs can only appear after the subject.

2 Complete the sentences with 原来, 果然 or 竟然.

1 天气预报说今天有暴风雪，现在 _____ 就下起雪来了。

2 早上还是晴天，没想到中午 _____ 下起雨来了。

3 他学中文才一年就说得这么好，_____ 是天天跟中国朋友聊天的结果。

4 这道菜是这个餐馆的招牌菜，味道 _____ 很好。

5 _____ 你一直在骗(deceive)我！我 _____ 相信了你这么多年，我真是太傻了！

| **Expressing personal judgments with** | 算（是） |

1 Look at the sentences.

Topic	算（是）+ judgment
你	算（是）问对人啦。
他不来麻烦我们	就算（是）帮了我们的忙了。
他只不过请我看了场电影，	不算（是）约会吧。
在我去过的地方里，西安	算（是）历史比较悠久的城市。
这个宾馆的条件	还算（是）比较好的。

Now check the correct explanations.

☐ 1 算 means "to be considered as" or "to count as". As a verb, it introduces the speaker's subjective judgment about a person, a thing or an event.

☐ 2 算 prevents a judgment, positive or negative, from sounding absolute.

☐ 3 Adverbs like 就, 也 and 还 often follow 算（是）.

☐ 4 是 is optional.

2 Work in pairs. Talk about the following topics.

1 一个只在网络上写文章、从来没出过书的人，能算是作家吗？

2 什么样的工作算是好工作？什么样的工作不算好工作？

3 怎样的生活方式才算是健康的生活方式？

▶ Turn to page 191 for grammar reference.

Lesson 2　Unit 8　111

LESSON 3

Communication activity

Work in groups of four.

Student A: You are an office worker who wants to quit the job, but you are not sure what to do next. Ask your friends for help. Listen to their suggestions and choose the best one.

Student B, C and D: You are friends of A. Each choose one idea from below, and explain to A why it is good.

1 Staying with the current job while searching for his/her genuine passion for life.
2 Taking one year off and travelling around the world.
3 Starting his/her own business.

Now act out a group conversation to the class. Vote for the best one.

> Turn to pages 174 and 180 for more speaking practice.

Cultural corner

Yunnan Province

Yunnan is a province located in the furthest southwestern part of China. Its capital and largest city is Kunming. The region is very mountainous and rich in natural resources, and there is a great diversity of plant life. 34% of Yunnan's population is made up of ethnic minority groups, the largest percentage among all Chinese provinces, with the Yi and Bai peoples being the most significant. The Old Town of Lijiang and the South China Karst are recognized as UNESCO World Heritage sites. Yunnan cuisine is a mixture of Han Chinese and ethnic ingredients and cooking styles, with emphasis on spices, plants and mushrooms. Yunnan also has several tea-growing regions that produce the famous Pu'er (普洱) tea.

Review and practice

1 Complete the sentences with the words in the box.

> 讨厌　似乎　放弃　名不虚传
> 怀疑　来不及

1 早就听说这家公司生产的产品质量非常好，果然_____。
2 离演出开始只剩十五分钟了，你现在回去换衣服肯定_____了。
3 他_____一点儿也不在乎别人的看法。
4 你怎么能_____她这么诚实的人呢？
5 千万别让我唱歌，我最_____唱歌了。
6 这个项目我们都研究了一年多了，现在怎么能_____呢？

2 Complete the passage with the words in the box.

> 四季如春　值得　文化　享受　后悔
> 世外桃源　印象　特点　欣赏　地道
> 停止

　　云南有一个美称，叫"彩云之南"。云南_____游览的地方特别多，每个地方都有自己的_____。昆明是个_____的城市，又名"春城"。在这里你不仅能吃到_____的傣家菜，还能_____到优美的傣族舞。丽江是一个可以让你慢下来的小城，很多人都说在这里时间是_____的，品茶、散步、聊天、发呆，要想_____生活，这里再好不过了。还有香格里拉，这里像是一个_____，如画的风景、神秘的雪山、独特的藏族_____，一定会给你留下最深的_____。总之，来云南看一看吧，你一定不会_____的。

3 Choose the correct words to complete the sentences.

1 A：这些照片都是你拍的吗？太漂亮了！你真厉害！
   B：_____，我也就是业余水平。
   a 哪里哪里　　b 可以可以　　c 什么什么

2 他们正在办公室里开会，_____停电了。
   a 果然　　b 忽然　　c 然后

3 这个小区的房价虽然贵了一点儿，但是环境比我_____中的好多了。
   a 相信　　b 想象　　c 体会

4 _____多么难的项目，到了她的手里都变得容易了。
   a 尽管　　b 既然　　c 不论

5 我忘了借一本书，还得再去一_____图书馆。
   a 趟　　b 家　　c 场

4 Read the blog entry and answer the questions.

1 什么季节适合去大理旅游？
2 大理有什么风景值得看？
3 白族有什么特点？
4 大理给人什么样的印象？

Now match the words with their meanings.

5 山茶花	a elegant
6 古朴	b camellia
7 优雅	c peaceful, tranquil
8 宁静	d of aged simplicity

5 Write an entry for a travel journal about the most impressive trip you have ever taken. Include:

- 你对那里的印象
- 那里的自然风景、文化特点、当地人的生活
- 你在那里遇到了什么人，聊了些什么
- 在那里难忘的事情
- 你的心情和感受

不能不去的地方：云南大理

这里四季如春、风景如画。苍山的雪、洱海的月、五颜六色的山茶花、古朴优雅的大理古城，处处是绝美的风景。大理是白族的故乡，白族的歌舞、服饰、建筑、美食、传统节日，都是那么独特。如果说昆明让人觉得温暖，丽江让人觉得放松，那么大理会让人觉得宁静而又浪漫。

主页　新状态

个人资料
关注 (1260)
粉丝 (1820)
相册 (5)

Vocabulary review

Fill in the blanks.

爱好者	àihàozhě		buff, enthusiast
白领	báilǐng	n.	white-collar worker
___	bìxū	adv.	must
程度	chéngdù	n.	degree
辞职	cízhí	v.	resign
典型	diǎnxíng	adj.	typical
发呆	fādāi	v.	stare blankly
放弃	fàngqì	v.	___
风景如画	fēngjǐng rú huà		picturesque landscape
高原反应	gāoyuán fǎnyìng		altitude sickness
___	guǒrán	adv.	sure enough
后悔	hòuhuǐ	v.	___
___	hūrán	adv.	all of a sudden
怀疑	huáiyí	v.	___
激动	jīdòng	adj.	excited
___	jìjié	n.	season
竟然	jìngrán	adv.	to one's surprise
来不及	láibují	v.	have no time to do sth
___	lǎn	adj.	lazy, sluggish
名不虚传	míngbùxūchuán		live up to one's name
年轻人	niánqīng rén		young people
啤酒	píjiǔ	n.	___
___	qí	v.	ride (an animal / a bike)
群	qún	measure word	group, flock
___	sècǎi	n.	certain sentiment; colour
摄影	shèyǐng	v.	take a photograph
___	shēngyīn	n.	sound, voice
失眠	shīmián	v.	suffer from insomnia
十分	shífēn	adv.	___
实在	shízài	adv.	indeed, really
世外桃源	shìwài-táoyuán		fictitious land of peace
___	sìhū	adv.	seemingly; as if
趟	tàng	measure word	(used for a round trip)
___	tǎoyàn	v.	dislike, loathe
特点	tèdiǎn	n.	___
提到	tídào		mention
体会	tǐhuì	v./n.	experience
体面	tǐmiàn	adj.	decent, respectable
天堂	tiāntáng	n.	heaven
___	tíngzhǐ	v.	stop
危险	wēixiǎn	adj./n.	___
温暖如春	wēnnuǎn rú chūn		as warm as springtime
享受	xiǎngshòu	v.	enjoy
想象	xiǎngxiàng	v.	___
___	xiāoxi	n.	news
原来	yuánlái	adj./adv.	former; as it turns out
___	zhǎi	adj.	narrow
最爱	zuì ài	n.	favourite
傣族	Dǎizú	n.	Dai ethnic group
葫芦丝	húlusī	n.	cucurbit flute
昆明	Kūnmíng	n.	Kunming
丽江	Lìjiāng	n.	Lijiang
石林	Shílín	n.	the Stone Forest
香格里拉	Xiānggélǐlā	n.	Shangri-La
雨崩村	Yǔbēng Cūn		Yubeng Village
云南	Yúnnán	n.	Yunnan Province
藏族	Zàngzú	n.	Tibetan ethnic group

Review 2

Vocabulary

1 Match the words to make phrases.

1	布置	a	上司
2	解决	b	会议
3	召开	c	问题
4	把握	d	机会
5	请示	e	任务
6	享受	f	生活

2 Circle the odd words out.

1 批评　威胁　怀疑　糟糕
2 诚恳　夸奖　佩服　答谢
3 程度　请柬　提纲　讲稿
4 合作　业务　竟然　友谊
5 高材生　爱好者　年轻人　讲信用

3 Complete the sentences with the idioms in the box.

名不虚传　尽力而为　世外桃源
心想事成　手忙脚乱

1 A: 事情太多了，实在让我 _____。
　B: 没关系，你只要 _____ 就行了。

2 我刚去了新西兰的皇后镇（Queenstown），果然 _____，真是个 _____！

3 祝你新年快乐，_____！

4 Choose the correct words to complete the sentences.

1 我要好好 _____ 我的假期。
　a 享受　　　b 欣赏　　　c 表扬

2 我打算从今天开始 _____ 准备下个月的考试。
　a 全体　　　b 完全　　　c 全力

3 你别怪他了！他不过是个小孩子罢了，当然会 _____ 祸。
　a 犯　　　　b 闯　　　　c 做

4 我们希望能和贵公司有进一步的 _____。
　a 配合　　　b 会议　　　c 合作

5 _____ 你告诉了我这个方法，解决了我失眠的问题。
　a 多亏　　　b 幸运　　　c 不然

6 你这个四川人 _____ 不能吃辣的！真是没想到！
　a 果然　　　b 竟然　　　c 实在

7 下面我们 _____ 一下公司在过去三年中取得的成绩。
　a 回顾　　　b 复习　　　c 表达

5 Match the words with their opposites.

1	夸奖	a	安全
2	讨厌	b	批评
3	危险	c	喜欢
4	谦虚	d	怀疑
5	信任	e	宽
6	窄	f	骄傲

Review 2　115

Grammar

1 Choose the correct words to complete the sentences.

1 他 _____ 能过春节都不回家呢？
   a 怎么   b 要不   c 怎么样

2 昨天的风雪还不 _____ 严重，我们这儿每年冬天都有好几次暴风雪。
   a 是   b 算   c 挺

3 你们 _____ 别以为安排行程很简单！
   a 可是   b 是   c 可

4 在客服部实习，压力 _____ 是没有别的部门大，不过工资也比较少。
   a 却   b 不   c 倒

5 我们的新产品看起来还是不错的，但_____ 能不能让客户满意呢？
   a 究竟   b 还是   c 毕竟

6 不管 _____ 高原反应，他都要去爬雪山。
   a 有   b 多么   c 有没有

7 这本书对昆明的介绍 _____ 详细不过了。
   a 再   b 还   c 更

8 _____ 他已经道歉了，你就原谅他吧。
   a 既然   b 虽然   c 因为

2 Complete the sentences with the words in the box.

| 到底 | 后来 | 然后 |
| 原来 | 竟然 | 果然 |

1 A: 怎么可能？我们公司的订单 _____ 被取消了！_____ 是怎么回事？

B: 现在还不清楚，马克正在问。

2 A: 我昨天很晚才下班，总算把欢迎宴会的事情安排好了。

B: _____ 昨天那个加班的人是你啊。

3 A: 咱们部门的例会时间怎么又变了？

B: 是啊，以前月初开，_____ 改成月中开，最近又变成月末开。

4 A: 你知道吗，周详已经申请去销售部了。

B: 他 _____ 不喜欢在客服部啊。

5 A: 明天的例会什么流程？

B: 各组先汇报，_____ 王经理作总结。

3 Complete the conversations with the words in brackets.

1 A: 什么季节到英国旅游比较好？

B: _____（不论）

2 A: 我实习结束后会留在这家公司工作。

B: 你真厉害！_____（要是……就好了）

3 A: 我要不要把客户的意见告诉经理呢？

B: 我看你还是不要说了，_____（反正）

4 A: 我从来没去过云南，你去过吗？

B: 我去过两次。

A: _____（既然……那……）

5 A: 我今天吃饭的时候想跟小张聊一聊，可是他好像根本不想跟我说话。

B: 你别生气，他这个人其实挺好的，_____（不过……罢了）

Integrated skills

1 Listen to the speech and choose the best answers to the questions.

1 发言的主要内容是 _____。
   a 实习待遇
   b 实习注意事项
   c 实习工作前景

2 实习生应该 _____。
   a 遵守上下班时间
   b 多犯错误
   c 尽量独立工作

3 表现优秀的实习生，会 _____。
   a 有机会成为公司正式员工
   b 拿到更多的工资
   c 实习得很愉快

2 Listen again and complete the sentences.

1 发言的人叫 _____，是 _____ 部的。

2 虽然实习生的 _____ 很强，可是态度一定要 _____。

3 一名合格的员工，不但要能独立完成任务，还要有 _____，能和同事很好地 _____。

4 实习生不要怕 _____，开会的时候可以积极 _____。

3 Work in pairs. Look at the pictures and make up a coherent story.

4 Complete the passage with the words in the box.

负责	无论	解决	谦虚	导致
请教	道歉	忙碌	好好	高材生
陪同	闯祸	合作	请示	做不完

在实习中，我学到的第一件重要的事情是：_____。实习以前，我一直是学校

里的_____，所以有一点儿骄傲。可是实习以后才知道，经验和知识是不一样的。工作中一定要多向前辈和同事_____，遇到问题要向上司_____，不能自己想怎么做就怎么做。

　　第二，要懂得_____的重要性。工作中有太多事情是需要大家一起努力才能完成的。如果大家既能把自己_____的事情做好，又能_____配合同事，那么一切都会很顺利。

　　第三，别怕犯错。实习既_____又充实，每天都有_____的事情。有些事情比较容易，比方说订酒店、订机票、_____客户参观工厂；而有些事情就非常复杂，比如为会议做翻译、为来访的代表团准备礼物等等。_____是容易的事情还是复杂的事情，都可能出错，甚至_____。犯了错误，一定要想办法马上_____，并通过真诚地_____求得上司或客户的谅解，不然只会_____更严重的后果。

5 Look at the questions. Choose one and write a passage expressing your opinions.

1 如果"谦虚"意味着向别人请教，那别人会不会觉得这个人能力差？

2 如果跟你一起做事情的人没有合作精神，你会怎么办？会不会怪他？

3 如果你做错了事，道了歉，别人却不愿意原谅你，你该怎么办？

Enjoy Chinese

恋：love, long for

忘：forget

感：feel; feeling

恨：hate, regret

Ancient Chinese people believed that the heart was the organ that dominated people's minds, and people used their hearts to think, feel and love. The 心 radical also has a variant form 忄, which is called the "vertical heart radical" and used as the left part of a character. Can you find 心 and 忄 in the following characters?

爱恋	志愿
忘怀	愉快
感恩	恐怕
悔恨	思想

UNIT 9

Qiúzhī-bùdé
求之不得!

Only too glad to!

LESSON | 1

Vocabulary and listening

1 Find pairs of opposites in the sentences.

1 谦虚使人进步，骄傲使人落后。
2 失败是成功之母。
3 输赢不是关键，重要的是参与。
4 比赛的日期马上就要到了，不知道现在报名还来得及来不及？

2 Work in pairs. Talk about the feelings of participants before and after a match or competition. Use the words in the box to help you.

> 比赛　获奖　赢　输　紧张　放松
> 担心　害怕　得意　谦虚　骄傲

Now ask and answer the questions.

1 如果参加一个比赛，是不是一定要赢？
2 比赛能够帮助参赛者提高水平吗？

3 Steve is having a video chat with Wang Yu. He shows her the photos he took in Yunnan. Listen to the conversation and answer the questions.

1 史蒂夫为什么又黑又瘦？
2 王玉喜欢史蒂夫拍的照片吗？为什么？
3 史蒂夫为什么犹豫是否参加摄影比赛？

4 Check the true statements.

☐ 1 由于高原反应，史蒂夫进了医院。
☐ 2 史蒂夫不光用照相机拍照。
☐ 3 王玉不希望史蒂夫参加比赛。
☐ 4 史蒂夫最后决定参加比赛了。

王玉：史蒂夫，你看起来好像黑了，也瘦了。
史蒂夫：是不是也更帅了？
王玉：哈哈，还行吧。
史蒂夫：我刚从云南回来，那边温度不高，但紫外线很强。在梅里雪山的时候，我的高原反应很厉害，差点儿进了医院，所以现在又黑又瘦的。
王玉：好在你没事，否则就太不值了。
史蒂夫：就算生病也值啊！云南太让我流连忘返了！
王玉：那快发两张得意的照片给我看看。
史蒂夫：照相机里的照片我还没来得及整理，先给你发两张手机里的吧。
王玉：你拍的雪山，有一种让人安静的力量。
史蒂夫：如果亲眼看到，你会觉得更

5 Choose all the correct answers to the questions.

1. 史蒂夫为什么问"是不是也更帅了"？
   a 他觉得自己更帅了。
   b 他不确定自己是不是更帅了。
   c 他只是跟王玉开个玩笑。
2. 史蒂夫对去云南有什么看法？
   a 如果会生病，云南就不值得去。
   b 即使会生病，云南也值得去。
   c 云南让他流连忘返。
3. 哪句话是王玉夸奖史蒂夫的摄影水平的？
   a "你拍的雪山，有一种让人安静的力量。"
   b "我这次拍的照片质量确实不错……"
   c "……快赶上专业摄影记者了。"

美。不过我这次拍的照片质量确实不错，不谦虚地说，快赶上专业摄影记者了。

王玉：是吗？那你可以试试给旅游杂志投稿啊。

史蒂夫：其实，我在考虑是否参加一个摄影比赛，主题就叫作"我看云南"。

王玉：多好的机会啊，你还有什么好犹豫的？

史蒂夫：截止日期快到了，我担心来不及选照片。再说，高手那么多，要得奖肯定很难。

王玉：你刚才不是还说自己够专业吗，怎么，害怕失败，不敢跟高手比了？

史蒂夫：我才不怕呢。输赢又不是关键，重在参与！

王玉：得了奖要请我吃饭！

史蒂夫：求之不得！

New words

hēi 黑	dark, tanned	gǎnshang 赶上	catch up with
wēndù 温度	temperature	zázhì 杂志	magazine
zǐwàixiàn 紫外线	ultraviolet ray	tóugǎo 投稿	submit for publication
chàdiǎnr 差点儿	nearly	yóuyù 犹豫	hesitant
hǎozài 好在	fortunately	jiézhǐ rìqī 截止日期	deadline
fǒuzé 否则	otherwise	dé jiǎng 得奖	win an award
liúlián wàng fǎn 流连忘返	enjoy so much as to forget to go home	hàipà 害怕	be afraid of, fear
		shībài 失败	fail
déyì 得意	proud, pleased	gǎn 敢	dare
zhàoxiàngjī 照相机	camera	shū 输	lose
láidejí 来得及	have enough time to do sth	guānjiàn 关键	crux; crucial
lìliàng 力量	power, effect	cānyù 参与	participate in
qīnyǎn 亲眼	with one's own eyes	qiúzhī-bùdé 求之不得	more than one could wish for
zhìliàng 质量	quality		

Lesson 1 Unit 9 121

6 You are going to hear a conversation between two amateur photographers. Look at the statements they make and predict what they are talking about.

- "我对色彩的运用的确有我的理解。"
- "我觉得技术比器材更重要。"

Now listen to the conversation and choose the correct words to complete the sentences.

1 对于女士的夸奖，男士表现得_____。
 a 不谦虚　　b 不理解　　c 不开心

2 "对摄影爱好者来说，天气就像空气和水一样"，这句话的意思是_____。
 a 天气是多变的
 b 好天气是必需的因素
 c 天气是大自然决定的

3 女士认为，要想成为摄影高手，应_____。
 a 努力提高摄影水平
 b 在网站上写摄影方面的文章
 c 买很贵的高级摄影器材

7 Listen again and complete the table.

影响摄影的因素	为什么重要
1 颜色	
2	如果天气不好，_____
3 器材	
4	一个摄影师，如果水平很高，不管_____

Now work in pairs. Check your answers and talk about what you think are the most important factors for taking a photograph.

Pronunciation and speaking

1 Listen to the sentences. Notice how they imply either encouragement or confidence.

1 快发两张得意的照片给我看看。
2 不过我这批照片质量确实不错，不谦虚地说，快赶上专业摄影记者了。
3 我对色彩运用有我的理解。
4 得了奖要请我吃饭！

Now repeat the sentences.

2 Work in pairs. Complete the conversations with encouragement or confidence.

1 A: 我假期去旅游了，写了好几篇文章，还发了很多照片。
 B: _____

2 A: 真没想到你做菜做得这么好。
 B: _____

3 A: 下个星期五我们要给客户举办一个欢迎宴会。你负责选酒店，行吗？
 B: _____

4 A: 我们球队马上就要去比赛了，祝我们好运吧。
 B: _____

3 Work in pairs. Talk about the benefits of taking part in a competition.

CHINESE TO GO
Daring responses

Wǒ cái bú pà ne
我 才 不 怕 呢。   I'm not scared at all.

Qiúzhī-bùdé
求之不得！   Only too glad to!

LESSON 2

Reading and writing

1 Look at the meanings of the characters and complete the word map with the meanings of the words.

获 win　　　奖 award
参 take part in　赛 match, competition

摄影爱好者 _____

参赛者
_____

者

获奖者
_____

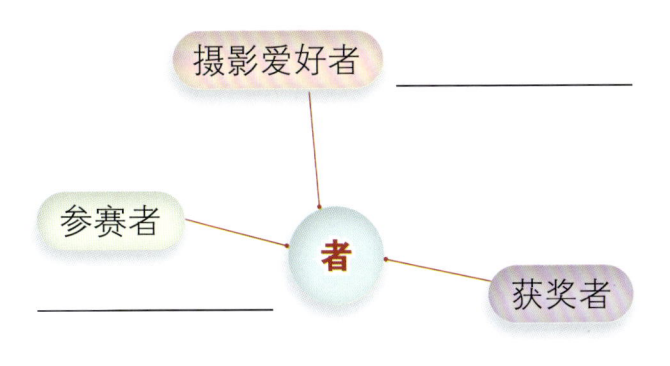

Now work in pairs. Write as many words with 者 as possible.

2 Match the formal expressions with their meanings.

1 须	a 是
2 为	b 没有
3 未	c 到
4 至	d 都
5 均	e 必须
6 起	f 还有
7 及	g 开始

Now make sentences with two pairs of the expressions.

所有的老师和学生都必须准时出席开学仪式。

全体师生均须准时出席开学仪式。

3 Match the words to make phrases.

1 发表	a 责任
2 展现	b 证书
3 举办	c 作品
4 颁发	d 魅力
5 承担	e 比赛

Now make sentences using three of the phrases.

🔊 2-17

4 Read the announcement about the photography competition on page 124 and write down the reasons why the competition is being held.

举办摄影比赛的目的：

1 _____
2 _____
3 _____

Lesson 2　Unit 9　123

"我看云南"摄影比赛征稿启事

为向广大摄影爱好者提供交流作品的平台，通过摄影作品展现云南的魅力，推动云南省旅游业的发展，《云南旅游》杂志社和云南摄影家协会决定联合举办主题为"我看云南"的摄影比赛。

一、活动时间

1 投稿：即日起至2023年7月31日截止
2 评审：投稿截止后三周
3 结果公布：《云南旅游》2023年9月刊

二、征稿办法

1 比赛面向所有摄影爱好者。
2 作品须为2020年6月之后在云南拍摄，风格不限。
3 每人限投6张照片，每张照片须有名称和拍摄信息（包括拍摄时间、地点和照片的内容）。
4 参赛者须寄送纸版照片投稿，入选后按要求发送电子版。照片须为原始图像，未作任何修改。
5 作品须为未发表过的原创作品。作品的一切法律责任均由投稿者本人承担。参赛者须同意并遵守以上规定。

三、奖项设置

一等奖：1名，奖金5000元
二等奖：5名，奖金2000元
三等奖：10名，奖金500元
所有获奖者均将获得由云南摄影家协会颁发的证书及《云南旅游》2022年全年杂志。

四、投稿地址

云南省昆明市《云南旅游》杂志社"我看云南"大赛项目组

邮政编码：650000

参赛者请写明姓名和联系方式。

云南摄影家协会
《云南旅游》杂志社
2023年5月15日

New words

征稿	zhēnggǎo	solicit contributions
启事	qǐshì	notice, announcement
广大	guǎngdà	numerous
作品	zuòpǐn	works (of literature and art)
平台	píngtái	platform
展现	zhǎnxiàn	show
魅力	mèilì	charm, glamour
推动	tuīdòng	push forward, promote
旅游业	lǚyóuyè	tourism
协会	xiéhuì	association
联合	liánhé	united; unite
即日	jírì	this very day
评审	píngshěn	judge and determine
公布	gōngbù	make public, announce
刊	kān	issue (periodical)
面向	miànxiàng	be geared to the needs of
风格	fēnggé	style
纸版	zhǐbǎn	hard copy
电子版	diànzǐbǎn	electronic version
原始	yuánshǐ	raw, original, primitive
图像	túxiàng	image
修改	xiūgǎi	revise, amend
发表	fābiǎo	publish
原创	yuánchuàng	originate, initiate
承担	chéngdān	bear, assume
奖项	jiǎngxiàng	prize
设置	shèzhì	set up
奖金	jiǎngjīn	prize money, bonus
获得	huòdé	win, acquire
颁发	bānfā	award, confer, issue
证书	zhèngshū	certificate
邮政	yóuzhèng	
编码	biānmǎ	postcode

5 Choose all the correct answers to the questions.

1 参加这个比赛可以在什么时候投稿？
   a 七月　　b 八月　　c 九月

2 哪组照片不能参加比赛？
   a 2018年2月在云南拍的照片
   b 2020年11月在云南拍的照片
   c 2020年9月在内蒙古拍的照片

3 哪组照片可以参加比赛？
   a 以前参加过别的比赛，但是没得奖也没在杂志上出现过的照片。
   b 以前参加过比赛，得了奖也在杂志上出现过的照片。
   c 以前没参加过比赛，也没在杂志上出现过的照片。

4 如果照片出了法律问题，谁承担责任？
   a 参赛者本人　b 云南摄影家协会
   c 《云南旅游》杂志社

5 二等奖会得到什么奖品？
   a 1000元奖金　b 500元奖金
   c 2000元奖金　d 5000元奖金
   e 一年的《云南旅游》杂志

6 Find the sentences in the announcement with the same meanings.

1 为了让许许多多喜欢摄影的人有展示、交流照片的机会……
2 投稿日期从现在开始到2023年7月31日。
3 照片应该是2020年6月以后在云南照的，什么风格都可以。
4 参加比赛的人必须同意上面提到的规定，而且也要遵守这些规定。

7 Write an email to a photographer friend and encourage him/her to take part in a photo competition. Include:

- 你认为他/她满足参赛的条件
- 参加这个比赛的好处
- 你对他/她的鼓励

Language in use

Expressing "seem to be" with 看起来

1 Look at the sentences.

Subject	看起来	Predicate
你	看起来	好像黑了，也瘦了。
那个地方的人	看起来	都很友好。
这件衣服	看起来	不如那件漂亮。
他	看起来	挺年轻的。
她	看起来	和你差不多高。

Now check the correct explanations.

- [ ] 1 看起来 is used to express "it looks like …" or "somebody / something seems to be …".
- [ ] 2 The subject should follow 看起来.
- [ ] 3 The predicate after 看起来 indicates what the subject appears to be like.
- [ ] 4 Usually the predicate contains adjectives which may appear with adverbs of degree or in different comparative structures.
- [ ] 5 看起来 has a connotation of objective descriptions and comparisons; therefore it does not indicate how the observer feels.

2 Work in pairs. Compare two things using 看起来.

Expressing "nearly" with 差点儿

1 Look at the sentences.

	差点儿 （就）+ verb phrase	
在梅里雪山的时候，我	差点儿	进了医院。
他昨天晚上睡觉的时候	差点儿	从床上掉下去。
我们	差点儿	就误会她了。
他跟我下棋的时候	差点儿	赢了我。
我们跟广州那家公司的生意	差点儿	就谈成了。

Now check the correct explanations.

- [ ] 1 差点儿 literally means "differing a little bit". It is an adverb and means "nearly", expressing that an event or action almost happened (but did not).
- [ ] 2 If the action or event is good and desired by the subject, 差点儿 implies that "it nearly happened, and it was a pity that it didn't".
- [ ] 3 If the action or event is bad and not desired by the subject, 差点儿 implies that "it nearly happened but luckily it didn't".

2 Choose the correct results for each of the statements.

1 我差点儿忘了做功课。
   a 我忘了做功课。　　b 我没忘做功课。
2 她差点儿就喝醉了。
   a 她喝醉了。　　　　b 她没喝醉。
3 昨天他排队排了一个多小时，差点儿买不到电影票。
   a 他买到了电影票。　b 他没买到电影票。

126 • Unit 9 Lesson 2

Exclamations with 多……(啊)

1 Look at the sentences.

	多 + adj. ……(啊)	
	多好的机会啊，	别犹豫了！
所以说天气因素	多重要啊。	
	多可爱的小猫，	我们把它抱回家吧。
他每个周末都在家待着，哪儿也不去，	多无聊！	
这里的风景	多美啊！	太值了！

Now check the correct explanations.

- [ ] 1 多 and 啊 are used together to intensify an adjective. This forms an exclamation and expresses a strong feeling on behalf of the speaker.
- [ ] 2 Adjectives or noun phrases that are modified by adjectives should be placed between 多 and 啊.
- [ ] 3 In this structure, 多 is optional, but 啊 is not.
- [ ] 4 多……(啊) is usually used in oral expressions when the speaker expresses feelings or impressions about something.

2 Complete the conversations with 多……(啊).

1 A: 请进，随便坐吧。屋子有点儿乱，不好意思啊。
   B: _____

2 A: _____
   B: 好啊，咱们去香山吧。

3 A: 她的父母嫌她的男朋友年龄大，想让他们分手。
   B: 开什么玩笑？_____

4 A: 你看，马克新买的自行车，才三百块，_____
   B: 是够便宜的，我也买一辆吧。

Expressing "whether or not" with 是否

1 Look at the sentences.

	是否	Verb phrase
我在考虑	是否	参加那个摄影比赛。
他们还在犹豫	是否	要跟我们公司合作。
你	是否	觉得我们都对他很不客气？
我不去想我	是否	能够成功，我只努力把每一件事情都做好。

Now check the correct explanations.

- [ ] 1 是否 means "whether or not".
- [ ] 2 是否 is used either in a question or in a clause that serves as the object of verbs like 考虑, 犹豫 or 想.
- [ ] 3 是否 is always placed before the verb phrases that it modifies.
- [ ] 4 是否 is usually used in formal written language.

2 Work in pairs. Translate the following wedding vows into formal Chinese.

(妻子、丈夫、婚姻、是否、无论……都……)

1 X, are you willing to take Y to be your husband?
2 Y, are you willing to take X to be your wife?
3 Do you promise to be true to her/him in good times and in bad, in sickness and in health, to love her/him and honour her/him all the days of your life?
4 Is this both of your understanding of marriage?

▶ Turn to page 192 for grammar reference.

LESSON 3

Communication activity

1 Work in groups of four as editors of a photography magazine. Discuss an announcement to solicit contributions for four columns of your magazine from writers and photographers. Include:

- themes of the columns;
- deadlines for submissions;
- requirements for submissions of both photos and articles;
- compensation for accepted submissions;
- address for submissions;

2 Present your announcement to the whole class and vote for the best one.

> Turn to pages 175 and 181 for more speaking practice.

Review and practice

1 Complete the sentences with the words in the box.

> 得意　亲眼　赶上　犹豫　充分　公布

1. 我还在 _____ 是选历史专业，还是选法律专业。
2. 今年获得奖学金的学生名单将在明天 _____ 。
3. 我哥哥在学习、运动、工作上，样样都特别厉害，我是不可能 _____ 他了。
4. 大卫刚才在路上给几个中国人指路，他们说大卫中文好，他现在可 _____ 了。
5. 他的新房子特别棒，温度、光线、电器都可以用声音控制。你一定要去 _____ 看一看。
6. 客户可以在 _____ 了解产品信息以后再决定买不买。

Cultural corner

Four-character idioms in Chinese

Four-character idioms abound in Chinese, and account for more than 95% of all Chinese idioms. Though many are quite ancient, they remain frequent in modern Chinese, where they can emphasize a point, give a vivid description, or lend a more literary or formal touch. The sources of such idioms include ancient scripts (see 名不虚传), historical events (see 后顾之忧), fables (see 南辕北辙), metaphors (see 风景如画) and folk wisdom. A four-character idiom can be a noun phrase, a verb phrase, or an adjective phrase, but it is completely fixed in its structure, and changes cannot be made to any part of it. Because four-character idioms are fixed in structure, rich in meaning, and loaded with historical references—and because there are so many of them—they are hard for learners of Chinese to become proficient in.

2 Choose the correct words to complete the sentences.

1 我觉得什么钱都可以省，只有吃饭的钱_____不能省。
   a 果然　　b 绝对　　c 竟然

2 他的手机和小王的一样，他_____就把小王的手机拿走了。
   a 差不多　　b 差点儿　　c 几乎

3 A: 听说你的车被撞了。你没事吧？
   B: 没事，_____撞我的那辆车车速不快，我没受什么伤，不过我的车得修一修。
   a 好像　　b 好在　　c 正好

4 周末是我好朋友的婚礼，可是我得加班，不能_____她的婚礼了。
   a 参加　　b 参访　　c 参观

5 这真是个_____的好机会。
   a 尽力而为　　b 心想事成　　c 求之不得

3 Complete the passage with the words in the box.

写明	害怕	关键	寄送	通过
电子版	证书	发表	风格	奖金
面向	展示	主题

摄影比赛

我参加过各种各样的摄影比赛。这些比赛一般都会_____所有的摄影爱好者。比赛一般要求参赛者提交多张照片，还要_____每张照片的拍摄信息，包括拍摄时间、地点和照片要表现的_____等等。虽然很多比赛不限_____，但是参赛者必须使用未_____过的原创作品。随着科技的发展，越来越多的比赛已经不再要求参赛者_____纸质照片了，而只需要_____照片。很多比赛奖品丰厚，除了获奖_____以外，还会有_____和其他奖品。有的人可能_____失败，不敢参加比赛。其实我觉得比赛输赢并不是_____，重在参与。这些比赛不但向广大摄影爱好者提供了_____作品的平台，而且也让大家_____比赛提高了摄影水平。

Now check the true statements.

☐ 1 很多摄影比赛允许所有的摄影爱好者参加。
☐ 2 这些比赛对照片是否为原创没有要求。
☐ 3 很多比赛都既要求提供纸质照片也要求提供电子版照片。
☐ 4 比赛并不能帮助摄影爱好者提高摄影水平。

4 Write an announcement about a Chinese speech contest next year. Include the following:

中文演讲比赛通知

- 比赛的主题
- 目的及组织者
- 比赛时间
- 比赛办法
- 奖项设置
- 组织者的联系方式

Vocabulary review

Fill in the blanks.

颁发	bānfā	v.	award, confer, issue
参与	cānyù	v.	participate in
差点儿	chàdiǎnr	adv.	nearly
承担	chéngdān	v.	bear, assume
得奖	dé jiǎng		_____
得意	déyì	adj.	proud, pleased
电子版	diànzǐbǎn	n.	electronic version
___	fābiǎo	v.	publish
风格	fēnggé	n.	_____
___	fǒuzé	conj.	otherwise
赶上	gǎnshang	v.	catch up with
___	gǎn	v.	dare
公布	gōngbù	v.	make public, announce
关键	guānjiàn	n./adj.	crux; crucial
广大	guǎngdà	adj.	numerous
___	hàipà	v.	be afraid of, fear
好在	hǎozài	adv.	fortunately
黑	hēi	adj.	_____
获得	huòdé	v.	win, acquire
即日	jírì	n.	this very day
奖金	jiǎngjīn	n.	_____
奖项	jiǎngxiàng	n.	prize
截止日期	jiézhǐ rìqī		deadline
刊	kān	n.	issue (periodical)
来得及	láidejí	v.	have enough time to do sth
___	lìliàng	n.	power, effect
联合	liánhé	adj./v.	united; unite
流连忘返	liúlián wàng fǎn		enjoy so much as to forget to go home
旅游业	lǚyóuyè		tourism
魅力	mèilì	n.	charm, glamour
面向	miànxiàng		be geared to the needs of
平台	píngtái	n.	platform
评审	píngshěn	v.	judge and determine
启事	qǐshì	n.	notice, announcement
亲眼	qīnyǎn	adv.	_____
求之不得	qiúzhī-bùdé		more than one could wish for
设置	shèzhì	v.	set up
___	shībài	v.	fail
输	shū	v.	_____
投稿	tóugǎo	v.	submit for publication
图像	túxiàng	n.	image
推动	tuīdòng	v.	push forward, promote
___	wēndù	n.	temperature
协会	xiéhuì	n.	association
修改	xiūgǎi	v.	_____
邮政编码	yóuzhèng biānmǎ		postcode
犹豫	yóuyù	adj.	hesitant
原创	yuánchuàng	v.	originate, initiate
原始	yuánshǐ	adj.	raw, original, primitive
杂志	zázhì	n.	_____
展现	zhǎnxiàn	v.	show
照相机	zhàoxiàngjī	n.	camera
征稿	zhēnggǎo	v.	solicit contributions
证书	zhèngshū	n.	certificate
纸版	zhǐbǎn	n.	hard copy
___	zhìliàng	n.	quality
紫外线	zǐwàixiàn	n.	ultraviolet ray
作品	zuòpǐn	n.	_____

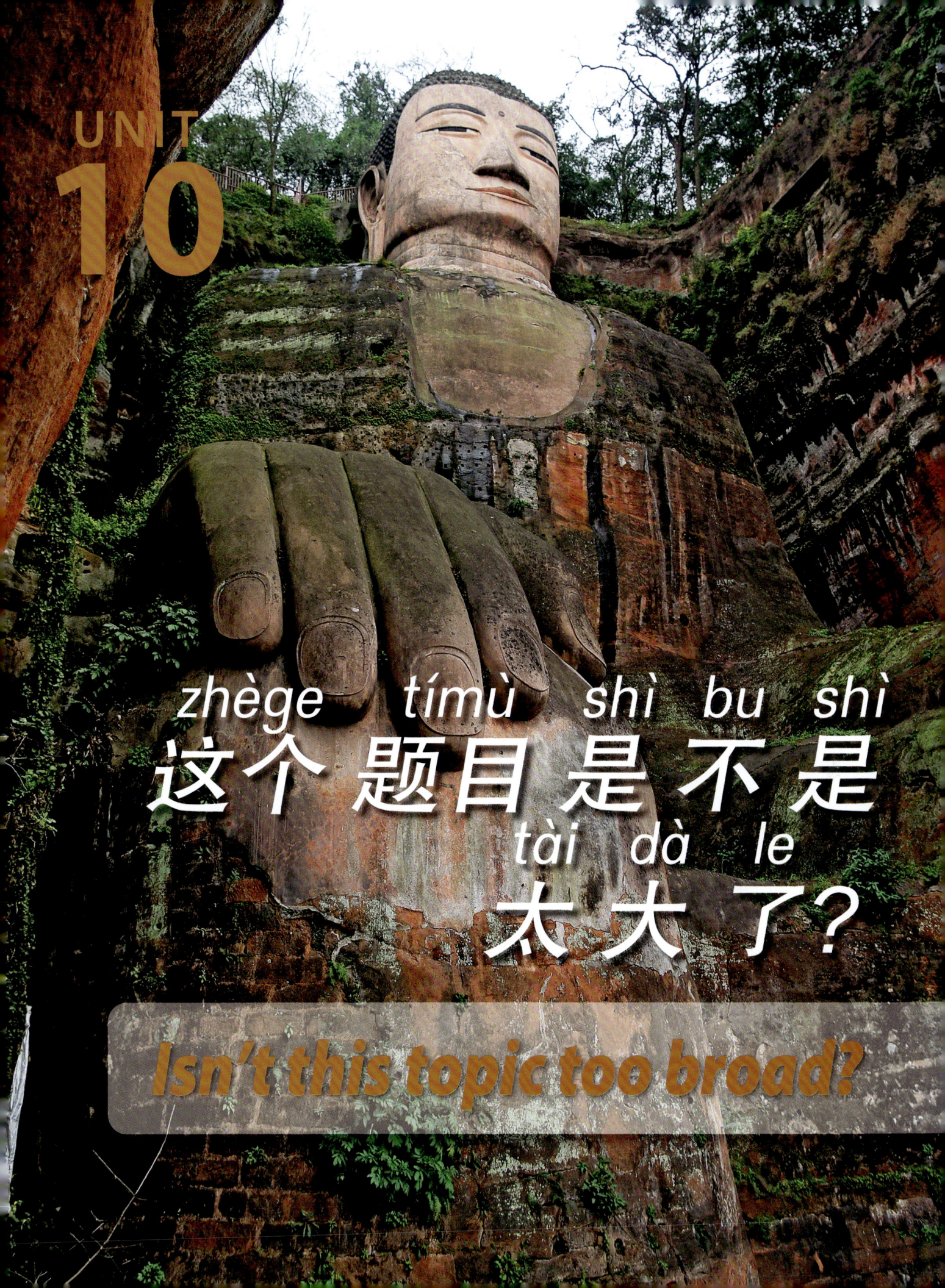

UNIT 10

zhège tímù shì bu shì tài dà le
这个题目是不是太大了?

Isn't this topic too broad?

LESSON | 1

Vocabulary and listening

1 Work in pairs. Talk about the topics below and order them in terms of difficulty for use in a speech.

a 为什么学中文
b 科技发展与现代生活
c 网络对生活的影响
d 金钱可以带来幸福吗

2 Look at the meanings of the words and complete the sentences.

1	看来看去：look back and forth 想来想去：think about something over and over 走来走去：walk to and from	The meaning of ……来……去 is _____.
2	说出来：speak (it) out 走出来：walk out 拿出来：take (it) out	The meaning of ……出来 is _____.
3	说下去：go on speaking 做下去：continue to work on (it) 听下去：keep on listening	The meaning of ……下去 is _____.

3 Yeong-min and Xiaowen are planning the upcoming contests for the campers. Listen to the conversation and answer the questions.

1 永民和小文在讨论什么事情？
2 在今天跟永民聊天之前，小文想出了几个题目？永民觉得这些题目怎么样？
3 永民为什么觉得"金钱可以带来幸福吗？"这个题目好？
4 永民觉得小文的性格怎么样？

永民：这里挺凉快的，咱们坐这儿吧。

小文：好的。永民，演讲和辩论赛的题目，我想来想去才想出来三个。第一个是"我为什么学中文"，这对夏令营的同学来说应该不算太难，他们肯定有话可说。

永民：但是有话可说并不能保证他们一定感兴趣。咱们的题目得让参赛的同学愿意说、观众也愿意听才行。你还想出了什么题目？

小文：第二个题目是"科技发展与现代生活"。你觉得怎么样？

永民：这个题目是不是太大了？即使同学们有想法，也不见得能用中文说清楚。稍微具体一些比较好吧。

小文：那第三个题目挺具体的："网络对生活的影响"。我记得开营那天，有几个同学知道没太多机会上网，好像很失望。这个题目还不错吧？

永民：嗯，的确比前两个好多了，不过……

小文：哎呀，这也不行，那也不行，这么讨论下去三天也弄不出个结果！

永民：小文，你先别急，听我说完。我觉得这个做演讲比赛的题目很不错，但作为辩论赛的题目还不够有争议性。

小文：这倒是没错。有了！这个怎么样："金钱可以带来幸福吗？"

永民：这个问题什么样的回答都有可能，没有固定结论，不管什么立场都有话可说，我看行！

小文：真的？对不起啊永民，我刚才有点着急，我的脾气不太好……

永民：我跟你的看法相反，我觉得你的性格直来直去，有什么说什么，挺可爱的！

4 Match the topics with Yeong-min's comments.

1 "我为什么学中文"	a 同学们有话可说
	b 同学们可能不感兴趣
	c 观众不一定愿意听
2 "科技发展与现代生活"	d 题目太大了
	e 同学们很难用中文说清楚
3 "网络对生活的影响"	f 不够有争议性

生词 New words

liángkuai 凉快	nice and cool	shīwàng 失望	disappointed
yǎnjiǎng 演讲	make a speech	nòng 弄	manage to get
biànlùn 辩论	debate	zhēngyìxìng 争议性	contestability
lái……qù…… 来……去……	(doing something) over and over	jīnqián 金钱	money
		huídá 回答	answer
bǎozhèng 保证	guarantee	gùdìng 固定	fix
jíshǐ 即使	even if	jiélùn 结论	conclusion
xiǎngfǎ 想法	idea, opinion	lìchǎng 立场	stand, position
bújiàndé 不见得	not necessarily	xiāngfǎn 相反	opposite
shāowēi 稍微	slightly		

Lesson 1　Unit 10　133

5 Work in pairs. List the aspects that Yeong-min thinks should be considered when choosing topics for the debate.

6 Look at the table and predict what you are going to hear.

Now listen to the conversation and complete the table.

辩题：	
正方 the Affirmative	反方 the Negative
1 金钱可以买到喜欢的东西	
2	表达感情＿＿＿＿＿＿ ＿＿＿＿＿＿＿＿＿
3 金钱越多，经历越多，快乐也越多。	
4	没有钱也可以帮助别人。

7 Listen again and choose all the correct answers to the questions.

1 金钱买不到什么？
   a 亲情   b 友情   c 爱情
2 哪件事情不花钱也可以做到？
   a 去电影院看电影
   b 去很远的地方旅行
   c 看一本从图书馆借的书
3 什么事情可能会让人感到快乐？
   a 满足自己的需要
   b 有新鲜的、特别的经历
   c 帮助别人
4 正方觉得反方实际上讨论的是哪个问题？
   a 没有金钱也可以快乐
   b 金钱不能带来快乐
   c 金钱可以带来快乐

Pronunciation and speaking

1 Listen to the sentences expressing disagreement or objection.

1 但是有话可说并不能保证他们一定感兴趣。
2 这个题目是不是太大了？即使同学们有想法，也不见得能用中文说清楚。
3 这个的确比前两个好多了，不过作为辩论赛的题目还不够有争议性。
4 我跟你的看法相反。
5 你说的有一定道理，可是帮助别人有很多种方法，不一定都需要钱。

Now repeat the sentences.

2 Make appropriate responses to the following statements using the underlined words from Activity 1.

1 照顾小孩子，最重要的是让他们吃得健康，身体好。
2 他已经学了三年英文了，去英国生活肯定没问题。
3 我觉得在现代社会中男人比女人更辛苦。

3 Write four main points to support your response to one of the statements in Activity 2.

Now work in pairs. Exchange your ideas.

CHINESE TO GO
Responses to frustrations

Zhè yě bù xíng   nà yě bù xíng
这也不行，那也不行！
Nothing works!

Yǒu le   Zhège zěnmeyàng
有了！这个 怎么样？
I've got a new idea! How about this one?

Wǒ kàn xíng
我看行！
I like this one!

134 ◆ Unit 10   Lesson 1

LESSON 2

Reading and writing

1 Work in pairs. Talk about your own experience of social networking. Use the words to help you.

登录	社交网站	更新状态
消息	陌生人	评价

2 Match the words with their opposites.

1 亲近   a 熟悉
2 陌生   b 有趣
3 无聊   c 疏远
4 结束   d 开始
5 具体   e 个人
6 集体   f 大概

Now work in pairs. Talk about social networking using the words.

A：我觉得社交网络会让人们变得更亲近。
B：我不这么想，我认为它让人们变得疏远了。

3 Look at the words and the sentences.

安静 → 安安静静地

图书馆里非常安静。

他坐在那里安安静静地看书。

Now make two sentences using each of the words in the box.

仔细　高兴　开心　舒服

4 Read the essay from the Summer Camp on page 136 and answer the questions.

1 为什么说互联网是"我"最好的朋友？
2 没有网络的夏天，"我"的生活发生了哪三个变化？
3 夏天结束的时候，"我"对网络的看法发生了什么变化？

暑期项目					输入关键字，如：获奖、夏令营
夏令营首页	活动风采	论坛	辩论赛	演讲赛	**优秀作文**

当前位置： | 第四届国际中学生夏令营优秀作文＞没有网络的夏天

没有网络的夏天

过去我认为，互联网是我最好的朋友，有了网络我可以做任何事情。比方说，我几乎天天在网上看体育节目；每隔一段时间就登录社交网站更新自己的状态，顺便了解朋友们的最新消息；去饭馆吃饭之前先看看网上的评价；要去陌生的地方，会事先在网上查好地图；出远门之前，会在网上看天气、买机票、订酒店等等。

这次来参加夏令营，我住的地方不方便随时上网。我本来以为这个夏天一定会过得很无聊。然而夏令营结束的时候，我发现，没有网络虽然有一点儿不方便，可是我的生活也发生了很多积极的变化。

首先，我参加了很多集体活动，亲近了大自然，跟同学和老师之间的交流也多了很多。这不但让我们建立了很深的感情，也让我的中文有了很大的进步。其次，由于登录社交网站不太方便，所以我给在美国的朋友们寄了有中国特色的明信片，这让他们特别开心，因为他们能看到我手写的祝福。另外，由于不能上网听音乐、看视频，我反而多了很多时间可以安安静静地专心看书了。

这个夏天的经历使我明白，网络在给我们的生活带来很多方便的同时，也使我们与真实的世界疏远了很多。现在，虽然我的生活还是离不开网络，但是我不会把时间都浪费在网上。我不再让网络支配我的时间，而是要让它更好地为我服务。

在线用户

熊猫先生
+关注TA

小Q
+关注TA

人在中国
+关注TA

评论

一 祝贺你走出网络世界，走进现实生活！

二 语言简洁、结构清楚、观点明确，是一篇好作文！

三 不再让网络限制生活，而是让它更好地为我们服务，这个结论太好了！

New words

jiémù 节目	programme	qīnjìn 亲近	get close to
gé 隔	every other; separate	jiànlì 建立	establish
dēnglù 登录	log in	shēn 深	deep, intimate
shèjiāo 社交	social intercourse	gǎnqíng 感情	feeling, emotion
gēngxīn 更新	update	shìpín 视频	video clips
zhuàngtài 状态	status, condition	fǎn'ér 反而	on the contrary
shùnbiàn 顺便	conveniently, in passing	zhuānxīn 专心	focused
píngjià 评价	judgement; judge	shǐ 使	make, enable
mòshēng 陌生	strange, unfamiliar	tóngshí 同时	same time; in addition
chū yuǎnmén 出远门	go out on a long trip	shūyuǎn 疏远	alienate, become distant
yǐwéi 以为	think, consider (incorrectly)	lí bu kāi 离不开	cannot do without
guò 过	spend time	làngfèi 浪费	waste
wúliáo 无聊	boring	zhīpèi 支配	control, arrange
rán'ér 然而	however	fúwù 服务	serve
jítǐ 集体	group, collective		

5 Match the activities with when or how often they take place.

1 看天气、买机票、订酒店
2 看看网上的评价
3 在网上看体育节目
4 登录社交网站
5 查好地图

a 几乎天天
b 每隔一段时间
c 去饭馆吃饭之前
d 去陌生的地方之前
e 出远门以前

6 Choose all the correct answers to the questions.

1 没有了网络，"我"觉得怎么样？
 a 很无聊
 b 有一点儿不方便
 c 生活变得更积极了

2 参加集体活动对"我"有什么好处？
 a 跟别人的交流变多了
 b 想念网络
 c 有了更多亲近大自然的机会

3 夏令营期间，"我"给在美国的朋友们寄了什么？
 a 明信片
 b 证书
 c 杂志

4 在夏令营期间，"我"把更多时间花在了什么事情上？
 a 听音乐　　b 看视频　　c 看书

7 Complete the passage.

　　以前，我认为_____，有了网络_____。现在我明白了网络在_____的同时，也使_____。以后，虽然我的生活还是_____，但是我不会_____。

8 Write a passage on the influence of the Internet on your life. Use examples to support your arguments. Include:

• 网络的好处
• 网络的坏处
• 网络生活和现实生活
• 离开网络，我的生活会怎样

Language in use

Continual repetition of an action with Verb 来 verb 去

1 Look at the sentences.

Subject	Verb 来 verb 去	(Adv.) + verb + complement + (object)
我	看来看去	也看不明白她的意思。
我	想来想去	才想出来三个题目。
他	找来找去	还是没找到。
他	说来说去	也说不清楚去博物馆应该怎么走。
他们	商量来商量去，	终于商量出来一个办法。

Now check the correct explanations.

☐ 1 Verb 来 verb 去 is used to express continual repetition of an action.

☐ 2 来 and 去 have lost their meanings as indicators of direction, and instead indicate the performance of a certain action over and over again.

☐ 3 Very often a verb-complement structure follows Verb 来 verb 去 in order to indicate the result of the repeated action.

☐ 4 The complement can be either a resultative complement, or the negative form of a potential complement.

☐ 5 If there is an object of the verb, it should be inserted between the verb and its complement.

2 Work in pairs. Talk about the following experiences using ……来……去.

1 你有没有碰到熟人时突然忘了他/她的名字的情况？你后来想起来了吗？
2 在你看过的书里，哪本书最难懂？
3 你给别人解释一件事情的时候，他们总是能明白你的意思吗？

Indicating a continuing action with the complement 下去

1 Look at the sentences.

	Verb (不) 下去	
我们这么	讨论下去，	三天也讨论不出个结果。
这儿我一个人都不认识，要是继续	住下去，	我肯定会无聊死的。
不管多么困难，我们都要	坚持下去。	
这个演讲太无聊了，我	听不下去	了。
她说着说着，就	说不下去	了，然后哭了起来。

Now check the correct explanations.

☐ 1 下去 literally means "going down". It can be used as a directional complement. It also has a more abstract meaning which indicates a continuing action.

☐ 2 As a complement, 下去 follows the action verb.

☐ 3 讨论下去 means "continue the discussion" while 讨论不下去 means "cannot continue the discussion".

2 Work in pairs. Ask and answer the questions.

1 你愿意在你现在的城市生活下去吗？
2 你认为最难坚持下去的三件事情是什么？
3 有没有哪部电影或哪个电视节目，你看了几分钟就看不下去了？

Talking about disposal of time / money / energy with 把

1 Look at the sentences.

	把	Time / Money / Energy	Verb + 在……上
我不会	把	时间	都浪费在网上。
他	把	时间	都花在打游戏上了。
你不能	把	钱	浪费在没有用的东西上。
父母希望	把	钱	用在孩子的教育上。
她	把	精力	都放在找工作上了。

Now check the correct explanations.

☐ 1 把……verb 在……上 is used to express how one disposes of one's time, money or energy.

☐ 2 The verb can only be 花, 用, or 浪费 in this structure.

☐ 3 The phrases that are inserted between 在……上 can be either nouns or verbs.

2 Work in pairs. Complete the conversation.

A: 昨天我花了500块钱买游戏机，我的父母很不高兴。
B: 为什么？
A: 因为他们觉得_____很不值得。
B: 我同意你父母的看法。
A: 可是我真的非常喜欢那个游戏机。
B: 我觉得你应该_____，或者_____。

Expressing "even if" with 即使……也……

1 Look at the sentences.

（即使）clause 1	（也）clause 2
即使他们有想法，	也不见得能用中文说清楚。
即使没时间参加她的生日聚会，	你也该给她发条短信祝她生日快乐。
即使明天下大雨，	我也要去看那个演出。
即使输掉了一切，	她也会微笑着面对。

Now check the correct explanations.

☐ 1 The conjunctive structure 即使……也…… means "even if …, still …". It is used to express that even if the condition in the first clause were realized, the situation in the second clause would not change.

☐ 2 即使 is placed at the beginning of the first clause.

☐ 3 If there is a subject in the second clause, it should be placed after 也.

☐ 4 即使……也…… has the same meaning and function as 就算……也……, but it is more formal than the latter.

☐ 5 即使 is different from 虽然 because 虽然 introduces a fact while 即使 introduces a hypothetical condition.

2 Work in pairs. Complete the conversation.

A: 你最想做的工作是什么？
B: 我最想_____。
A: 如果这个工作需要经常加班，你还做吗？
B: 即使_____，我也会做。
A: 如果_____，你还做吗？
B: 即使_____，我也会做。
A: 看来你是真的喜欢这个工作。祝你美梦成真！

▶ Turn to page 193 for grammar reference.

Lesson 2　Unit 10　139

LESSON | 3

Communication activity

Work in groups of three. Brainstorm ideas for a business plan competition for students.

- **Student A:** You are creative. You come up with some ideas very quickly and discuss them with B and C. You show your impatience at times during the discussion.
- **Student B:** You are cautious and foresee risks and want to avoid pitfalls. You show your cautiousness at times in your discussion with A and B.
- **Student C:** You are a peacemaker. You weigh pros and cons and help A and B to reach an agreement.

Now present the process of your discussion and final plan to the class and vote for the best one.

> Turn to pages 175 and 181 for more speaking practice.

Review and practice

1 Complete the sentences with the words in the box.

> 稍微　争议性　评价
> 然而　亲近　专心

1 她是这个时代最有_____的人物，有人说她是艺术家，有人说她是疯子。
2 我向总经理汇报了我对新项目的想法，_____他却不是很看好。
3 你别打电话了，开车的时候就要_____开车，一边开车一边打电话多危险啊！
4 上个学期我的课特别多，每天都忙得不得了，这个学期_____好一点儿了。
5 去动物园不但可以_____动物，还可以学到很多知识。
6 人们对这家店的_____很差。

Cultural corner

The four great inventions

Known as "the four great inventions", the compass, gunpowder, papermaking and printing only became known in Europe hundreds of years after they were first invented in China. These inventions changed not only China, but eventually the whole world. Paper provided a convenient and cheap material for writing and recording human knowledge; the invention of printing spread knowledge faster and easier; the emergence of the compass led to a boom in maritime exploration; and the invention of gunpowder brought modern war. The four great inventions represent the scientific and technological advantage that the Chinese enjoyed over other civilizations for many centuries. However, while Europe was going through a scientific revolution in the 18th and 19th centuries, the development of science and technology in China gradually fell behind.

2 Choose the correct words to complete the sentences.

1 我觉得她很眼熟，可是想来想去也_____在哪儿见过她。
   a 想不出去   b 想不起来   c 想不下去

2 我一定要去爬梅里雪山，_____可能会有很严重的高原反应，我也不能错过这次机会。
   a 既然   b 依然   c 即使

3 风不但没停，_____越来越大了。
   a 反正   b 反而   c 然而

4 要是每天都能有一段时间安安静静_____看看书就好了。
   a 地   b 的   c 得

5 这次的旅行_____让我体会到了大自然的魅力。
   a 经验   b 经历   c 经过

3 Read the essay and answer the following questions.

1 什么是"手机病"？得了这种病的人有什么表现？
2 哪些例子能说明现代人得了"手机病"？
3 请根据这些例子检查一下，你是不是也得了"手机病"？你的"手机病"严重吗？
4 你觉得手机限制了你的生活还是让你的生活更方便了？

手机病

你可能有这样的经历，跟朋友一起吃饭的时候，大家不是在热闹地聊天儿，而是都低着头忙着看自己的手机。

你用手机查邮件、看电子书、听音乐，甚至拍下每顿饭的照片再上传到网上。

你的室友就住在你隔壁的房间，可是你们并不面对面地交流，而是用发短信的方式告诉对方这个星期该你打扫卫生了。

要是有一天你的手机不小心丢了，你会非常难过，因为你的生活真的不能没有手机。

手机在为你服务的同时，也限制了你的生活。没错，你已经得了很严重的"手机病"。

什么是手机病？这是一种只有现代人才会得的病。

得了这种病的人一离开手机就会觉得很紧张，他们必须一直把手机拿在手里或者放在身边，并且每隔几分钟就要看一看是不是有电话、短信或者别的信息。

4 Write down your argument with supporting examples for the topic below.

题目：金钱可以带来快乐吗

• 我的看法_____
• 我的例子（正，反）

1_____
2_____
3_____

Now write a complete passage to demonstrate your points.

Vocabulary review

Fill in the blanks.

保证	bǎozhèng	v.	_____	___	mòshēng	adj.	strange, unfamiliar
辩论	biànlùn	v.	debate	弄	nòng	v.	_____
不见得	bújiàndé	adv.	not necessarily	评价	píngjià	n./v.	judgement; judge
出远门	chū yuǎnmén		go out on a long trip	亲近	qīnjìn	v.	get close to
登录	dēnglù	v.	_____	然而	rán'ér	conj.	however
反而	fǎn'ér	adv.	on the contrary	稍微	shāowēi	adv.	slightly
___	fúwù	v.	serve	社交	shèjiāo	n.	social intercourse
感情	gǎnqíng	n.	_____	___	shēn	adj.	deep, intimate
隔	gé	v.	every other; separate	失望	shīwàng	adj.	disappointed
更新	gēngxīn	v.	update	使	shǐ	v.	_____
固定	gùdìng	v.	fix	视频	shìpín	n.	video clips
___	guò	v.	spend time	疏远	shūyuǎn	v.	alienate, become distant
___	huídá	v.	answer	顺便	shùnbiàn	adv.	conveniently, in passing
___	jíshǐ	conj.	even if		tóngshí	n./conj.	same time; in addition
集体	jítǐ	n.	group, collective	无聊	wúliáo	adj.	boring
建立	jiànlì	v.	establish	相反	xiāngfǎn	adj.	_____
节目	jiémù	n.	programme	想法	xiǎngfǎ	n.	idea, opinion
结论	jiélùn	n.	_____	演讲	yǎnjiǎng	v.	make a speech
___	jīnqián	n.	money		yǐwéi	v.	think, consider (incorrectly)
……来……去	…lái…qù		(doing something) over and over	争议性	zhēngyìxìng		contestability
浪费	làngfèi	v.	_____	支配	zhīpèi	v.	control, arrange
离不开	lí bu kāi		cannot do without	专心	zhuānxīn	adj.	_____
立场	lìchǎng	n.	stand, position	状态	zhuàngtài	n.	status, condition
凉快	liángkuai	adj.	_____				

142　Unit 10　Vocabulary

UNIT 11

Huí jiā de gǎnjué zhēn hǎo
回家的感觉真好！

It feels so good to be back home!

LESSON 1

Vocabulary and listening

1 Work in pairs. Check what you are most likely to talk about with a friend whom you have not seen for a long time. Add more to the list.

- ☐ 1 自己最近的情况
- ☐ 2 对方最近的情况
- ☐ 3 家人的情况
- ☐ 4 两人共同的朋友

2 Steve is meeting up with Wang Yu, who has just come back to Beijing. Listen to the conversation and answer the questions.

1 王玉对回国的感觉怎么样？
2 史蒂夫为什么不能把照片放在自己的社交网站上？
3 史蒂夫为什么说"我欠你一顿饭"？

史蒂夫：王玉，没想到你这个时候回国啊，挺突然的。
王玉：放假了，周围的同学都走了，我一个人待着特别无聊。回家的感觉真好！每天想吃什么就吃什么，想睡到什么时候就睡到什么时候。
史蒂夫：这半年你一个人在异国他乡，挺不容易的吧？
王玉：刚去的时候不太适应，流了不少眼泪。说真的，生活上、学习上，苦点儿累点儿都能应付；最难克服的是那种孤单、寂寞的感觉。由于有时差，也不能随时跟家人通电话。高兴的事情没人分享，难过的时候常常要一个人默默忍受。
史蒂夫：其实你可以随时给我打电话。虽然我帮不上你什么忙，但至

王玉：我知道。不过最难熬的那段时间已经过去了。别光说我了，你怎么样？摄影比赛的结果出来了吗？

史蒂夫：哈哈，我有个好消息要告诉你。我得了二等奖，是唯一获奖的外国人。

王玉：太棒了，祝贺你！快让我看看你的作品！……照片真好看，怎么没放到你的社交网站上呢？

史蒂夫：不是我不想放。这批照片的版权已经被一家图片公司买下来，不属于我了。我们说好了的，我欠你一顿饭，正好也给你接风。说吧，想吃什么？

王玉：我刚好也饿了，现在特别馋火锅，咱们去吃火锅吧！顺便也庆祝你得奖！

（前文）……少可以做一个忠实的听众。

New words

tūrán 突然	sudden	tīngzhòng 听众	listener
yìguó-tāxiāng 异国他乡	foreign land	nán'áo 难熬	hard to bear
liú yǎnlèi 流眼泪	shed tears	wéiyī 唯一	only
kǔ 苦	bitter; hard	shǔyú 属于	belong to
yìngfu 应付	deal with	qiàn 欠	owe
gūdān 孤单	lonely	dùn 顿	measure word (for meals)
shíchā 时差	time difference	jiēfēng 接风	give a dinner of welcome
fēnxiǎng 分享	share (in)	gānghǎo 刚好	it so happens that
mòmò 默默	silently	è 饿	hungry
rěnshòu 忍受	bear	chán 馋	be gluttonous; hunger for
bāng bu shàng 帮不上	cannot help	huǒguō 火锅	hotpot
zhōngshí 忠实	loyal		

3 Check the true statements.

☐ 1 史蒂夫觉得王玉这个时候回国很突然。

☐ 2 对王玉来说，学习上的辛苦比孤单更难克服。

☐ 3 王玉再回美国的时候就不会觉得日子太难熬了。

☐ 4 这次摄影大赛，除了史蒂夫以外，没有别的外国人获奖。

☐ 5 王玉想吃火锅。

4 Choose all the correct answers to the questions.

1 王玉为什么回国？
 a 她很想家。
 b 她想回来看史蒂夫的摄影作品。
 c 周围的同学都走了，她一个人很无聊。

2 在异国他乡，王玉是怎样应付孤单的？
 a 她常常跟家里通电话。
 b 她一个人默默忍受。
 c 她跟身边亲近的朋友交流。

3 对于王玉的孤单，史蒂夫表示他可以怎么帮助她？
 a 他随时给她打电话、跟她聊天儿。
 b 他随时接听她的电话，听她讲她的事情。
 c 他能帮她解决所有的问题。

5 Check the situation of Wang Yu about her life in the US.

☐ 1 很顺利
☐ 2 感觉真好
☐ 3 不太适应
☐ 4 想吃什么就吃什么
☐ 5 高兴的事情没人分享
☐ 6 很孤单
☐ 7 难过的时候只能默默忍受

6 You are going to hear an interview. Look at the questions and predict what it is about.

☐ 1 是怎么决定参加这次比赛的？
☐ 2 是不是第一次参加摄影比赛？
☐ 3 怎样拍出照片？
☐ 4 如何选出照片？
☐ 5 比赛前的心情如何？
☐ 6 获奖后的心情如何？

Now listen to the interview and check the three questions asked.

7 Listen again and check the true statements.

☐ 1 记者一眼就认出了史蒂夫，因为这里只有他一个外国人。
☐ 2 史蒂夫觉得自己的水平还不够高，所以一直在犹豫是否参赛。
☐ 3 主题鲜明是史蒂夫的摄影作品获奖的重要原因。
☐ 4 史蒂夫觉得从大量照片中选出6张不容易。
☐ 5 史蒂夫想用他的照片表现出云南人的生活、文化和故事。
☐ 6 史蒂夫接到电话通知的时候，他的耳朵正好出了点儿问题，所以他不相信自己听到的。

Pronunciation and speaking

1 Listen to the greetings between friends.

1 这半年你一个人在异国他乡，挺不容易的吧？
2 其实你可以随时给我打电话，虽然我帮不上你什么忙，但至少可以做一个忠实的听众。
3 我请你吃饭，为你接风！说吧，想吃什么？
4 别光说我了，你怎么样？

Now repeat the sentences.

2 Complete the conversation with the sentences in Activity 1.

A: 真高兴你回来了。_____
B: 是啊，所有的事情都得自己做决定，有的时候真不知道该怎么办。
A: _____
B: 谢谢你。_____
A: 我挺好的，不算太忙。一会儿一起吃饭吧，_____
B: 你决定吧，吃什么都好。

3 Work in pairs. Talk about the biggest change in your life, including:

• 你当时的感觉
• 跟谁分享了这件事情
• 用了多长时间适应这个变化

CHINESE TO GO
Showing frankness

Shuō shízài de
说 实在 的，…… — To be honest, …

Wǒmen shuōhǎole de
我们 说好了 的。 — We made a deal.

LESSON 2

Reading and writing

1 Work in pairs. Choose the three most important things in an award winner's profile and explain why.

1. 身高、长相
2. 生活环境
3. 以前的经历
4. 参加比赛的原因
5. 参加比赛的经历
6. 对自己影响最大的人
7. 获奖以后的心情
8. 未来的打算

2 Look at the explanations for these three measure words.

次 → emphasizes the frequency of the action
遍 → emphasizes the course and thoroughness of the action
趟 → measures trips to somewhere

Now complete the sentences with the correct measure words.

1. 这个电影我看了三 _____。
2. 他一个月去三 _____ 中国城。
3. 你打算什么时候回一 _____ 国？
4. 那个地方我跟你提过一 _____。
5. 你的解释我没有听清楚，麻烦你再说一 _____。
6. 他只去了一 _____ 就记住路了。

3 Work in pairs. Compare the verbs and the verb phrases.

认：identify	认出：recognize
爱：love	爱上：fall in love with
留：leave	留下：mark
提：bring up	提到：mention

Now write down more verb phrases with resultative complements.

4 Look at the example sentences and make the other two sentences with each of the given words which have more than one part of speech.

1. 鼓励
   - 我的好朋友鼓励我参加这次演讲比赛。
   - 受到老师的鼓励以后，我的中文越说越好了。

2. 握手
   - 跟总统握手让我很兴奋！
   - 他的握手很有力。

3. 兼职
   - 我在校外兼职。
   - 我辞去兼职了。

4. 考察
   - 代表团主要考察了我们公司今年的销售状况。
   - 今天的考察很顺利。

5. 记录
   - 父母常常用照片记录孩子的成长。
   - 这份会议记录非常详细。

5 Read the report about Steve and check the main points included.

☐ 1 外貌
☐ 2 在中国的经历
☐ 3 参加摄影比赛的经历
☐ 4 戴维斯对史蒂夫的影响
☐ 5 学习摄影的经历
☐ 6 他的家庭情况
☐ 7 来中国以前的经历

"我看云南"摄影大赛 获奖者专访

足迹

特约记者/小爱

在民族大学附近的傣家饭馆，我一眼就认出了我的采访对象史蒂夫，一个来自英国伦敦的小伙子，也是"我看云南"摄影大赛中唯一获奖的外籍人士。他戴着一副近视眼镜，镜片后面的蓝眼睛亮亮的，总是带着笑意；他的握手真诚而有力；他的中文也很好，语速不紧不慢。

两年前史蒂夫大学毕业后，决定留在北京生活。这期间除了继续学汉语以外，他还在一家英国杂志社兼职做记者。史蒂夫最喜欢做的事情就是带着心爱的相机去中国各地旅游。长江、长城、嵩山少林寺、内蒙古大草原……他一路走，一路拍。用他自己的话说，他是以拍照的方式记录自己的足迹。

史蒂夫告诉我，他本来对参加"我看云南"比赛并不是很有信心，之所以决定参加，是因为受到了中国朋友的鼓励。对于获奖，史蒂夫感到特别高兴。他喜欢中国，更喜欢中国人。史蒂夫获奖的照片，就是以云南各地的不同人物为主题。这次云南之行，还让他认识了很多像他一样爱上云南的朋友。

在采访中，史蒂夫特别提到了一位英国人，戴维斯（H. R. Davis）。一百多年前，这名英国学者先后花了六年的时间，四次探访云南，对云南各地的气候、地理、物产、人文作了详细的考察，留下了珍贵的记录，包括文字和照片。"有机会我真的很希望能在云南生活一段时间，而不只是作为一个过客，看看风景、拍拍照就离开了。"史蒂夫说他有一个愿望，就是沿着戴维斯的足迹，重走一遍云南。

New words

足迹	zújì	footprint
特约记者	tèyuē jìzhě	special reporter
一眼	yì yǎn	at a glance
认出	rènchū	recognize
小伙子	xiǎohuǒzi	young fellow
外籍	wàijí	foreign nationality
人士	rénshì	person, people (formal)
戴	dài	wear
近视	jìnshì	nearsighted
镜片	jìngpiàn	lens
亮	liàng	bright, shining
握手	wòshǒu	shake hands
真诚	zhēnchéng	sincere
有力	yǒulì	powerful
兼职	jiānzhí	moonlight; part-time job
长江	Cháng Jiāng	Yangtze River
长城	Chángchéng	Great Wall
对于	duìyú	as to
探访	tànfǎng	visit, investigate
地理	dìlǐ	geography
物产	wùchǎn	produce
人文	rénwén	humanities
珍贵	zhēnguì	valuable
过客	guòkè	passing guest
愿望	yuànwàng	wish
沿着	yánzhe	along
重	chóng	again, afresh
遍	biàn	(for actions) once through

6 Write down the words and phrases used to describe the journalist's first impression of Steve.

1 样子 ....
2 握手 ....
3 语言 ....

7 Choose all the correct answers to the questions.

1 记者觉得史蒂夫是个什么样的人？
  a 严肃   b 热情   c 真诚

2 史蒂夫大学毕业以后做了什么？
  a 留在北京继续学汉语
  b 为一家杂志社兼职做记者
  c 在中国各地旅游、拍照

3 史蒂夫获奖照片的主题是什么？
  a 云南各地的风景
  b 云南各地的人物
  c 爱上云南的人们

4 对史蒂夫来说，拍照意味着什么？
  a 只不过是他的业余爱好而已
  b 是记录自己在中国的足迹的方式
  c 是他留在中国的原因

5 将来史蒂夫可能会做什么事情？
  a 去云南生活一段时间
  b 更深入地了解云南
  c 沿着戴维斯走过的路再走一遍云南

8 Complete the table about H. R. Davis.

戴维斯	
国籍	
时代	
经历	
对史蒂夫的影响	

9 Write a short biography of an important historical figure. Include:

- 生活经历
- 成就（achievements）
- 趣事
- 他/她的影响

Lesson 2   Unit 11   149

Language in use

Expressing "as one pleases" with 想……就……

1 Look at the sentences.

Subject 1	想+ verb + question word	Subject 2	就+ verb + question word
我	每天想吃什么		就吃什么。
我	想睡到什么时候		就睡到什么时候。
你	周末想玩到几点	我	就陪你玩到几点。
你	想怎么庆祝，	我们	就怎么庆祝。

Now check the correct explanations.

☐ 1 想……就…… can be used to express that someone can do something as he/she pleases.

☐ 2 The "verb + question word" or "question word + verb" following 想 and 就 must be the same.

☐ 3 The question word in this structure is used as an indefinite reference.

☐ 4 The subjects preceding 想 and 就 cannot be the same.

2 Complete the conversations with 想……就…….

1 A: 我们晚上看什么电影？
   B: _____

2 A: 周末去博物馆，咱们几点出发？
   B: _____

3 A: 我从中国带回来的纪念品，应该送给谁呢？
   B: _____

4 A: 咱们一会儿去哪个饭馆吃饭？
   B: _____

Emphasizing a particular manner of carrying out an action using Verb 1 着 + verb 2

1 Look at the sentences.

Subject	Verb 1 着（object 1）	Verb 2（object 2）
他	经常带着心爱的相机	去中国各地旅游。
他	总是笑着	跟人说话。
老师	抱着很多书	走进来。
你	别站着	说话，快坐下吧。
孩子们	每天都背着很重的书包	去上学。

Now check the correct explanations.

☐ 1 Verb 1 着+ verb 2 is used to express "to conduct an action in a particular manner or state".

☐ 2 Verb 1 着 (object) is not the main action, but is used to indicate a particular manner or state.

☐ 3 Verb 2 (object) is the main action, which is conducted in the particular manner expressed in verb 1 着 (object).

☐ 4 Both verb 1 and verb 2 are main actions.

2 Describe what people are doing in the pictures using verb 1 着 + verb 2.

a

b

Emphasizing the reason for a result with 之所以……是因为……

1 Look at the sentences.

Subject	之所以……	是因为……
史蒂夫	之所以最后决定参加比赛，	是因为受到一位中国朋友的鼓励。
写作	之所以重要，	是因为它可以锻炼人的思维。
这部小说	之所以能成功，	是因为它反映了社会现实。
她	之所以会爱上他，	是因为他幽默风趣。
他	之所以放弃这次机会，	是因为他不想离家太远。

Now check the correct explanations.

☐ 1 之所以……是因为…… is used to show result and reason.

☐ 2 是因为…… indicates the reason, and 之所以…… introduces the result.

☐ 3 Compared with 因为……所以……, 之所以……是因为…… is an informal expression and often appears in colloquial speech.

☐ 4 The subject should go after 之所以.

2 Rewrite the following sentences using 之所以……是因为…….

1 因为他们热情地帮助了我们，所以我们非常感谢他们。
2 他不喜欢那家公司的企业文化，所以离开了那家公司。
3 他的父母认为研究艺术没有前途，所以反对他选择艺术史专业。
4 由于弄错了数据，结果这个项目的研究报告完全不可信。

Expressing "to regard A as B" using 以……为……

1 Look at the sentences.

Subject	以 A	为 B
史蒂夫的照片	以云南各地的不同人物	为主题。
服务当然要	以用户	为中心。
我们	以北京时间	为标准。
英国	以英里、码、英尺、英寸	为长度单位。

Now check the correct explanations.

☐ 1 以……为…… is used to express "to regard A as B". For example, "以北京时间为标准" means "to regard Beijing time as the reference".

☐ 2 以……为…… is an informal expression. Its formal counterpart is "把 A 当作 B".

☐ 3 以……为…… means "assumed wrongly".

2 Work in pairs. Talk about the meanings of the following Chinese sayings.

1 民以食为天。
2 与人相处应以和为贵。
3 物以稀为贵。

3 Work in pairs. Ask and answer the questions.

1 一个公司的发展应该以什么为中心？
2 如果你负责主办一次摄影展览，你想以什么为主题？
3 你的国家，以什么为标准长度单位？以什么为标准重量单位？
4 你学习汉语，是以什么为目标？

▶ Turn to page 194 for grammar reference.

LESSON | 3

Communication activity

1 Work in groups of three.

Student A: You are a journalist from a Chinese TV station. Prepare a list of questions to ask the participants. They may have won or lost.

Student B: You won the first prize in the competition. Answer A's questions.

Student C: You participated in the competition but did not win anything. Answer A's questions.

2 Act out the interview in front of the whole class and vote for the best.

> Turn to pages 176 and 182 for more speaking practice.

Review and practice

1 Complete the sentences with the words in the box.

> 随时　属于　受到　鼓励　不紧不慢

1 他的脾气就是这样_____，我们都在为毕业论文着急，他却在休息。

2 要不是林教授一直_____我继续这项研究，我肯定早就放弃了。

3 这是我的手机号，有事_____跟我联系，别怕麻烦我。

4 她父母是医生，哥哥和姐姐也是医生，_____家人的影响，她也决定学医。

5 王心来到这座城市已经三年了，但她一直是孤身一人，没有朋友。这座城市很大，却没有一个_____她的地方。

Cultural corner

The modern "Marco Polo"

Marco Polo, the famous Italian explorer and merchant who travelled to China during the Yuan Dynasty, is so well known to the Chinese that his name has long been synonymous with any European in China. Early travellers to China were mostly missionaries, explorers, merchants and scholars. Modern-day "Marco Polos" came to China after 1979. Initially, there were very few people from overseas in China. Over the past several decades, as China has become a major economic force in the world, more and more foreigners have been attracted to China to study, to work, and to do business. Now the presence of people from overseas is becoming common in major Chinese cities, and more and more expatriates have started to live like the local Chinese.

2 Choose the correct words to complete the sentences.

1 你有什么困难就说出来，就算我 _____ 什么忙，也可以帮你出出主意。
   a 帮不上   b 帮不下   c 帮不出

2 他是这所学校 _____ 参加过国际马拉松比赛的学生。
   a 只有   b 只   c 唯一

3 这 _____ 产品的质量没有之前的好。
   a 段   b 批   c 遍

4 她很喜欢这个电视节目，每个星期都要看，绝对是最 _____ 的观众。
   a 忠实   b 诚实   c 真诚

5 开会的时候，经理特别 _____ 两年前的一份订单。
   a 提出   b 提到   c 提高

3 Complete the passage with the words in the box.

作为　探访　之所以　先后
是否　是因为　详细

听说过戴维斯的人可能很多。他本来是一个英国军官，_____ 去了中国云南，_____ 1894年英国政府派他带队去考察修建一条从缅甸通往云南的铁路 _____ 可行，当时他才29岁。他 _____ 花了六年时间，四次徒步 _____ 云南，对云南多地的气候、物产、人文、地理作了 _____ 的考察和记录，这些内容后来都被收录在他1909年出版的游记中。除了文字以外，他的书中还附有大量珍贵的照片。虽然他的书并不是学术研究著作，但是 _____ 第一个详细记录云南风土人情的西方人，他为我们讲述了他所看到的那个时代的云南故事。

Now choose the correct answers to the questions.

1 戴维斯最后离开云南大概是在哪一年？
   a 1894年   b 1900年   c 1909年

2 戴维斯为什么会去云南考察？
   a 英国政府派他去的
   b 他对云南的风土人情很感兴趣
   c 他是一个研究人文地理的学者

3 为什么戴维斯的书很重要？
   a 他的书是第一本关于云南的学术研究著作
   b 他的书是用中文写的
   c 他的书是西方人详细记录云南的最早的珍贵资料

4 Interview a person who lives overseas. Ask about:

- 他/她的身份
- 他/她在这个地区生活了多长时间，生活得怎么样
- 他/她的特别经历
- 他/她的愿望

Now write a passage about his/her life.

Vocabulary review
Fill in the blanks.

Chinese	Pinyin	Part	Meaning
帮不上	bāng bu shàng		cannot help
___	biàn	measure word	(for actions) once through
馋	chán	v.	be gluttonous; hunger for
___	chóng	adv.	again, afresh
戴	dài	v.	wear
地理	dìlǐ	n.	geography
对于	duìyú	prep.	___
___	dùn	measure word	(for meals)
饿	è	adj.	hungry
___	fēnxiǎng	v.	share (in)
刚好	gānghǎo	adv.	it so happens that
孤单	gūdān	adj.	___
过客	guòkè	n.	passing guest
火锅	huǒguō	n.	hotpot
兼职	jiānzhí	v./n.	moonlight; part-time job
接风	jiēfēng	v.	give a dinner of welcome
近视	jìnshì	adj.	___
镜片	jìngpiàn	n.	lens
___	kǔ	adj.	bitter; hard
___	liàng	adj.	bright, shining
流眼泪	liú yǎnlèi		shed tears
默默	mòmò	adv.	silently
难熬	nán'áo	adj.	hard to bear
欠	qiàn	v.	owe
人士	rénshì	n.	person, people (formal)
人文	rénwén	n.	humanities
忍受	rěnshòu	v.	___
___	rènchū		recognize
时差	shíchā	n.	time difference
属于	shǔyú	v.	belong to
探访	tànfǎng	v.	visit, investigate
特约记者	tèyuē jìzhě		special reporter
听众	tīngzhòng	n.	___
突然	tūrán	adj.	sudden
外籍	wàijí	n.	foreign nationality
___	wéiyī	adj.	only
握手	wòshǒu	v.	shake hands
物产	wùchǎn	n.	produce
小伙子	xiǎohuǒzi	n.	young fellow
沿着	yánzhe		along
一眼	yì yǎn		at a glance
异国他乡	yìguó-tāxiāng		foreign land
应付	yìngfu	v.	deal with
有力	yǒulì	adj.	___
愿望	yuànwàng	n.	wish
珍贵	zhēnguì	adj.	valuable
___	zhēnchéng	adj.	sincere
忠实	zhōngshí	adj.	___
足迹	zújì	n.	footprint
长城	Chángchéng	n.	___
长江	Cháng Jiāng		___

UNIT 12

Yǒu fùchū,
cái yǒu shōuhuò.
有付出，
才有收获。

No pain, no gain.

LESSON | 1

Vocabulary and listening

1 Work in pairs. Talk about who you like best in *Discover China* and why. Use the words in the box to help you.

> 勇敢　粗心　马虎　成熟
> 漂亮　帅　可爱　热情

我觉得 ____ 很 ____，比方说 ____。

2 Work in pairs. Talk about the questions.

1 老朋友聚会有哪些常聊的话题？
2 聚会总是会让人愉快吗？

3 The four friends are reunited in the summer. Listen to the conversation and answer the questions.

1 哪四个人参加了聚会？
2 在过去的一年中，大家都去了哪些地方，做了些什么事？
3 永民宣布了什么好消息？
4 你认为谁的收获最大？为什么？

永民：咱们上次聚在一起是去年夏天吧？转眼就一年了！

王玉：是啊。大家看起来好像都成熟了不少。

史蒂夫：我想大家这一年都有些经历吧，不如都讲讲？

马克：我先来！其实你们都知道了，我去了深圳实习。虽然偶尔也觉得很辛苦，可是学到了不少东西，还改掉了马虎、粗心的毛病。经理还说欢迎我毕业后去正式工作呢。

史蒂夫：马克，你真厉害！

马克：别光表扬我了，你才了不起呢，旅游的时候随便拍几张照片都能获奖！

王玉：马克，你这么说我反对。史蒂夫可不是随便拍的，他一直都在努力提高摄影水平。有付出，才有收获。

史蒂夫：谢谢你，王玉。你也很不容易，孤身一人在美国，什么都要自己来。

王玉：在美国的时候我常常梦见你们，醒了就觉得很失落。可现在我们不是又聚在一起了！永民，你怎么样？

永民：说来惭愧，我只是去了学校的夏令营帮忙。不过我有个好消息：和我一起在夏令营工作的小文现在是我的女朋友了！

马克：你太让我们吃惊啦，永民！快说说，你是怎么追女孩儿的，不许保密！

永民：男人嘛，勇敢一点儿就行了！

史蒂夫：你真行，永民！今天怎么没把小文带来啊？

永民：她有点儿不好意思，下次吧。

王玉：看来大家的收获都不小！

马克：我看还是永民的收获最大！

4 Check the true statements.

☐ 1 大家成熟了是因为又长了一岁。
☐ 2 大家聊起了这一年各自的经历。
☐ 3 马克觉得他的实习很轻松。
☐ 4 大家没想到永民已经有女朋友了。
☐ 5 小文不知道他们要聚会，所以这次没来。

5 Choose all the correct answers to the questions.

1 马克去深圳实习的收获是什么？
 a 他学到了不少东西。
 b 他改掉了马虎、粗心的毛病。
 c 他得到了一份正式工作的邀请。

2 王玉认为史蒂夫为什么会获奖？
 a 他随便拍了几张照片就获奖了。
 b 他一直在努力提高摄影水平。
 c 他去旅游了。

3 王玉在美国的生活怎么样？
 a 她每天都跟同学聚会。
 b 她非常想念她的朋友们。
 c 她孤身一人，很不容易。

4 永民是怎么追小文的？
 a 他保护了小文。
 b 他把自己的秘密告诉了小文。
 c 他勇敢地向小文表达了自己的感情。

New words

jù 聚	gather	cūxīn 粗心	careless, thoughtless	gūshēn yì rén 孤身一人	all on one's own	bùxǔ 不许	not allow, must not
zhuǎnyǎn 转眼	in a flash	máobìng 毛病	defect	mèng 梦	dream	bǎomì 保密	keep secret
chéngshú 成熟	mature	biǎoyáng 表扬	praise, commend	xǐng 醒	wake up	yǒnggǎn 勇敢	brave
ǒu'ěr 偶尔	occasionally	fǎnduì 反对	object, oppose	shīluò 失落	feel lost		
gǎidiào 改掉	give up, drop	nǔlì 努力	hard-working; make an effort	cánkuì 惭愧	ashamed, abashed		
mǎhu 马虎	careless, sloppy	fùchū 付出	pay, expend	chījīng 吃惊	be surprised/ astonished/shocked		

6 Complete the table.

人物	事情	收获
(photo)		
(photo)	去云南旅游，参加摄影比赛	
(photo)		
(photo)		交了一个女朋友

7 You are going to hear three schoolmates at their reunion. Predict what they will talk about.

Now listen to the conversation and check the correct statements.

☐ 1 他们每年聚一次。
☐ 2 阿风大学毕业后没有换过公司。
☐ 3 小爱写过很多人物采访报道。
☐ 4 小爱在大学时就是校报的记者。
☐ 5 陈博发现自己不喜欢做饭。
☐ 6 陈博的餐厅已经开业了。

8 Listen again and complete the table.

	大学时的梦想/做过的事情	现在的梦想/在做的事情
阿风		
小爱		
陈博		

Now work in pairs and check your answers.

Pronunciation and speaking

1 Listen to the sentences used for exchanging praise or feelings.

1 别光表扬我了，你才了不起呢！
2 谢谢你。你也很不容易。
3 你太让我们吃惊啦！我看你的收获最大！

2 Complete the conversations in an appropriate way.

1 A: 你太厉害了！这么多人参加的比赛，你都能获奖！我真佩服你。
   B: _____

2 A: 我听说你一个人把这些东西拿回来的，你太辛苦了。
   B: _____

3 A: 我要宣布一个好消息：我已经被去年实习过的公司正式录用了！
   B: _____

4 A: 你是我见过的最努力的人。你不管做什么事情，都特别认真。
   B: _____

Now work in pairs. Act out the conversations using the correct intonations.

3 Work in pairs. Talk about two or three improvements that you have made in learning Chinese and praise each other.

CHINESE TO GO
Chit-chat

Wǒ xiān lái
我 先 来！ — I'll go first.

Kuài shuōshuo
快 说说，…… — Quickly, tell me...

Bùxǔ bǎomì
不许 保密！ — Don't keep it to yourself!

Nánrén ma yǒnggǎn yìdiǎnr jiù xíng le
男人 嘛，勇敢 一点儿 就 行 了！
Man, just be brave!

LESSON | 2

Reading and writing

1 Work in pairs. Talk about a reunion with your former schoolmates and how you felt.

激动　难过　伤感　吃惊　兴奋　惭愧　幸运　失落　……

2 Describe your best friend. Use three words from the box and give some examples.

细心　乐观　积极　努力
勇敢　粗心　成熟　活泼

3 Match the words to make phrases.

1 突破	a 意见
2 坚持	b 眼界
3 走遍	c 世界
4 开阔	d 自我

Now work in pairs. Make sentences with the phrases you have made.

4 Look at the characters on the left and write down the meanings of the words on the right.

| 聚: meet, assemble, gather | 聚会:
聚在一起:
聚餐:
每两年聚一次: |
| 离: part, separate, leave | 离开:
离去:
离别:
距离:
分离: |

5 Read Wang Yu's blog post on page 160 about the reunion. Check the main ideas.

☐ 1 聚会那天的天气
☐ 2 聚会的地点
☐ 3 聚会的时候吃了什么
☐ 4 重逢时的心情
☐ 5 朋友们的最新情况
☐ 6 朋友们对自己的影响
☐ 7 自己今后的打算

八月的重逢

这个夏天北京很闷热，已经是八月下旬了，温度还迟迟降不下来。今天早上下了一场雨，总算凉快了一点儿，有了秋天的意思。

今天去参加朋友聚会以前，我的心情很复杂。能跟老朋友见面让我很激动，可是一想到很快就要去美国，不知道下次什么时候才能再聚，心里又有点儿难过。聚会的时候，有朋友提议大家每两年聚一次，可以在地球上的任何地方，这让我的心情一下子就变好了。是啊，离别是为了下一次的重逢，我又何必这么伤感呢！

在美国求学并不容易，这半年来流过的汗水和泪水都不少。可每当我想到这几个朋友，就有了勇气和力量。几年前他们刚到中国的时候，也都是孤身一人，语言不通、饮食不习惯，还要面对各种各样的文化冲击，但他们都很快就适应了。现在，M打算毕业后在中国长期工作；S参加了一个中国杂志的摄影比赛，获了奖；Y找了个中国女朋友。他们每个人都有很大的收获，而且中文也都突飞猛进！

他们最值得我学习的地方，就是一直保持乐观、开放的心态，乐于接受新事物。比方说，他们都热爱旅游。在中国短短两三年时间，去过的地方比我还多。别说深圳、西安这样的大城市，就是内蒙古和云南这样比较远的地方也有他们的足迹。他们还打算走遍全中国呢！

很幸运自己有这样的朋友，可以激励我不断地突破自我。我也要更积极、乐观地面对生活中的困难和问题。即使我不能走遍世界，也要尽可能地多看一看、走一走，开阔自己的眼界。

大家又聚在一起了，真好！我想死你们了，下次聚会我一定要参加！

阿曼达，我们也都很想你！说不定下次聚会我们就去巴西找你了！

New words

chóngféng	重逢	meet again
mēnrè	闷热	muggy, sultry
xiàxún	下旬	last ten days of a month
chíchí	迟迟	slow
jiàng	降	lower, drop, fall
chǎng	场	spell, period
jùhuì	聚会	gathering; get together
dìqiú	地球	earth, globe
yíxiàzi	一下子	all at once
líbié	离别	part, leave, bid farewell
hébì	何必	there is no need
shānggǎn	伤感	sentimental
hànshuǐ	汗水	sweat
yǒngqì	勇气	courage
bù tōng	不通	be obstructed
miànduì	面对	face
chōngjī	冲击	impact
chángqī	长期	long term
tūfēi-měngjìn	突飞猛进	make great progress
lèyú	乐于	be happy to
shìwù	事物	thing, object
zǒubiàn	走遍	travel all over
jīlì	激励	inspire, encourage
búduàn	不断	unceasingly
tūpò	突破	break through
jǐn kěnéng	尽可能	to the best of one's ability
kāikuò	开阔	broaden; wide
yǎnjiè	眼界	field of vision
shuōbudìng	说不定	perhaps

6 Match the words with their meanings.

1. 一下子
2. 迟迟
3. 不断
4. 尽可能
5. 说不定
6. 长期

a. to the best of one's ability
b. perhaps, possibly
c. unceasingly
d. long term
e. all at once
f. slow

7 Choose all the correct answers to the questions.

1. 王玉和朋友们下次聚会可能会在哪里？
   a 巴西　　b 美国　　c 哪里都可能

2. 王玉的朋友们去过哪些地方旅游？
   a 一些大城市
   b 一些比较远的地方
   c 走遍了全中国

3. 朋友们给王玉的启发是什么？
   a 要热爱旅游
   b 乐于接受新事物
   c 保持乐观、开放的态度

4. 王玉打算做什么？
   a 走遍全中国
   b 走遍全世界
   c 尽量开阔眼界

8 Check the difficulties that Wang Yu faces in the US.

☐ 1 孤身一人
☐ 2 天气很难适应
☐ 3 毕业以后很难找工作
☐ 4 语言不通
☐ 5 饮食不习惯
☐ 6 要面对各种文化冲击
☐ 7 出去旅游的机会不多

9 Write a post summarizing your experiences or main achievements last year. Include:

• 你当时的心情
• 它对你的启发或影响
• 你对未来的期望

Language in use

Expressing an emphatic tone using 才……呢

1 Look at the conversations.

	Subject + 才……呢
A：马克，你真棒！	B：你才了不起呢！
A：今天的球赛挺有意思的。	B：昨天的球赛才有意思呢！你没看太可惜了。
A：西安的天气真好。	B：昆明的天气才叫好呢！
A：去他家看他，不带礼物好吗？	B：没关系，他才不在乎呢。
A：你真不给她打电话解释一下吗？	B：我才没时间理她呢。

Now check the correct explanations.

☐ 1 才……呢 is used when the speaker wants to emphasize a fact or situation in response to a question or statement.

☐ 2 才 as an adverb should go after the subject.

☐ 3 才……呢 can only be used to emphasize the positive form of an adjective or verb.

2 Work in pairs. Complete the conversations using 才……呢.

1. A：你的中文说得真流利。
   B：_____

2. A：最新的这部《007》大家都说不好看，你觉得呢？
   B：最新的这部还算不错，_____

3. A：王玉的生日聚会你不去，没关系吗？
   B：_____

4. A：你就帮我这一次吧，最后一次，还不行吗？
   B：又是"最后一次"？_____

Expressing unnecessariness using 何必……呢

1 Look at the sentences.

Clause 1	何必……呢
离别是为了下一次的重逢，	我又何必这么伤感呢？
你跟他是这么多年的朋友，	何必为了一点小事情吵架？
既然你不相信我说的话，	何必还来问我呢？
你家楼下不是就有卖水果的吗？	何必跑去远处的超市？
反正我也没时间见他，	何必让他白来一趟呢？

Now check the correct explanations.

☐ 1 何必……呢 is used in a rhetorical question to express that "there is no need to do something" or "it's not necessary to do something".

☐ 2 The clause preceding 何必……呢 introduces a reason or premise which explains why there is no need to do the thing.

☐ 3 If there is a subject in the second clause, the subject should follow 何必.

☐ 4 呢 can never be dropped.

2 Work in pairs. Talk about how you feel about the following using 何必……呢.

1. 衣服的款式、质量、品牌、价格
2. 餐馆的味道、服务、环境、价格

A：去餐馆吃饭，你觉得环境重要吗？
B：我觉得只要饭菜的味道好就行了，何必在乎环境呢？

| Expressing "let alone" with | 别说A，就是B，也/都…… |

| Indicating "constantly" or "non-stop" with | 一直 or 不断(地) |

1 Look at the sentences.

	别说A	就是B	也/都 + comment
	别说深圳、西安这样的大城市，	就是内蒙古和云南这样比较远的地方，	也已经有他们的足迹了。
毕业以后，	别说每年聚一次，	就是五年一聚，	都不容易。
他的成绩这么好，	别说上普通大学了，	就是上最好的大学，	也肯定没有问题。
	别说外国，	就是北京、上海，	我奶奶都没去过。
这么难看的衣服，	别说一百块钱，	就是十块钱，	我也不买。

Now check the correct explanations.

☐ 1 别说 means "let alone", "not to mention".

☐ 2 Topics A and B are related, but A is a more extensive case than B in terms of the comment following 也/都.

☐ 3 If the comment can be applied to topic B, then the comment can also be applied to A.

☐ 4 If there is a subject, it should be placed after 也 or 都 in the comment clause.

2 Work in pairs. Complete the conversations.

1 A: 这个地方交通不方便。

   B: 是啊，_____

2 A: 你听得懂中文新闻吗？

   B: 我的中文水平，_____

3 A: 你喝过普洱茶吗？

   B: _____

1 Look at the sentences.

	一直/不断(地)	Verb phrase
他	一直	都在努力提高摄影水平。
他们	一直	保持着乐观、开放的心态。
他们激励我	不断地	突破自己。
这个地区的人口近年来	一直在 / 不断地	增长，带来了很多环境问题。

Now check the correct explanations.

☐ 1 Both 一直 and 不断 are adverbs used to indicate that the action is continuous, and they always apply to the same context.

☐ 2 一直 means "all along" or "all the time", expressing the continuation of an action or an unchangeable circumstance within a certain period of time. The verbs or adjectives modified are usually durative. It can also be used together with structures indicating ongoing actions such as V 着 or 在 V.

☐ 3 不断 literally means "non-stop" or "unceasingly". The verbs modified usually express a single occurrence, so 不断 is used to express that the action is repeated over and over again.

☐ 4 一直 and 不断 cannot be used together.

2 Complete the sentences with 一直 or 不断(地).

1 我 _____ 想知道古时候的厕所是什么样的。

2 他 _____ 给一些报社打电话，希望他们能报道他的故事。

3 从七月到现在，气温 _____ 都是三十多度。

4 在研究中，我 _____ 发现新问题。

5 我今年 _____ 忙得不得了。

▶ Turn to page 195 for grammar reference.

LESSON 3

Communication activity

1 Work in pairs. Tell each other about a friend who has inspired you most in the past year. Ask and answer questions for more details. Include:

- basic information about the friend;
- his/her story or experience;
- why he/she is so inspiring to you;

Now discuss and decide whose story you would like to tell the whole class.

2 Tell the story to the class and vote for the best.

> Turn to pages 176 and 182 for more speaking practice.

Cultural corner

Review and practice

1 Choose the correct words to complete the sentences.

1 你觉不觉得他这一年 _____ 更成熟了？
 a 变　　　b 变得　　　c 变成

2 既然他不喜欢你，你又 _____ 把时间浪费在他身上？
 a 不必　　b 必要　　　c 何必

3 A: 你做的蛋糕真好吃！
 B: 我也就是比业余水平高一点点，人家蛋糕店里卖的 _____ 好吃呢。
 a 才　　　b 就　　　　c 还

4 小王，你女朋友今天 _____ 没跟你一起来？
 a 怎么　　b 什么　　　c 怎样

5 没想到快到十月了，温度还这么高，老是 _____ 。
 a 不能降　b 没降下来　c 降不下来

2 Complete the sentences with the words in the box.

| 偶尔 | 改掉 | 坚持 |
| 面对 | 提议 | 尽可能 |

Chinese symbols of good fortune

There are many symbols in Chinese culture that are associated with good fortune, which are widely used in the design and displayed during holidays and on special occasions:

- The colour red symbolizes prosperity. Red envelopes (红包) containing money are given out as gifts, and red is the traditional colour of Chinese weddings.
- The pronunciation of the number eight (八) sounds very similar to the word meaning "becoming rich (发财)". Many Chinese like their phone number or address to contain 8 as many times as possible.
- Double Happiness (囍) is a famous ornamental design used in Chinese weddings. It is almost always red.
- The Chinese character for good fortune (福) is used as ornamental symbol during Chinese New Year.
- The bat (蝙蝠) and the magpie (喜鹊) are auspicious animals because of their phonetic association with the character 福 and the character 喜. The animals are widely used as decorative symbols in charms and textiles.

1 有人 _____ 下次聚会我们应该一起去黄山旅游。
2 晚睡、久坐、暴饮暴食（overeating），这些都是需要 _____ 的坏习惯。
3 在现代社会中，很多人每天都 _____ 着巨大的学习压力或工作压力。
4 你放心，我会 _____ 在最短的时间内把这件事情做完。
5 伦敦的地铁一般来说是很可靠的，不过 _____ 也会出问题。
6 锻炼身体不是一天两天的事情，一定要每天都 _____ 才能看到效果。

3 Put the sentences into the correct order.

泰瑞·福克斯

a 1980年4月12日，泰瑞出发了。他每天大约跑28英里，一共跑了143天，共3339英里，最后他一共募到了2400万加元。

b 一直到现在，每年9月的第二个周末，全世界很多国家的人会聚在一起参加"希望马拉松"，继续为癌症研究筹款。

c 然而事实并不是这样。手术以后，他装上了假肢、穿上了跑鞋。他打算从加拿大的最东边跑到最西边，为癌症研究筹款。他的这项计划叫作"希望马拉松"。

d 他是加拿大人。他本来只是一个很普通的青年，热爱生活、热爱运动。

e 你也许从来没听过泰瑞·福克斯这个名字，可是他却是对我影响最大的人。

f 故事说到这里，很多人会猜，他可能从此以后就生活在痛苦中了。

g 令人难过的是，他没能跑到加拿大的最西边就倒下了，癌症夺去了他的生命。尽管如此，他的精神和勇气却感动了许许多多的人。

h 不幸的是，18岁的时候，他被查出得了骨癌，疾病使他失去了右腿。

1 _____ 2 _____ 3 _____ 4 _____
5 _____ 6 _____ 7 _____ 8 _____

Now match the words with their meanings.

9 癌（ái）症	i bone cancer
10 骨癌	j cancer
11 筹（chóu）款	k marathon
12 马拉松	l raise money
13 夺（duó）去	m courage
14 勇气	n take away

4 Read the story in Activity 3 again and choose all the correct answers to the questions.

1 泰瑞·福克斯是哪一年进行募款长跑的？
 a 1979年 b 1980年 c 1981年
2 泰瑞在得了骨癌并失去了一条腿之后做了什么事情？
 a 每天都生活在痛苦中
 b 装上了假肢
 c 跑"希望马拉松"
3 他跑了多远？
 a 28英里 b 3339英里
 c 从加拿大最东边跑到了最西边
4 泰瑞对人们有什么样的影响？
 a 很多人为癌症研究捐款。
 b 很多人参加"希望马拉松"。
 c 很多人继续为癌症研究筹款。

5 Write a journal report introducing someone who has influenced you or inspired you. Include:

• 他/她的简介
• 他/她的经历对你有什么启发
• 你在哪些时候想到了他/她

Lesson 3　Unit 12　165

Vocabulary review

Fill in the blanks.

保密	bǎomì	v.	keep secret	聚	jù	v.	gather
___	biǎoyáng	v.	praise, commend	聚会	jùhuì	n./v.	gathering; get together
不断	búduàn	adv.	___	开阔	kāikuò	v./adj.	broaden; wide
不通	bù tōng		be obstructed	乐于	lèyú	v.	be happy to
___	bùxǔ	v.	not allow, must not	离别	líbié	v.	part, leave, bid farewell
惭愧	cánkuì	adj.	ashamed, abashed	马虎	mǎhu	adj.	___
长期	chángqī	adj.	___	毛病	máobìng	n.	defect
场	chǎng	measure word	spell, period	闷热	mēnrè	adj.	muggy, sultry
成熟	chéngshú	adj./v.	mature		mèng	v./n.	dream
___	chījīng	v.	be surprised/ astonished/ shocked	面对	miànduì	v.	___
迟迟	chíchí	adv.	slow	___	nǔlì	adj./v.	hard-working; make an effort
冲击	chōngjī	v.	impact	偶尔	ǒu'ěr	adv.	occasionally
重逢	chóngféng	v.	meet again	伤感	shānggǎn	adj.	sentimental
___	cūxīn	adj.	careless, thoughtless	失落	shīluò	adj.	feel lost
地球	dìqiú	n.	earth, globe	事物	shìwù	n.	thing, object
反对	fǎnduì	v.	___	说不定	shuōbudìng	adv.	___
付出	fùchū	v.	pay, expend	突飞猛进	tūfēi-měngjìn		make great progress
改掉	gǎidiào		give up, drop	突破	tūpò	v.	break through
孤身一人	gūshēn yì rén		all on one's own	下旬	xiàxún	n.	last ten days of a month
___	hànshuǐ	n.	sweat		xǐng	v.	wake up
何必	hébì	adv.	there is no need	眼界	yǎnjiè	n.	field of vision
激励	jīlì	v.	inspire, encourage	一下子	yíxiàzi		all at once
降	jiàng	v.	lower, drop, fall	勇敢	yǒnggǎn	adj.	___
尽可能	jǐn kěnéng		to the best of one's ability		yǒngqì	n.	courage
				转眼	zhuǎnyǎn	v.	in a flash
				走遍	zǒubiàn		travel all over

166 Unit 12 Vocabulary

Review 3

Vocabulary

1 Match the words to make phrases.

1 忠实的		a 礼物
2 珍贵的		b 天气
3 孤单的		c 听众
4 闷热的		d 态度
5 犹豫的		e 生活

2 Circle the odd words out.

1 失落　伤感　惭愧　赶快
2 专心　粗心　爱心　开心
3 孤单　无聊　难熬　忍受
4 帮不上　来得及　离不开　说不定
5 修改　设置　刊登　平台

3 Complete the sentences with the idioms in the box.

求之不得	流连忘返
突飞猛进	异国他乡

1 A: 第一年在 _____ 生活，你一定非常想家吧？
　B: 我可不想家。这儿的生活丰富多彩，让我 _____。

2 A: 去美国留学，你的英文水平一定会 _____。
　B: 那我真是 _____！

4 Choose the correct words to complete the sentences.

1 这首歌是他的 _____ 作品吗？
　a 原创　　b 原始　　c 原来

2 没有得到这份工作，让我很 _____。
　a 失败　　b 失望　　c 寂寞

3 他的研究终于有了重大的 _____。
　a 突破　　b 突然　　c 修改

4 上了大学，你应该学会自己 _____ 自己的时间。
　a 支配　　b 支持　　c 花费

5 她虽然不漂亮，可是非常有 _____，所以喜欢她的人特别多。
　a 力量　　b 魅力　　c 能力

5 Match the words with their opposites.

1 反对		a 经常
2 偶尔		b 批评
3 坚持		c 支持
4 表扬		d 放弃
5 无聊		e 熟悉
6 陌生		f 有趣
7 集体		g 个人
8 疏远		h 亲近

Grammar

1 Choose the correct words to complete the sentences.

1 没得到大奖，他 _____ 很失落。
   a 听出来　　b 看起来　　c 看出来

2 这份旅游杂志办得这么好，应该继续办 _____。
   a 下来　　b 上去　　c 下去

3 这些玩具你想跟谁分享 _____。
   a 就跟谁分享　b 就跟谁　c 跟谁

4 她的眼睛不太好，总是得戴 _____ 眼镜上 _____ 课，要不然就看不清楚。
   a X……着　　b 着……X　　c 着……着

5 客服部的人找来找去，终于找 _____ 了出错的订单。
   a X　　b 到　　c 下

6 别把钱都 _____ 在买衣服上。
   a 用　　b 控制　　c 支配

7 _____ 生命只剩下一天，我们也应该好好把握每一分钟。
   a 虽然　　b 即使　　c 既然

2 Complete the sentences with the words in the box.

一直　是否　不断　差点儿

1 A: 昨天的辩论比赛，阿曼达表现得怎么样？
   B: 她表现得很好，不过对方也非常厉害，她 _____ 就输了。

2 A: 对您来说，坚持梦想 _____ 意味着有的时候要面对困难和孤独？
   B: 确实是这样，我相信所有坚持梦想的人都是有勇气的人。

3 A: 马克和安迪的关系很好吗？
   B: 是的，他们俩从高中起就 _____ 是好朋友。

4 A: 我们 _____ 地向对方公司保证我们会按时交货，可是他们还是不相信。
   B: 那还是让经理来处理吧。

3 Complete the conversations with the words given.

1 A: 她父母本来说周末来给她过生日，可是今天又突然说不能来了。
   B: 那她该 _____ _____（多……啊）

2 A: 你的照片拍得真好！
   B: 哪里哪里，我的水平一般。_____（才……呢）

3 A: 你真的要去留学吗？如果你的家人都反对呢？
   B: _____ _____（即使……也……）

4 A: 你每年都来这里一趟吗？
   B: 怎么可能，_____ ___（别说……，就是……也……）

4 Rewrite the sentences using the words given.

1 他什么都不做，只打游戏。（把……V在……上）

2 这家餐厅的主题是棒球。（以……为……）

3 由于受到了戴维斯的影响，史蒂夫对云南有特殊的感情。（之所以……是因为……）

4 他根本不理解你的想法，你不用跟他解释。（何必……呢）

Integrated skills

1 Listen to the short speech and choose the correct answers to the questions.

1 发言的主要内容是 _____。
  a 怎么选择大学专业
  b 大学四年应该怎么过
  c 大学毕业以后找什么工作

2 "读万卷书，行万里路"的意思是 _____。
  a 为了开阔眼界，应该多看书，也应该去很多地方
  b 看很多书不如走很多路
  c 看书让人变得聪明，走路让人身体健康

3 王力决定去英国是为了 _____。
  a 换个工作
  b 开阔眼界，感受不同文化
  c 学会忍受寂寞，适应陌生环境

2 Listen again and check the true statements.

☐ 1 王力是一个刚毕业的人。

☐ 2 在王力看来，年轻人在面对选择时绝对不能犯错误。

☐ 3 王力在大学换了专业。他父母和老师开始都不支持他的决定，可是后来他们的看法改变了。

☐ 4 王力认为成功的人一定很幸福。

☐ 5 王力毕业以后去了一家世界知名的公司。

3 Work in pairs. Talk about what qualities a charismatic person should have and how to cultivate the qualities. You may begin with the adjectives in the box and come up with your own ones.

| 美丽 | 勇敢 | 幽默 | 努力 |
| 负责 | 成熟 | 积极 | 真诚 |

Now write down a coherent paragraph using the words you have chosen.

我认为一个有魅力的人首先要……，因为……，比方说……；其次，……

4 Complete the passage with the words in the box.

| 失败 | 得奖 | 分享 | 浪费 | 社交 | 孤单 |
| 坚持 | 改掉 | 流连忘返 | 突飞猛进 |

我是一个热爱网络游戏的人。刚开始我玩得不太好，后来我的水平_____，最近一年每次参加游戏比赛我都能_____。玩游戏能让我获得很多成就感。

可是我的父母却不理解我。他们总是说我把时间都_____在了虚拟世界里，说我必须_____玩游戏的坏毛病，否则我以后的人生会很_____。

可是我觉得虚拟世界也是我生活的一部分。现实生活中，我不太会_____，没有什么亲近的朋友，常常很_____，跟陌生人说话更让我紧张。然而在网络上，我有很多和我一样热爱游戏的朋友，他们佩服我、鼓励我，也跟我_____他们的感受。这也是为什么游戏世界那么让我_____。我的梦想是当一个职业游戏玩家或者游戏开发者。

我应该不应该_____这个梦想？

Now think about the following questions and write a passage expressing your opinions.

1 你对玩游戏是支持还是反对？
2 玩游戏对生活有什么影响？
3 以游戏为梦想值得鼓励吗？

Enjoy Chinese

Guess what the ancient Chinese characters resemble.

1　　　　　a 休
2　　　　　b 好
3　　　　　c 分
4　　　　　d 并
5　　　　　e 车
6　　　　　f 鸟

Now match the ancient characters with the modern ones.

Pair work activities for Student A

Unit 1

Read the following job description. Find six differences with Student B's job description.

让我们从这里 **开始**，
汉语教师 **招聘** 广告

》单位介绍

光华国际中学位于北京市朝阳区，是一所为外籍人士子女提供国际化教育的私立中学，共设六个年级，接受12岁到18岁的学生入校学习，使用美式教程和课本。现招聘用英文教授汉语的老师两名。每周课时为二十个小时。待遇从优。

》招聘要求

1. 英文水平高，TOEFL成绩为100分以上
2. 母语为中文
3. 大学及以上文化水平；教育专业、国际中文教育专业的毕业生优先
4. 性格活泼开朗、热爱教育、学习能力强
5. 有两年以上国际中文教学经验
6. 有中学教学经验的老师优先

联系方式   hr@discoverchinagh.edu   @

Unit 2

An educational company in China is looking for temporary summer employees to teach English in China. You are very interested in the position. Complete the table with your own information.

姓名	
年龄	
联系方式（电话/电子邮件）	
兴趣、爱好	
教育水平＆学校名称	
中文水平＆学中文多长时间	
有没有教外国人英文的经验？	
有没有教小孩子的经验？	
有没有教中学生的经验？	
有没有教成年人的经验？	
用三个词介绍你自己	

信息

Their HR manager, Student B, schedules an initial phone interview with you.

Act out the interview with Student B. Write down the questions Student B asks. At the end of the interview, you will be told if you will enter the second round of interview.

Unit 3

You are a travel agent who is helping a group of teenagers from Beijing to plan a one-week trip to your country. This will be their first trip abroad and they want to visit two cities. Student B is the group leader.

1 Pick four cities that you think are worth visiting and have many activities suitable for teenagers.

2 Research the routes and prices of round-trip flights between Beijing and a major city in your country. Make a list of choices.

3 Act out a conversation with Student B about the itinerary. Include:

- 往返时间
- 决定参观哪两个城市
- 在两个城市参观哪些景点，有哪些活动
- 从北京到目的地的往返机票

Unit 4

You and your partner, Student B, are stranded on an island. There is enough food and water but nothing else. Which personal items below do you wish you had brought with you? Explain why. You can choose six items only.

Unit 5

1 You are working for a consulting firm which advises their clients about business strategies in China. One of your clients, Student B, is seeking your advice about which gifts are suitable for their potential Chinese business partners. Here is your knowledge of gift-giving in China:

As in the West, gifts in China are given on special occasions and as an expression of gratitude. However, there are many differences which may complicate the exchange of gifts.

Firstly, it is usual for gifts to be presented and received with both hands, as this shows mutual respect. Gifts are commonly wrapped in red and gold, as these colours symbolize good luck.

Secondly, when giving gifts, there are certain taboos that should be avoided. For example, it is inadvisable to give knives or scissors, as this could be interpreted as a desire to "cut" a friendship. Other examples of unsuitable gifts include clocks and umbrellas, as the Chinese word for "clock" sounds similar to the word for "death" or "end", whilst the Chinese word for "umbrella" sounds similar to the word "lose".

If several gifts are given, it is important to note that six, eight and nine are lucky numbers.

Finally, in Chinese culture it is considered polite to return favours and kindnesses, so if given a gift, it is often best to show your appreciation by reciprocating. (See *Cultural corner* of Unit 6, *Discover China* 3)

2 Act out a conversation with Student B to help decide what gifts to give.

Unit 6

It has been ten years since you graduated from university. One week ago, you began working for an international organization in China. Tonight you are attending the organization's annual banquet. Because you do not know many people in the company, you feel a little bit bored. Then you bump into Student B, who was your classmate in university.

1 Imagine what has happened in your life (career and family) during the ten years after your graduation.

2 Act out a conversation with Student B. Start with questions about his/her family, his/her life experience after graduation, etc. Be prepared to answer some questions about your life experience too. Make sure you ask Student B about his/her experience with your current employer.

Unit 7

You are the academic director of an ESL school in China. A major part of your job is to deal with students' complaints about your ESL teachers, textbooks or curriculum. Here are some principles you stick to when getting complaints.

- Stay positive.
- Show your sympathy.
- Help the student to analyze the situation.
- Promise to get to the root of the problem and get back to the student quickly.

Now act out a conversation with Student B, who is a Chinese student of your school. Try to help him/her with his/her complaints. You will need to make apologies if necessary.

Unit 8

Student B and you are good friends. You have just graduated from college, and you have received two job offers. Right now you are tempted by the second one, but you want to consult Student B before making the final decision:

- The first one is a corporate job. The salary is good, but the location is in a big city where the living expenses are high. There will always be a lot of pressure and competition at work, but there is also great potential in terms of career development.

- The second one is at an educational institute. The salary is low, but the location is in the suburb of a big city where the living expenses are relatively low. It offers more stability than the first job, but there is less room for career development. You will have lots of free time if you take this job.

1. List the pros and cons of both positions.
2. Act out a casual discussion with Student B. You are trying to convince Student B that the second choice suits you better.

Unit 9

Look at the picture. Find differences with Student B's picture.

Unit 10

Look at the statements and check if you agree or disagree.

- ☐ 大城市比小城镇/郊区的生活更好。
- ☐ 出去旅游的时候不必省钱。
- ☐ 买二手的衣服比买新衣服更好。
- ☐ 网络让人和人的交流变得更少。
- ☐ 让孩子做家务活应该给钱。
- ☐ 学外语是为了有更多工作机会。

Now go through the statements with Student B, and mark the ones from which your opinions differ. Pick one and carry out a mini-debate with Student B. Support your opinions with examples.

Unit 11

You are passionate about other countries. You plan to travel the world and visit 20 countries. You think you can always support yourself by teaching English. Student B is a good friend of yours who likes to stay home. He/She thinks spending more than ten days on the road is unbearable.

1. Make a list of reasons why you love travelling to a foreign country and living there for an extended period of time.
2. Carry out a debate with Student B.

Unit 12

It has been _____ months/years since you started learning Chinese. You have been through many difficulties, but at the same time you have made substantial progress. It is time to reflect on your learning journey and share it with your teachers and classmates.

1. Talk about your learning experience with Student B, who is also a Chinese language learner. Find out what you had in common in learning Chinese. For example:

   - Did you have the same native language?
   - Did you encounter similar difficulties?
   - Did you both enjoy learning about Chinese culture?
   - Did you both find writing characters a challenging task?

   Add to the list more questions you want to ask.

2. Share the most rewarding/interesting experience you have had while learning Chinese.

Pair work activities for Student B

Unit 1

Read the following job description. Find six differences with Student A's job description.

让我们从这里 **开始**，
汉语教师 **招聘** 广告

》单位介绍

光华国际中学位于上海市碧云社区，是一所为外籍人士子女提供国际化教育的私立中学，共设六个年级，接受12岁到18岁的学生入校学习，使用美式教程和课本。现招聘用英文教授汉语的老师两名。每周课时为十五个小时。待遇从优。

》招聘要求

1. 英文水平高，TOEFL成绩为100分以上
2. 母语为中文
3. 大学及以上文化水平；中文专业、国际中文教育专业的毕业生优先
4. 性格活泼开朗、热爱教育、学习能力强
5. 有两年以上国际学校教学经验
6. 有海外留学经历者优先

联系方式　021-12344785

Unit 2

You are the HR manager of an educational company in China. You are looking for temporary summer employees to teach English in China. Below is a checklist of the credentials and characteristics the ideal candidate will have.

英语教师招聘要求

- 英文好，最好为母语
- 有教学经验
- 喜欢帮助别人
- 中文水平不错，可以跟中国人进行日常对话
- 性格独立，可以在中国独立生活
- 去过很多地方，适应新环境的能力很强

Student A is one of the many applicants for the position, and you will conduct an initial phone interview with him/her. Prepare a list of questions about the applicant's background information, past working experience and personality.

Act out the telephone interview with Student A. Take notes while Student A is answering your questions. Make a decision at the end of the interview and tell Student A if your company will invite him/her for a second interview.

Unit 3

You are the team leader of a group of teenagers from Beijing who are going to visit a foreign country for one week. This will be the group's first trip abroad and they want to visit two cities. Below is information about the group.

- 你带的团一共有十个学生，都是高中一年级的学生。
- 你们的钱不太多，希望飞机票尽量便宜，不一定要直飞。
- 除了参观景点以外，希望可以参观国外的高中，有机会跟当地的学生交谈。

Student A is a travel agent and will help you plan the trip. He/She will suggest four cities to visit, and routes and prices of round-trip flights. You will have to make decisions based on the information Student A provides and the budget/purpose of the group.

Act out a conversation with Student A about the itinerary. Include:

- 往返时间
- 决定参观哪两个城市
- 在两个城市参观哪些景点，有哪些活动
- 从北京到目的地的往返机票

Unit 4

You and your partner, Student A, are stranded on an island. There is enough food and water but nothing else. Which personal items below do you wish you had brought with you? Explain why. You can choose six items only.

Unit 5

1 Your company has decided to enter the Chinese market. A consulting firm is helping develop your company's business strategies in China. You are going to ask one of the consulting firm's associates, Student A, about which gifts are suitable for your potential Chinese business partners. Here is a list of items you have come up with. Complete the list with other gifts.

1 绿色的棒球帽
2 刀具
3 印有公司logo的伞
4 一瓶红酒
5 印有公司logo的T恤衫
6 一块手表
7 印有公司logo的笔、笔记本
8 _____
9 _____
10 _____

2 Act out a conversation with Student A, going over the items one by one. Make a decision about which gifts to take.

Unit 6

It has been ten years since you graduated from university. One week ago, you began working for an international organization in China. Tonight you are attending the organization's annual banquet. Because you do not know many people in the company, you feel a little bit bored. Then you bump into Student A, who was your classmate in university.

1 Imagine what has happened in your life (career and family) during the ten years after your graduation.

2 Act out a conversation with Student A. Be prepared to answer some questions about your life experience. Ask some questions about his/her family, his/her life experience after graduation. Make sure you ask Student A about his/her experience with your current employer.

Unit 7

You are a Chinese student who attends an ESL school to improve your English. Recently you have been unhappy about your class, because:

- Unlike the previous ESL teacher you had, the current teacher speaks too fast, and does not seem to focus on grammar much.
- The textbook is too difficult for your level.
- The teacher often puts you on the spot by asking for your opinions.
- You are not used to doing presentations in English in front of many people.

You may also add some other problems to the list.

Now act out a conversation with Student A, who is the academic director of the school. Choose three complaints and continue to complain until you are happy about Student A's solution.

Unit 8

Student A and you are good friends. Student A has just graduated from college, and he/she has received two job offers.

- The first one is a corporate job. The salary is good, but the location is in a big city where the living expenses are high. There will always be a lot of pressure and competition at work, but there is also great potential in terms of career development.
- The second one is at an educational institute. The salary is low, but the location is in the suburb of a big city where the living expenses are relatively low. It offers more stability than the first job, but there is less room for career development. He/She will have lots of free time if he/she takes this job.

1. List the pros and cons of both positions.
2. Act out a casual discussion with Student A. Student A is trying to convince you that the second choice suits him/her better, but you think Student A should definitely take the first offer and try to make him/her change his/her mind.

Unit 9

Look at the picture. Find differences with Student A's picture.

Unit 10

Look at the statements and check if you agree or disagree.

☐ 大城市比小城镇/郊区的生活更好。

☐ 出去旅游的时候不必省钱。

☐ 买二手的衣服比买新衣服更好。

☐ 网络让人和人的交流变得更少。

☐ 让孩子做家务活应该给钱。

☐ 学外语是为了有更多工作机会。

Now go through the statements with Student A, and mark the ones from which your opinions differ. Pick one and carry out a mini-debate with Student A. Support your opinions with examples.

Unit 11

You do not hate travelling but you prefer to be close to home. You think spending more than ten days on the road is unbearable. Student A is a good friend of yours who is passionate about other countries. It is his/her plan to travel the world and visit 20 countries. Student A thinks that he/she can always support him/herself by teaching English.

1 Make a list of challenges and practical difficulties that people face while travelling and living abroad, especially for an extended period of time.

2 Carry out a debate with Student A.

Unit 12

It has been _____ months/years since you started learning Chinese. You have been through many difficulties, but at the same time you have made substantial progress. It is time to reflect on your learning journey and share it with your teachers and classmates.

1 Talk about your learning experience with Student A, who is also a Chinese language learner. Find out what you had in common in learning Chinese. For example:

- Did you have the same native language?
- Did you encounter similar difficulties?
- Did you both enjoy learning about Chinese culture?
- Did you both find writing characters a challenging task?

Add to the list more questions you want to ask.

2 Share the most rewarding/interesting experience you have had while learning Chinese.

Grammar reference

Unit 1

Expressing "not at all", "not even one", "not a single" with 一……+ 都/也 + 不/没……

一……+ 都/也 + 不/没…… is used to express "not at all", "not a single" or "not even one". The phrase can either be "一点儿", which modifies uncountable nouns, or "一 + measure word", which precedes countable nouns. Sometimes, an object is moved to the very beginning of the sentence to serve as a topic, thus showing a strong emphasis.

Subject	一……	（Noun）	都/也	不/没……
	他	一点儿	休息的时间	都	没有。
从早上到现在	她	一点儿	水	也	没喝。
这些书，	我	一本		也	不想看。
在这里	他	一个	朋友	都	没有。
那些以前的事情，	他	一件		都	不记得了。

Emphasizing details of a past action using 是……的

是……的 is used to emphasize the time, method, place, purpose or agent of a particular action in the past. What the speaker wants to highlight should be put between 是 and 的. Sometimes, 是 can be omitted, but 的 can't.

1 她（是）昨天到的伦敦。（Time）
2 她（是）坐火车去的伦敦。（Method）
3 她（是）在伦敦学的建筑学。（Place）
4 她（是）为了学建筑学才去伦敦的。（Purpose）
5 （是）她的高中同学去车站接的她。（Agent）

Showing direction of movement with 回/进/上/下 + 来/去

回, 进, 上 and 下 can be combined with either 来 or 去 to show the direction of movement. That is, in words such as 回来, 上去, 下来, etc., 来 and 去 serve as directional complements. 来 indicates the action moves towards the speaker, while 去 indicates the action moves away from the speaker. If there is an object showing location or destination, it is placed between 回/进/上/下 and 来/去, e.g. 回北京来, 进房间去, etc.

	Verb	Object	Directional complement	
我父母上个星期就	回	家乡	去	了。
你觉得他明年还会	回	咱们公司	来	吗？
外面味道不太好，你快	进	屋里	去。	
我住在三层，你能不能	上	楼	来？	
这么高，你是不是有点儿害怕？要我帮你	下		去	吗？

Introducing an extreme case using (连)……都/也……

（连）……都/也…… means "even" and expresses that information or an event is unexpected or surprising. In order to express that something is unexpected or surprising, an extreme case is placed between 连 and 都/也.

	（连）	Extreme case	都/也	Verb
你真行！	连	唐诗	都	会背呀。
最近快要忙死了，	连	上厕所的时间	都	快没有了。
在伦敦生活了两年了，可是他	连	大英博物馆	也	没去过。

Grammar reference 183

	（连）	Extreme case	都/也	Verb
工作了一天，我爸累得	连	说话的力气	都	没有了。
你不是很喜欢音乐剧吗，怎么	连	《猫》	都	没听说过？

Unit 2

Indicating a very high degree of something with 不得了 (bùdéliǎo)

不得了 is a complement and is used to indicate a very high degree of an adjective or an emotional verb. They form the structure "adj./emotional verb 得不得了". The adjectives or emotional verbs can be either negative or positive in meaning.

	Adj. / Verb	得	不得了
屋子里没有空调，	热	得	不得了。
他的女朋友跟他分手了，他	难过	得	不得了。
那家饭馆儿的上海菜，	好吃	得	不得了。
听说周末要去钓鱼，小林	高兴	得	不得了。
她喜欢那个明星	喜欢	得	不得了。

Repeated actions with 再 (zài) or 又 (yòu)

Both 再 and 又 can serve as adverbs meaning "again", thus indicating the repetition of an action or activity. 再 indicates that an action which occurred in the past is to be repeated in the future. In contrast, 又 indicates that the repeated action has already occurred. In some circumstances, 又 can also be used to indicate the future recurrence of an action which can be expected or anticipated.

	再/又	Verb phrase
你能	再	给她发封邮件吗？
我们可以	再	给他一次机会。
我过几天	再	去他们学校一趟。
我和我哥昨天	又	看了一遍这个电影。
他	又	梦见父母了。
明天	又	要考试了。

Expressing "a little bit" using 一下 (yíxià) or 一点儿 (yìdiǎnr)

一下 and 一点儿 can both be used to moderate a statement to mean "a little bit". 一点儿 can be used as a qualifier to modify the object of the verb and denote that the quantity is small. 一下 is used in an imperative sentence or when the speaker wants to make a suggestion or request.

	Verb	一下 / 一点儿	Object	
这事儿我不太清楚，你还是	问	一下	别人吧。	
我能不能	借	一下	你的中文书？	
你好好跟他	解释	一下，		别再吵架了。
我	买了	一点儿	蔬菜和肉，	晚上咱们自己做饭吧。
他	知道	一点儿	中国的历史。	
去西班牙旅游，最好能	懂	一点儿	西班牙语。	

184 ❖ Grammar reference

Indicating the beginning of an action or the start of a new state with 起来 (qǐlái)

起来 is used after an action verb to indicate the beginning of an action or after an adjective to indicate the start of a new state. Even though 起来 still serves as a complement, its literal meaning of "upward movement" as a directional complement has been lost. If the verb takes an object, the object should be inserted between 起 and 来.

	Verb 起（object）来 / Adj. 起来
你不做功课，怎么	看起小说来了？
她的狗和邻居家的狗	打了起来。
他跟着音乐	唱起歌来。
一想到要在大家面前说话，他就	紧张起来。
看见又漂亮又好吃的蛋糕，孩子一下子就	高兴得跳起来了。

Unit 3

Introducing a new subject using 至于 (zhìyú)

至于 as a preposition means "as to" or "with regard to". It is used to introduce a new subject or raise a new topic. The new subject must be related to the topic of the previous statement, or be a new aspect of the previous topic. The new subject could be a noun phrase, a verb phrase, or a clause. 至于 and its new subject are followed by a further comment.

Previous statement	至于 + new subject matter	Further comment
听说他要离开公司了，	至于原因，	我不太清楚。
听说他要离开公司了，	至于什么时候离开，	现在还不太清楚。
听说他要离开公司了，	至于他以后去哪儿工作，	我就不知道了。

Previous statement	至于 + new subject matter	Further comment
那家餐馆，饭菜味道特别好，服务也很棒，	至于价格，	当然也是相当高的。
对我来说，能参加这次比赛就是很好的经历，	至于比赛成绩，	其实并不是很重要。

Comparative structures using 不如 (bùrú)

The comparative structure using 不如 means "A is not as … as B". If the adjectives appear at the start of the sentence, they do not need to be repeated at the end. If there is no specific adjective mentioned, the default meaning "(not as) good" applies.

Context	A	不如	B	Adj.
	香蕉	不如	苹果	好吃
	我工作	不如	他	努力
	我妹妹唱歌唱得	不如	我	好
他踢球踢得那么好，	我	不如	他。	
	坐飞机	不如	坐火车	

Expressing fractions and percentages with ……分之…… (fēn zhī)

……分之…… is used to express fractions or percentages. The order is the reverse of that used in English. So, when expressing a fraction, the denominator precedes 分之, while the numerator follows 分之, e.g. ¾ is read 四分之三. When expressing a percentage, the idea of "parts per hundred" is expressed first, with 百分之……, e.g. 25.9% is read 百分之二十五点九. "A 占 B 的……分之……" is a particular structure used to express fractions or percentages, often appearing in formal and written expression.

1 火车票差不多比飞机票便宜四分之三。
2 选择公共交通工具上下班的人占城市总人口的三分之一。
3 世界上约有五分之一的人喝不到干净的水。
4 地球上大约百分之九十七的水是咸水。
5 六十五岁以上的老人占伦敦总人口的百分之十三点七。

Moderating positive adjectives with 还 (hái)

还 as an adverb is used to moderate or weaken the positive tone of adjectives. As such, the meaning of 还 is similar to "quite" or "reasonably" in English. Even though 还 moderates the positive tone of adjectives, the speaker in fact still wants to convey a positive comment. If there are some other degree adverbs modifying the positive adjectives, they often follow 还 rather than precede it.

	还	Positive adjective
他觉得小林人	还	不错。
这家旅馆的服务	还	行。
共享单车月卡	还	算便宜。
昨天的考试	还	比较容易。
这附近就算到了晚上也	还	算安全。

Unit 4

"Verb + object" as a separable compound

"Verb + object" compounds (V-O compounds) are a group of verbs whose internal structure is "verb + object". A V-O compound is not a combination of two words; it is considered one word only, and the English translation is usually one word, e.g. 睡觉=sleep; 唱歌=sing. The V-O compounds can be separated by inserting the aspectual particles 了, 过, or 着, or by duration, frequency, and quantifiers. Because V-O compounds already contain an object, they cannot be directly followed by another object; this is why, e.g. *我要见面他 is ungrammatical and the correct expression is 我要跟他见面.

	Verb		Object	
为了复习，她昨天只	睡	了两个小时的	觉。	
我爸爸最喜欢给我和妹妹	照		相。	
你能不能过来	帮	一下	忙？	
他	毕	了	业	就搬到深圳去了。
天气太热了，他今天	洗	了五次	澡。	

通过 (tōngguò) as a preposition

通过 as a preposition means using a certain method to achieve a desired outcome. The structure is "通过 + method, subject + VP" or "Subject + 通过 + method + VP". The method introduced by 通过 should be a noun phrase or substantivized verb phrase.

	通过	Method	
	通过	社交网络，	年轻人之间进行着各种各样的交流。
年轻人之间	通过	社交网络	进行着各种各样的交流。
	通过	眼睛、耳朵、鼻子，	人们可以感受到外部世界。
人们	通过	眼睛、耳朵、鼻子，	可以感受到外部世界。
他们是	通过	别人的介绍	才认识的。
这里的人们喜欢	通过	唱歌或跳舞的方式	来表达他们心里的想法。

Introducing the agent or performer of an action

using 由 (yóu)

由 as a preposition is used to introduce and emphasize the agent or doer who performs a certain action. The structure is "topic + 由 + agent + verb". The agent introduced by 由 should be a noun or a pronoun indicating a person or an organization.

Object	由	Agent	Verb	
这次公司年会，	由	王经理	负责	。
1931年的科学考察队是	由	王教授	带领	的。
国家的未来应该	由	人民	决定	。
第32届夏季奥运会是	由	东京	主办	的。
旅行线路	由	你	安排	吧。

Disyllabic words that become monosyllabic in formal style

In written Chinese or formal speech, some disyllabic words like modal verbs, conjunctions, adverbs, etc. may appear in their monosyllabic form. The monosyllabic forms rarely appear in oral Chinese or informal style of writing.

	Disyllabic word	
我们	应（该）	把客户的需求放在第一位。
	如（果）	有任何需要，请及时联系我部门。
客户	可（以）	通过客服部跟我公司联系。
较少运动的人应少吃	或（者）	不吃甜食。
这些公园和艺术馆	已（经）	全部开放。

Unit 5

Concessive clauses with 倒 (dào)

倒 is an adverb that shows a turning point or concession in a sentence. 倒 may appear either in the first clause or in the second. If the first clause expresses negative comments, then the second clause uses 倒 to show the change in meaning and introduce positive comments. In contrast, if the first clause uses 倒 to show a concession to introduce positive comments, then the second clause should express negative comments. The comments in the second clause are what the speaker wants to emphasize or highlight. The second clause will often contain 不过, 但是, or 可是.

Clause 1（negative）	Clause 2（倒 positive）
在内蒙古当老师，收入的确不高，	不过马老师倒是很喜欢这里的生活方式。
你买的苹果有点儿小，	味道倒还不错。
我奶奶已经八十多岁了，牙掉光了，耳朵也不太听得见了，	不过精神倒很好。

Clause 1（倒 positive）	Clause 2（negative）
马老师倒很喜欢在内蒙古的生活方式，	不过她家人觉得她收入太低了。
你买的苹果味道倒还不错，	就是有点儿小。
我奶奶精神倒还好，	可是她牙掉光了，耳朵也不太听得见了，我们都很担心她。

Expressing "doing well" with 好好 (hǎohǎo)

好好 as an adverbial modifies the verb phrase which follows it, expressing the meaning of "doing something thoroughly" or "doing something as well as possible". Sometimes model verbs like 想 / 会 / 应该 / 得 / 要 appear before 好好 and help to emphasize the tone or the attitude of the speaker. In colloquial expression, the second "好 hǎo" changes to "hāo" and the "er" sound is also added, giving "hǎohāor".

Grammar reference 187

	好好 + verb phrase
这件事情，我们得	好好谈一谈。
请你们	好好考虑一下我的建议。
明天就是周末了，你也	好好放松放松吧。
我的朋友想	好好研究一下茶的历史和文化。
要想健康，一定要	好好锻炼身体。

Making deductions with 既然 (jìrán)

既然 is a conjunction used in the structure "既然 + fact / reason / premise, 那 / 就 / 为什么 + inference / suggestion". 既然 appears in the first clause to restate a known fact, reason or premise, while the second clause, as the main clause, presents a logical inference or suggestion deduced from the fact, reason or premise mentioned in the first clause. The second clause often has 那 or 就, meaning "then", to show the inference or suggestion is drawn naturally and logically. The second clause may also contain a rhetorical question, indicated by 为什么, to show a strongly questioning tone.

	Clause 1 (既然)	Clause 2
	既然小林喜欢画画，	他应该愿意去上画画课。
	既然这里的东西都不太合适，	我们还是去别的商店看看吧。
	既然你对那家公司很感兴趣，	为什么还不申请呢？
A：马克请我参加他的生日晚会，可是那天我太忙，怎么办呀？	B：既然你没时间，	那就别去了。
A：我父母不太希望我搬到广州住。	B：既然你父母不同意，	你就留在西安吧。

Stressing an extreme degree with 再……不过了 (zài... búguò le)

再……不过了 is used to stress an extreme degree, and means "nothing is more … than". The words inserted between 再 and 不过了 may be either adjectives or emotional verbs. The adjectives or emotional verbs usually have positive connotations.

	再……不过了	
这件衣服穿在你身上	再合适不过了。	
他说他很忙，恐怕没时间参加同学聚会。我觉得他的意思	再清楚不过了。	
用手机拍照片	再简单不过了。	
能把她请来唱歌	再好不过了。	
西红柿炒鸡蛋是一个	再普通不过	的菜。

Unit 6

Indicating an extreme degree with ……死了 (sǐ le)

死了 is used as a degree complement to intensify the adjectives preceding it, indicating an extreme degree of the adjectives in question. 死了 is similar to "deadly" or "… to death" in English. For example, 冷死了 means "deadly cold". Usually, the adjectives preceding 死了 have negative meanings, but occasionally, 死了 is used to intensify emotional adjectives with positive connotations, e.g. 高兴, 开心, 兴奋. In addition, if the speaker uses 死了 to express that they personally are affected to an extreme degree, 我 can be inserted in between 死 and 了.

	Adj. + 死了
楼上的音乐这么大声，真是	吵死了。
别买了，这家商店的水果	贵死了。
周末一直下大雨，哪儿都去不了，待在家里	无聊死了。
	郁闷死我了。

	Adj. + 死了
你给你妹妹买了这么漂亮的礼物，她一定	高兴死了。

Expressing wishes and hopes with 要是/如果……就好了

要是/如果……就好了 is a structure in the subjunctive mood which expresses a wish or hope. It is similar in meaning to "It would be great, if only …". Sometimes, 要是/如果 can be dropped.

	（要是/如果） clause	就好了
真可惜，	要是明天晚上你能来跟我们一起看球赛	就好了。
	如果我们的大学在同一个城市	就好了。
	明天没有考试	就好了。
	这件衣服便宜一点儿	就好了。
怎么下雨了？	要是出门的时候带上伞	就好了。

Expressing emphasis using 可

可 as an adverb is used to emphasize a statement. Without 可, the meaning of the statement doesn't change, but the tone of the statement is weakened. 可……了 can also be employed to intensify an adjective. It is similar to 很, but its tone is slightly stronger than 很. 可 as an emphatic adverb is mainly used in colloquial expression.

Subject	可	Verb phrase
坐火车	可	比坐飞机舒服。
你	可	别忘了交房租。
学中文	可	得注意声调。
她	可	不相信你说的这些话。
我	可	没有时间陪你逛街。

Subject	可	Adj. + 了
经理	可	生气了。
这个游戏	可	有意思了。

Justifying an opinion or decision using 反正

反正 as a modal adverb means "anyway" or "anyhow". The clause involving 反正 indicates a reason which is used to support the speaker's subjective attitude or judgment of a situation. The situation usually involves options or choices, e.g. 去 vs. 不去; 见面 vs. 不见面.

		反正+ justification	
A：没想到这门课这么难，怎么办呀？	B：反正现在后悔也来不及了，	好好学吧。
	B：那你就换一门别的课吧，	反正选课的时间还没过。	
	我们多买几种水果吧，	反正这些水果的价钱都是一样的，	只吃一种水果多没意思。
A：我想买个新照相机，可太贵了！	B：我看你还是别买了，	反正用手机也可以拍照片。	
	B：反正一部好照相机可以用很久，	贵点儿也值得。	

Unit 7

Expressing "how come" with 怎么

怎么 is a question word used to ask for a reason or explanation. 怎么 has a similar tone and connotation to "how come" in English. It not only asks "why", but also expresses a tone of surprise. 怎么 often appears after the subject of a sentence.

1 你怎么会在这儿？不是王云云来接我吗？
2 他怎么把他女朋友的生日忘了？
3 海鲜怎么越来越贵了？
4 她不来，怎么也不给我们打个电话？
5 你在北京住了四年，怎么还没去过长城？

Emphasizing an inquiry with 到底/究竟 (dàodǐ / jiūjìng)

到底 and 究竟 express an intensity or incredulity similar to the phrase "on earth". They are adverbs used to emphasize a question or to press the other speaker to give an answer or tell the truth. 到底 and 究竟 emphasize three question forms: questions beginning with wh-words; questions posed by a verb (V-not-V questions); and questions which offer an "either ... or ..." alternative. They can also be used in embedded questions. However, 究竟 is more formal than 到底.

1 究竟是什么原因让你对我们没有了信心？
2 很多大学生都想不清楚自己究竟应该选什么专业。
3 我们到底在哪个房间开会？
4 你到底认不认识他？
5 毕业以后，他到底想读研究生还是想马上工作？
6 两个都是他的好朋友，他实在不知道到底该帮谁。

Minimizing a situation with 不过/只不过/只+是……（罢了） (búguò / zhǐ búguò / zhǐ + shì … bàle)

不过/只不过/只+是……（罢了）is a pattern used to trivialize or downplay the thing, the situation, or the number they modify. 不过/只不过/只 means "merely". 罢了 is a modal particle which also means "merely". 罢了 either appears at the end of the clause or can be dropped.

	不过/只不过/只+是		罢了
这个菜其实不难做，	只不过（是）	比较花时间	罢了。
	不过是	一个小玩具，	坏了就坏了吧，没关系的。

	不过/只不过/只+是		罢了
他	只是	性格有点儿内向，	并不是不想跟你说话。
我还好，	只不过（是）	有点儿感冒	罢了，别担心。
哪里哪里，我哪有你说的那么厉害。我	只是	运气很好	罢了，要不然也进不了这么好的公司。

Indicating "not only …, but also …" with 不但/不只/不仅/不光……而且/还/也…… (búdàn / bùzhǐ / bùjǐn / bùguāng … érqiě / hái / yě …)

不但……而且…… is the most commonly used structure to express "not only …, but also …". Besides 不但……而且……, there are some other structures which are also used to express the same meaning. 不但 can be replaced by 不仅/不只/不光; 而且 can be replaced by 还/也. In addition, 而且 can also be used in conjunction with 还 or 也. Unlike their English counterparts, 不但/不只/不仅/不光 and 而且/还/也 can only be followed by an adjective or a verb phrase; they cannot be followed by a noun phrase. Thus, a sentence like *他会说不但法文，而且中文 is ungrammatical.

Subject	不但/不只/不仅/不光	而且/还/也
骑自行车	不但可以锻炼身体，	而且能保护环境。
他	不只记得大家的名字，	也知道每个人的生日和兴趣爱好。
这家超市的蔬菜	不但品种丰富，	而且价格也比别的超市要便宜。

Subject	不但/不只/ 不仅/不光	而且/还/也
这位医生	不仅医术好，	还很有耐心。
她	不光聪明，	还非常漂亮。

Unit 8

Comparing 后来 (hòulái) and 然后 (ránhòu)

后来 is a time noun referring to a certain period of time long ago in the past. 后来 can only be used to give the sequence of past events. It is similar to "afterwards" or "later on" in English.

Unlike 后来, 然后 is a conjunction and is often used together with 先 and 最后 to indicate the sequence of actions. It is similar to "and then" or "after that" in English. In addition, 然后 can be used to indicate the sequence of future actions as well as past ones.

Past event 1	后来 + past event 2
他刚认识小林的时候觉得小林不太爱说话，	后来才知道小林其实特别喜欢聊天儿。
我一年前刚进这个部门的时候还见过他几次，	后来就再也没见到，他是不是离开公司了？
这本小说一出来就非常受欢迎，	后来还被拍成了电影。

Action 1	然后 + action 2
我不能告诉你答案。你自己再仔细读一遍，	然后好好想一想吧。
先把这些菜切成小块儿，	然后再放进锅里炒一炒。
他们先去了哈尔滨，	然后又去了西安和丽江。

Expressing "no matter what / how / whether" with 无论/不论/不管……都…… (wúlùn / búlùn / bùguǎn ... dōu ...)

无论, 不论 and 不管 mean "no matter what / how / whether …" and appear in the first part of the sentence to introduce the circumstances. 都 appears in the second part of the sentence to emphasize that the result won't change. 无论/不论/不管 is always used with 1) wh-words, 2) questions which offer "either … or …" alternatives (是 X 还是 Y), or 3) questions in the "verb-not-verb" form. Among the three words, 无论 is the most formal and is generally used in written language; 不论 is less formal than 无论, and is used in both oral and written language; 不管 is the most informal, and generally used in oral language.

无论/不论/不管 + circumstances	都 + result
无论是科学还是艺术，	都离不开人类的思考。
无论放弃什么，	都不要放弃希望。
不论问题多么复杂，	他都能找到解决的办法。
不管你喜欢不喜欢他，	你都得承认他的话还是有一定的道理的。
不管谁找你，	你都不应该在上课的时候接电话。

Expressing tones with adverbs 原来 (yuánlái), 果然 (guǒrán), 竟然 (jìngrán)

原来 is used for recently discovered information. The tone is that of sudden realization.

果然 is used to confirm that the fact indeed corresponds to the previous statement, assumption or expectation.

竟然 is used to indicate that the fact or the situation is unexpected from the speaker's point of view, or is an unusual situation. 竟 is interchangeable with 竟然, but more literary than 竟然.

原来 can only be placed at the start of a clause. 果然 can be placed both at the beginning of a clause or after the subject. 竟然 can only appear after the subject.

原来

听说他特别高，昨天见了才知道，原来他还没有我高。

原来这种鱼就是三文鱼 (salmon) 啊，以前还真不知道。

我们都以为你已经下班回家了，原来你还没走啊。

果然

朋友说在那家店可以买到新手机，果然我就买到了。

我听说他不愿意和别人一起住，我去问他了，他果然不愿意搬来。

昨天我在地铁上看到一个人，很像小林，今天一问，那个人果然是他。

竟然

真不敢相信，一张邮票竟然卖到两万元。

偷走她鞋子的竟然是一只猫。

没想到他竟然能用粉笔画出这么美的画。

Expressing personal judgments with 算（是）suànshì

算 means "to be considered as" or "to count as". As a verb, it introduces the speaker's subjective judgment about a person, a thing or an event. 算 prevents a judgment, positive or negative, from sounding absolute. Adverbs like 就, 也 and 还 often precede 算. 是 is optional.

Topic	算（是）+ judgment
杭州	算（是）我去过的最漂亮的城市了。
这条鱼	还算（是）新鲜。
西红柿	能算（是）水果吗？
这会儿正堵车，他能一个小时赶过来，	也算（是）快的了。
对很多人来说，有工作、有食物、有住的地方，	就算（是）幸福了。

Unit 9

Expressing "seem to be" with 看起来 kàn qǐlái

看起来 is used to express "it looks like …" or "sb/sth seems to be …". The subject should precede 看起来. The predicate after 看起来 indicates what the subject appears to be like. Usually the predicate contains adjectives which may appear with degree adverbs or in different comparative structures. 看起来 has a connotation of subjective description and comparison; therefore it indicates how the observer feels.

Subject	看起来	Predicate
老师今天	看起来	挺累的。
这个项目	看起来	比去年那个项目困难多了。
我也不知道这辆车是什么牌子的。不过，它	看起来	并不是很贵。
你妈妈真年轻，她	看起来	就像是你的姐姐。
爱笑的人	看起来	更可爱。

Expressing "nearly" with 差点儿 chàdiǎnr

差点儿 literally means "differing a little bit". It is an adverb and means "nearly", expressing an event or action almost happened (but did not).

If the action or event was good and desired by the subject, 差点儿 implies that "it nearly happened, and it was a pity that it didn't". On the other hand, if the action or event was bad and not desired by the subject, 差点儿 implies that "it nearly happened, but luckily it didn't".

	差点儿	（就）+ verb phrase
父母	差点儿	忘了小女儿的生日。

	差点儿	（就）+ verb phrase
由于两天都找不到他，他的朋友们	差点儿	就报警了。
今天下午的课，我	差点儿	迟到了。
他	差点儿	没赶上火车。
为了让自己的宿舍和家里一样舒服，她	差点儿	把家里所有的东西都搬到宿舍。

	是否	Verb phrase
教授还在考虑	是否	要进行这次实验。
政府仍在犹豫	是否	要在本地新建一家医院。
你	是否	还把我当成最好的朋友？
参赛者如何知道自己	是否	得奖了？

Exclamations with 多……（啊） (duō a)

多 and 啊 are used together to intensify an adjective. This forms an exclamation and expresses a strong feeling on behalf of the speaker. Adjectives or noun phrases that are modified by adjectives should be placed between 多 and 啊. In the structure, 多 is necessary while 啊 is optional. 多……啊 is usually used in oral expressions when the speaker expresses feelings or impressions about something.

	多 + adj.……（啊）	
	多好的主意啊，	咱们就听他的吧。
	多地道的上海菜啊！	真没想到在伦敦也能吃到这么好吃的上海菜。
你弟弟	多独立，	他根本不需要你来照顾他。
坐地铁	多方便啊，	而且还很便宜。
你的宿舍	多干净啊。	我的宿舍可没你的好。

Expressing "whether or not" with 是否 (shìfǒu)

是否 means "whether or not". However, it is an adverb and is not always interchangeable with 是不是. 是否 is used either in a question or in a clause that serves as the object of verbs like 考虑, 犹豫, 想, etc. 是否 is always placed before the verb phrases that it modifies. It is often used in formal oral or written expression.

Unit 10

Continual repetition of an action with Verb 来 verb 去 (lái qù)

V 来 V 去 is used to express continual repetition of an action. Here 来 and 去 have lost their directional meanings, and instead they indicate that a certain action is done over and over again. Very often a verb-complement structure follows V 来 V 去 in order to indicate the result of the repetitive action. A complement may be either resultative, or the negative form of a potential complement. If the verb has an object, the object should be placed after the verb and its complement.

Subject	Verb 来 verb 去	(Adv.) + verb + complement + (object)
你	问来问去	也问不出什么结果的。
我	想来想去，	都想不明白。
我	想来想去，	也想不起来她叫什么名字。
他们	找来找去，	总算找到了那本书。
他	看来看去	也看不清楚黑板上究竟是什么字。

Indicating a continuing action with the complement 下去 (xiàqù)

下去 literally means "go down", and is often used as a directional complement. However, it has also developed a more abstract meaning, in which it serves as a complement to indicate a continuing action. The verbs that precede 下去 are action verbs which can continue (or not). For example, 讨论下去 means "to continue to discuss" or "to carry on discussing", while

讨论不下去 means "not able to carry on discussing".

	Verb（不）下去	
这件事情，我们不要再	讨论下去	了。
每个月挣多少钱才能在这座城市	生活下去？	
这个活动多有意义啊，应该	继续下去。	
只说了几句，她就	说不下去	了。
每天六点起来，真的太早了，我觉得我肯定	坚持不下去。	

Talking about disposal of time/money/energy with bǎ 把

把……V 在……上 is used to express how one disposes of one's time, money, or energy. In the structure, the verbs usually are 花, 用, 放 or 浪费. The phrases that are inserted between 在……上 can be either nouns or verbs.

Subject	把	Time/money/energy	Verb 在……上
他	把	时间	都浪费在看无聊的电视剧上了。
小林	把	时间	都用在学英语上了。
父母不让我	把	钱	浪费在买漫画书上。
我姐姐	把	钱	都花在买漂亮衣服上了。
她	把	精力	都放在交朋友上了。

Expressing "even if" with jíshǐ 即使……yě 也……

The conjunctive structure 即使……也…… means "even if ..., still...". It is used to mean that even if the condition in the first clause were realized, the situation in the second clause would not change. 即使……也…… has the same meaning and function as 就算……也……, but it is more formal than the latter. 即使 is different from 虽然 because 即使 introduces a hypothetical condition, while 虽然 introduces a fact.

	（即使）clause 1	（也）clause 2
这么多的内容，	即使他对你有好感，	也不见得就真的会爱上你。
	即使今天都记住了，	明天也会忘的。
	即使换一家公司，	也不一定轻松。
	即使在黑夜中，	这款相机也能拍出完美的照片。
	即使失败，	也不要放弃。

Unit 11

Expressing "as one pleases" with xiǎng 想……jiù 就……

"想+V+question word+就+V+question word" (or "想+question word+V+就+question word+V") is used to express that someone can do something as he/she pleases. The two "V+wh" (or "wh+V") structures following 想 and 就 must be the same and are necessary for both. The "question words" in this structure are used as indefinite references. The subjects preceding 想 and 就 may not be the same.

Subject 1	想+verb+question word	Subject 2	就+verb+question word	
你	想看什么表演，		就看什么表演。	
他	想几点回来，		就几点回来，	你不要管他。
你	想去哪儿，	我们	就去哪儿。	

	Subject 1	想+ verb+ question word	Subject 2	就+ verb+ question word
有钱的好处就是		想怎么花钱，		就怎么花钱。
	你	想选择谁，		就选择谁。

Emphasizing a particular manner of carrying out an action using Verb 1 着(zhe) + verb 2

"V1 着 (o1)+v2 (o2)" is used to mean "to conduct an action in a particular manner or state". "V1 着 (o1)" is not the main action, but is used to indicate a particular manner or state. "V2 (o2)" is the main action, which is conducted in the particular manner or state of "v1 着 (o1)".

Subject	Verb 1 着 (object 1)	Verb 2 (object 2)
他喜欢	站着	吃饭。
他们	追着那个明星	要他的签名。
她	抱着受伤的小狗	大哭起来。
给你推荐一本书，叫	《带着眼镜和心	去旅行》。
一群孩子	笑着闹着	跑进屋子。

Emphasizing the reason for a result with 之所以……(zhīsuǒyǐ) 是因为……(shì yīnwèi)

之所以……是因为…… is used to show result and reason. 之所以 introduces the result, which is caused by the reason introduced by 是因为. Compared with 因为……所以……, 之所以……是因为…… is a formal expression and often appears in written language. The subject or topic should go before 之所以.

Subject	之所以……	是因为……
这个地方	之所以会吸引大量的游客，	是因为它四季如春、风景如画。
他	之所以能在短短几年内取得这么大的成功，	是因为他从不害怕任何困难。
一个人	之所以会觉得累，	是因为对所有的事情都太过在乎。
这个国家的经济	之所以能快速发展，	是因为政府实行了比较有效的经济政策。
孩子	之所以可爱，	是因为他们简单又真诚。

Expressing "to regard A as B" using 以……(yǐ) 为……(wéi)

以……为…… is used to express "to regard A as B". For example, 以北京时间为准 means "to regard Beijing time as the reference". 以……为…… is a formal expression. Its informal counterpart is 把……当作…….

Subject	以 A	为 B
化学研究	以实验	为基础。
很多国家都	以毫米、厘米、分米、米、千米	为长度单位。
这所大学	以法律	为核心专业。
生活是否应该	以快乐	为目的？
这届夏令营	以"知行合一"	为主题。

Unit 12

Expressing an emphatic tone using 才……(cái) 呢(ne)

才……呢 is used to show that the speaker wants to emphasize a fact or situation when responding to the first speaker's question or statement. It can be used to emphasize both the positive form and the negative form of an adjective or verb.

Grammar reference 195

	Subject + 才……呢
A：这家店的咖啡可好喝了！	B：那家店的咖啡才好喝呢。
A：你们学校的体育馆真不错啊！	B：他们的体育馆才好呢！
A：昨天张老师批评你了吧？	B：张老师才不会呢，她对学生很好的。
A：你别相信他说的话。	B：我才不会相信他呢。
A：听说坐地铁去机场很不方便。	B：不会呀，坐地铁去机场才方便呢。

Expressing unnecessariness using 何必……呢 (hébì…ne)

何必……呢 is used in a rhetorical question to express the idea that there is no need to do something or that something is unnecessary. This is similar to the way we use "Why …?" in English. 何必……呢 appears in the second clause, where 何必 means "it's unnecessary", while the first clause introduces a reason or premise which explains why there is no need to do the thing. 呢 can sometimes be dropped.

Clause 1	何必……呢
我可以等下个星期有时间了再去邮局，	何必一定要这个星期去呢？
你不是已经通过那个考试了吗？虽然分数有点儿低，	可是何必再考一次呢？
既然他已经跟你分手了，	你何必还跟他联系呢？
你不是住三楼吗？	我们走楼梯就行了，何必等电梯？
想了解苗族，去北京的中华民族园就可以，	何必非要去一趟云南。

Expressing "let alone" with 别说A, 就是B, 也/都…… (biéshuō jiùshì yě dōu)

别说 means "let alone", "not to mention". The structure indicates that in most cases if the comment can be applied to topic B, then the comment can also be applied to topic A.

	别说A	就是B	也/都 + comment
我爷爷说，他小的时候，	别说电脑和网络，	就是好看的书，	也没有多少。
这个房间绝对安全，	别说是人了，	就是蚊子，	也进不来。
	别说走一个小时，	就是走六个小时，	他都没问题。
这么奇特的水果，	别说吃了，	就是见，	我都没见过。
只要让我跟你们一起去云南，	别说为你们开车，	就是帮你们做更多的事情，	我也愿意。

Indicating "constantly" or "non-stop" with 一直 or 不断 (yìzhí búduàn) (地) (de)

Both 一直 and 不断 are adverbs used to indicate that the action is continuous. But they do not always apply to the same context. 一直 means "all along" or "all the time", which expresses the continuation of an action or an unchangable circumstance within a certain period of time. The verbs or adjectives modified by 一直 are usually durative; 一直 can also be used together with structures indicating ongoing actions such as 在 V or V 着.

However, 不断 literally means "nonstop" or "unceasingly". The verbs modifed by 不断 are usually those that express a single occurrence, so 不断 is used to indicate that the action is repeated again and again.

In addition, 不断 often requires the adverbial particle 地 to follow it, while 一直 does not. If 一直 and 不断 appear in one sentence, 一直 goes before 不断.

Subject	一直/不断（地）	Verb phrase
这些年来，她	一直	把李娜当成自己的姐姐。
这个国家	一直	非常重视儿童的教育。
亚深公司	不断地	把货物从深圳运到全国各地。
他的做法	不断	受到别人的批评。
人的一生，要	一直不断地	进行各种各样的选择。

English translations

Unit 1

❖ Vocabulary and listening

Mark: Yeong-min, how was your vacation?

Yeong-min: Very good. I went back to South Korea to see my parents and friends. It was so good to be with my parents. I binged and have put on some weight. How about you? Where did you go during your vacation?

Mark: I didn't go anywhere. I just stayed at school studying Chinese. Next week I have an interview to attend.

Yeong-min: What kind of interview? Are you looking for a job?

Mark: Just a post for an internship. Since I want to stay and work in China after graduation, I would like to gain some work experience in China by interning during the summer vacation.

Yeong-min: Excellent! You've made such an early start in preparing for job hunting. What are the company and the post like?

Mark: It's an international trading company, and their Customer Service Department are looking for an interpreter. I have people skills and understand Chinese culture, which I hope will meet their requirements.

Yeong-min: You are quite capable. With good preparation, it shouldn't be a problem.

Mark: Thanks for your encouragement. However, they say that a lot of people are applying for this post, and the competition is fierce. I have no confidence at all.

Yeong-min: Don't worry. You'll be fine. Where did you see the information for the job?

Mark: On a website. I'll send you the link this evening. Oh yes, Amanda went back to Brazil. Did you know?

Yeong-min: She sent me an email. Ah, so many friends have left Beijing. Wang Yu has also gone to the States to study.

Mark: Yes. Anyway, we can still contact them online. Recently I came across a line from a classical Chinese poem: "A bosom friend afar brings a distant land near".

Yeong-min: Great, you even know classical Chinese poetry!

❖ Reading and writing

Home   Job search   Company search   Print

Current page: Yashen International Trading Co Ltd
Industry: import and export
Size: 100–150 employees
Location: China
Company description: Yashen International Trading Co Ltd specializes in the import and export of children's toys and clothing products. Founded in 2000, the company has branches in Beijing, Chongqing and Shenzhen.

Position	Location	Issue date
1 Customer service intern	Shenzhen	28 March
2 Branch sales manager	Chongqing	15 March

Home   Job search   Company search   Print

Current page: Interpreter intern, Customer Service Department, Yashen International Trading Co Ltd (2)

Location: Shenzhen (frequent business trips required)

Duties: Assist in receiving American and European customers; provide interpretation service in Chinese and English; assist in arranging work schedules, visits and sightseeing activities for customers.

Requirements: Undergraduate students; having strong communication skills and ability of articulating; priority will be given to those majoring in English, economics or management and those who have experience of English-Chinese translation or of secretarial work.

Benefits: Free accommodation and internship wages (negotiable); those with an excellent standard of performance during the internship may become employees after graduation.

How to apply: Please send your CV to the company's mailbox; notice for the interview will be issued in one week.

Contact person: Miss Wen

The International Exchange Centre is looking for summer volunteers

Number of people required: 2

Project: The 4th International Secondary School Students' Summer Camp

Time period: 15 July to 15 August

Location: Beijing and Harbin

Duties: Assist the International Exchange Centre in organization and student management at the International Summer Camp for Secondary School Students.

Benefits: Food, accommodation and transport during the summer camp will be provided by the International Exchange Centre; there will also be a living allowance.

Applicant requirements: International students of the university (all nationalities welcome) must speak fluent English and Chinese, with strong communication skills.

Application method: Fill in and submit the application form to Mr Wang at room 203 of the International Exchange Center before 30 March; interview notice will be issued by 20 April.

Telephone number: 62351234

Unit 2

Vocabulary and listening

Wang Yu: Mark! How's the interview preparation for the company you last mentioned going? Do you want me to help you practise it again?

Mark: No, thanks, Wang Yu. The interview ended last Wednesday, and since then I have been waiting for the outcome.

Wang Yu: How do you feel about it?

Mark: Not too bad, and I'm fairly satisfied with my performance.

Wang Yu: What kind of questions did they ask you?

Mark: What they were most interested in is why, as a foreigner, I want to stay and work in China. Then they asked me to present my previous work experience and my plans for the future. In general, they didn't ask any complicated questions.

Wang Yu: How did you present your work experience?

Mark: I said I had helped my classmates translate some papers, and I worked as a volunteer in a rest home during high school in Australia.

Wang Yu: Did you emphasise your adaptability and conscientious attitude to work?

Mark: I didn't say that directly, but they should be able to sense that. When the interview was coming to an end, they were already talking about the benefits of the internship with me.

Wang Yu: Your chances are good! By the way, can you work in China while you hold a student visa?

Mark: Oops! I forgot to ask. Thanks for reminding me. Tomorrow I will write an email to ask about this. Enough about me. How are you finding living in the States?

Wang Yu: I still haven't got used to it. I miss my home very much. My Chinese stomach doesn't seem to be able to consume American food. Besides, with the huge pressure from studying and trying to cope with my inadequate English, my feelings are quite complicated.

Mark: Don't worry. All these difficulties are just temporary. I felt the same way as you when I first arrived in Beijing. But now hasn't everything turned out well? I've made lots of new friends, and I have also fallen in love with Chinese food. Now I even want to stay and work here. I think you will definitely get used to your new life soon.

Reading and writing

Dear Miss Wen,

How are you? I would like to thank you for taking the time to read my application letter.

My name is Mark, and I am from Australia. I am an international student of Beijing Foreign Studies University, and will graduate next year. I am hoping that I can stay and work in China after graduation, so I would like to gain some relevant work experience during the summer vacation. I'm very interested in the interpreter intern post in the Customer Service Department in your company. I believe I can adapt to the job and become a competent interpreter very quickly.

My mother tongue is English, but my current major is Chinese, with a minor in economics. In the last two years, I have helped my classmates translate various types of articles. Although I haven't had a chance to work as a business interpreter formally, I did help arrange the journey for my Australian friends who came to China to explore business development.

I have an open and optimistic personality, and I love sports and travelling. I'm sympathetic and rest, and enjoy dealing with various people. In high school, I spent two years as a volunteer in a rest home in Brisbane, mainly helping with sorting out documentation, recording notes for meetings, and organizing a lot of activities. While working on this job, I honed my abilities in planning, organization and communication, and formed the habit of performing tasks with diligence and detailed planning. During the several years I have spent studying and living in China, I have learnt a great deal not only about Chinese history and culture, but also about cultural differences between the East and the West. I think all these have helped to qualify me for the role of an interpreter in the Customer Service Department in your company.

I really hope I get the opportunity to work as an intern at your company. Attached please find my CV.

I'm looking forward to hearing from you.

Regards,
Mark
2 April, 2023

Unit 3

Vocabulary and listening

CSO = Customer Service Officer   YM = Yeong-min

CSO: Hello, Qingfeng Travel Service Ticket Centre. How may I help you?

YM: Hi, I'm from Beijing Foreign Studies University. Our university will have a group with about 15 people travelling from Beijing to Harbin in mid-July. I want to know how much plane tickets and train tickets will probably cost during that period of time.

CSO: Wait a minute, and I will check that for you. May I know your surname, please?

YM: My surname is Jin.

CSO: Mr Jin, because July is the peak season for tourism, the plane tickets will almost be full price. As for the train tickets, you have a lot more choices. You can choose an express train or a high-speed train, a sleeping berth or a hard seat.

YM: Excuse me, could you explain more in detail?

CSO: Certainly, Mr Jin: an express train from Beijing to Harbin takes from 10 to 19 hours, and a ticket for a sleeping berth is two or three times that of a hard seat. A hard seat is of course not as comfortable as a sleeping berth, but the price is much cheaper. A high-speed train is a bullet train, and the fastest one takes only 5 hours to get to Harbin. There are only seats on a high-speed train, but the seats are more comfortable than those on an express train. A first-class ticket for a high-speed train is nearly half of the full price for an air ticket, while a second-class ticket is cheaper than a first-class ticket by about a third.

YM: Train tickets are indeed not very expensive. However, I still need to discuss it with our team leader. By the way, is there any discount for group tickets?

CSO: Mr Jin, I suggest you allow our travel consultant to help you. They will make the most economical and sensible travel plan to suit your requirements, including your tickets, food and accommodation, and any other arrangements for the trip. That way, you can enjoy a worry-free trip. Shall I put you through to our travel consultant?

YM: That would be great! Thank you!

Reading and writing

> **Four-Day Trip from Beijing to Harbin during Summer**
>
> Price: RMB 2000*
>
> Departure date: Every Tuesday and Friday from 1 July to 15 September
>
> Main transport: train   Departure: Beijing
>   Destination: Harbin
>
> Local transport: air-conditioned coach
>
> Day 1:
> – Take the train from Beijing Railway Station to Harbin
>
> Day 2:
> – Climb the highest steel tower in Asia—the Dragon Tower, and take in a bird's-eye view of Harbin.
> – See the Saint Sophia Cathedral and Square, and visit the Harbin Municipal Architectural Art Museum.
> – Stroll along the longest pedestrian precinct in Asia—the Central Street. Walk on the cobblestone pavement, appreciate the European-style buildings and get a sense of the last hundred years of history.
>
> Day 3:
> – Visit Heilongjiang Provincial Museum and learn about the history and culture of Northeast China.
> – Free time in the afternoon. You can go for a walk along the Songhua River, enjoy the shows at Harbin's Summer Concert, or go shopping in the downtown area and try some of the local cuisine.
>
> Day 4:
> – Visit the Sun Island summer resort, a national AAAAA scenic place of interest. You can also buy a ticket to visit the largest indoor ice and snow art gallery in Asia, and view the beautiful ice lanterns and snow sculptures.
> – Take the train at night and get back to Beijing the next morning.

Notes for visiting Harbin in summer:

1 The temperature difference between day and night is substantial, so please make sure that you bring enough clothes to avoid getting cold.

2 The sunshine is strong in summer, so make sure you apply sun cream to avoid getting sunburnt.

* Price includes transport, accommodation, breakfast and lunch each day, tickets for places of interest and a tour guide. Personal activities, dinner and travel insurance are not included in the price.

Unit 4

Vocabulary and listening

Teacher Qian: Hello, everyone, welcome to the Beijing Foreign Studies University International Summer Camp for Secondary School Students. I'm your team leader, and my surname is Qian. Today is our camp's opening ceremony. First of all, let's welcome Director Wang of the International Exchange Centre to make a welcome speech and announce the opening of the camp.

Director Wang: All students from far and wide, on behalf of the Beijing Foreign Studies University International Exchange Centre, I welcome you here to attend the International Summer Camp for Secondary School Students. Beijing Foreign Studies University is a very famous higher education institution for language majors in China, and it is also one of the first universities to provide a programme to teach Chinese as a foreign language. We have already held three summer camps for international secondary school students. The theme of this year's camp is using Chinese to tell Chinese stories. I believe, through the rich and diverse language practice activities, your Chinese proficiency will be much improved by the time you leave the camp, and your understanding of China will be much enriched, just like the students of the previous three camps. I hereby announce the International Summer Camp for Secondary School Students formally open!

Teacher Qian: Thank you very much, Director Wang, for the speech. Next, I would like to introduce you to the two assistants who will stay with you for the duration of the summer camp. Both of them are students at our university: Sun Xiaowen and Jin Yeong-min.

Xiaowen: Hello everyone, I'm Xiaowen. I'm very happy to have the opportunity to stay with you for your summer in China.

Yeong-min: I'm Yeong-min, how are you doing? I hope you have an enjoyable and very productive stay at the camp. Feel free to contact me whenever you need anything!

Reading and writing

Summer Camp Rules

1. Follow the instructions and arrangements of the camp staff. Strict observation of daily schedules is required.
2. Take good care of your personal belongings, and if there's the loss of valuables, report to the team leader or assistant immediately.
3. Be mindful of food and water hygiene and sudden weather changes. Report immediately to the team leader or assistant if you feel ill, and go to see the doctor in their company.
4. Go to class on time. If you cannot attend the class because of illness, ask the teacher for time off in advance.
5. Finish your homework on time. If you have any questions about the lessons, you may raise them with the teacher on duty during the evening self-study class.
6. Try your best to speak Chinese. Do not speak other languages, or speak them less.
7. Take an active part in all the activities. If you have a special reason for not attending, inform the team leader or assistant in advance.
8. No unaccompanied activities will be allowed during free time. Try to avoid going to places you are not familiar with. Remember the emergency telephone numbers, and if an emergency occurs, make the phone call immediately.
9. Cooperate with other members of the camp, and carry on team spirit by caring for and supporting each other.

Emergency telephone numbers:
Police service: 110   Fire service: 119
Ambulance service: 120

Daily schedule

08:00–10:00	Language lesson
10:00–12:00	Culture lesson
12:00–14:00	Lunch and noon break
14:00–17:30	Extracurricular activities, tours and sightseeing
17:30–19:30	Dinner and free time
19:30–21:30	Evening self-study

Things needed for the Harbin tour:
- summer clothes (you are also advised to bring long-sleeved shirts and trousers)
- sun protection (sun cream, hat and sunglasses)
- personal medicines
- toiletries for personal use
- watch, torch, mug, umbrella, notebook, pen
- cash (RMB)

Unit 5

Vocabulary and listening

Mark: Manager Tang, were you looking for me?

Tang Yu: Mark, come here. Sit on the sofa. How's it going? How are you coping with the work in the first week of your internship?

Mark: Thanks for your concern. I love my job and I've learnt a lot from my colleagues since I first came to the company.

Tang Yu: That's great. Talk to your colleagues if you have any questions. In the next two weeks, we are going to receive an inspection team from Australia, and you will be accompanying them everywhere and will be responsible for the main interpretation work.

Mark: Oh… I will try my best.

Tang Yu: But there's no need to be nervous, since the other colleagues in the Customer Service Department will help you in every way possible. I have seen your CV, and have confidence in you.

Mark: Thank you for your trust. It is a lot of pressure, but it is a good opportunity for me to practise. I will make good use of it.

Tang Yu: Good. There are two more things on which I need your advice. We plan to hold a welcome dinner banquet for the inspection team. Which do you think is more appropriate, Western food or Chinese food?

Mark: I think since they have come to China, wouldn't they like to try local Chinese cuisine?

Tang Yu: Sounds reasonable. In addition, we want to give each of them some souvenir. Do you have any suggestions?

Mark: I don't think it is necessary to give something expensive. Oh wait, I saw in our company a panda toy made from environmentally friendly materials, which not only reflects our company's mission to protect the environment, but also looks very Chinese. We could not find a better gift than that! What do you think?

Tang Yu: Yes, that sounds good, too. Let's further discuss the issues concerning this inspection team at Thursday's regular meeting.

Mark: OK, Manager Tang. I will think about whether there are other issues to consider. If there's nothing else, I will go back to work.

Tang Yu: OK.

Reading and writing

Memo

Mark,
Manager Tang has asked you to go to her office when you get back. It's mainly about arrangements for receiving the Australian inspection team. In addition, the company's invitation card needs an English version. Please translate with reference to the Chinese invitation card on your desk. Please send me the translation via email no later than noon tomorrow. Thank you.

Xie Yue
10:15 am, 27 June

Meeting Notice

The Customer Service Department is going to have the regular monthly meeting on 30 June (Thursday), with the following arrangements:

Time: registration starts from 9:50 am, meeting begins at 10:00 am.

Venue: the major conference room beside the General Manager's office

Participants: all staff of the Customer Service Department

Meeting agenda:
1) Team leaders report on this month's work progress and the work plan for next month. Need to include an analysis of any unfinished work and propose specific suggestions for improvement.
2) Manager Tang delivers the summary of the Customer Service Department's work.
3) Discuss arrangements for the reception of the Australian inspection team.
4) Discuss customer feedback on the new customer service system.

Yashen (Shenzhen) Customer Service Department
27 June

Invitation card

Dear (Mr/Ms) _____ ,

Yashen International Trading Co Ltd Shenzhen Branch requests the pleasure of your company

At an event for _____

On _____ (date and time)

At _____ (address)

Telephone: _____

Li Shuqing, General Manager
_____ (D/M/Y)

Unit 6

Vocabulary and listening

Xie Yue: Mark, you did a good job today!

Mark: Thanks! Actually I was very nervous and afraid of missing important information because I had misheard or hadn't translated accurately.

Xie Yue: Really? No one could tell.

Mark: That's good. Fortunately, Zhou Xiang had prepared the material for me in advance, or I would have performed very badly today.

Zhou Xiang: You are too modest, Mark. Colleagues are supposed to help each other.

Xie Yue: Yes, you two have cooperated very well.

Zhou Xiang: Thanks for the compliment. Mark, I really admire you: you have learnt Chinese so well! If only I could speak English as well as you speak Chinese.

Mark: Your English is already very good. I would like to learn about international trade

Xie Yue:	from you.
Xie Yue:	Yes, Zhou Xiang is a very talented student majoring in foreign trade studies. You two can certainly learn from each other and improve together.
Mark:	We should really learn from you and others in the company who have so much experience. Practical experience is more important than information learnt from books.
Zhou Xiang:	That's absolutely right. Xie Yue, have you been working in the Customer Service Department since you joined the company?
Xie Yue:	No, when I first came here I worked in the Sales Department. But later I found that I was more suited to customer service work, so less than a year later I was transferred to the current department.
Zhou Xiang:	I see. If there is an opportunity, I would also like to intern in the Sales Department.
Xie Yue:	Really? Then I will recommend you for a position there to gain experience at some point.
Zhou Xiang:	That would be great!
Xie Yue:	How are you both feeling? Are you tired? Do you still have the energy to sing karaoke?
Mark:	Now? Zhou Xiang, it's up to you. If you go, I will go.
Zhou Xiang:	Tomorrow is the weekend anyway, and there's no need to go to sleep early. Let's go. Afterwards, I will take you out for a night snack.

❖ Reading and writing

Mark,

Attached are two documents for the evening banquet the day after tomorrow, one being the individual arrangements and agenda for the banquet, the other the outline of the General Manager's speech. The General Manager's speech is not long this time and there's no need to prepare a speech draft, so there is only an outline. Please let me know immediately if there is anything else you need, and I will help you prepare it.

Zhou Xiang

Attachment 1: Evening banquet arrangements and agenda.doc   view   download
Attachment 2: General Manager's speech (outline).doc   view   download

Evening banquet arrangements and agenda for the Australian inspection team
Time: 18:30–22:00, 12 July 2023
Venue: Banquet Hall, ground floor, Shenzhen Hotel
Received by: Reception team, Customer Service Department
Interpreter: Mark
Hostess: Tang Yu

18:30 Guests of the banquet start to arrive, and reception staff lead them to their seats.
18:45 Members of the Australian inspection team and the main leaders of the company take their seats.
19:00 The hostess introduces the company leaders and VIPs.
19:10 The General Manager makes a welcome speech.
19:20 The Australian delegation makes a speech of thanks in response.
19:30 The evening banquet formally begins, interspersed with performances of Chinese folk music.
22:00 The evening banquet ends.

Evening banquet welcome speech (outline)

1 Opening speech: "Dear delegates from Australia, colleagues from Shenzhen, ladies and gentlemen, good evening. On behalf of all the staff of Yashen Company Shenzhen Branch, I would like to extend our warmest welcome to the Australian inspection team here to visit our company!"

2 A simple review of the history of Yashen's development; focus on introducing Shenzhen Branch's current main business and international partners.

3 Introduce the company's plan for business development and seeking new partners in Australia in the next two years. Wish the inspection team great success in its visit to China.

4 Concluding remarks: "Lastly, I would like to propose a toast to our friendship and future cooperation, and to all the ladies and gentlemen present. Cheers!"

Unit 7

Vocabulary and listening

Xie Yue: Mark, you are the only one left in the office. Why haven't you left? Are you going to work overtime?

Mark: Ah, working overtime might not be enough to solve the problem.

Xie Yue: Do you want to talk about it with me?

Mark: OK. I received a phone call from the factory yesterday, saying that one of our customers' order cannot be completed on time. I then sent an email to the customer informing them of the situation. Unexpectedly, they were very angry, and criticized us for not keeping our promise, saying that they would cancel the order. Have I caused a lot of trouble?

Xie Yue: Don't worry. Relax and calm down first. What exactly is the reason why the factory cannot complete the order on time?

Mark: They say that recently they have not been able to find enough qualified workers in the labour market.

Xie Yue: Hmm, that is quite possible. Did you mention any solutions in your email?

Mark: No, I just explained the situation.

Xie Yue: Dealing with this kind of problem does require experience, so don't put the blame all on yourself. But if I were the customer, I would think that you were just finding excuses.

Mark: Then what should I do now?

Xie Yue: "The customer is always right." You should not only apologize sincerely to the customer, but also propose solutions, for example, shortening the delivery time, or giving the customer a discount, and so on. However, you should consult Manager Tang on how to handle this specifically. Remember, if you come across similar problems in the future, do consult your supervisor immediately.

Mark: Thank you very much. Do you think Manager Tang will forgive me?

Xie Yue: Don't worry about it. Just leave off work first.

Reading and writing

Wang Yu,

How are you doing?

Nowadays people are used to sending emails and chatting online, and basically do not write letters any more. But I still think writing letters by hand is very engaging, and by doing this I can also practise my handwriting.

I have been working as an intern in the Shenzhen company for more than one month. Being at work feels very different from being at university. I leave home early and return late, with endless amounts of information to check, emails to reply to and phone calls to make. In addition, my colleagues often come to ask me questions about English and about cultural differences. My brain doesn't stop working even after work, and it is always excited! But I feel myself becoming smarter because the busy schedule every day gives me many opportunities to learn new things.

For example, last week I went on a business trip for the first time, accompanying a customer on a visit to the factory. I had to handle everything by myself, from booking the hotel, buying the plane tickets and arranging the itinerary to interpreting. Although I'm in a flurry, doing these things is really helping me to exercise my skills.

I consider myself very lucky. My leader and colleagues are very kind to me, and I can consult them whenever I have questions. Just yesterday, I made a not-so-small mistake due to my lack of experience. My leader not only didn't criticize me, but also gave me some very good suggestions. This meant a lot to me. I really hope I can continue working for this company after graduation.

Also, I often sing karaoke with my colleagues in my spare time. Already I can sing a few Chinese songs. Next time you come back, we can go and sing songs together.

Enclosed, please find a photo I took. It's a street view of Shenzhen. This city is full of energy, and I like it very much.

How are you doing in the States? Have you made many new friends? Write to me when you have time.

Hoping everything goes well, and may all your wishes come true.

Your friend, Mark

24 July, Shenzhen

Unit 8

❖ Vocabulary and listening

Steve: Hello! My name is Steve. How should I address you?

Da Liu: You can call me Da Liu. Your Chinese is very good! Is this the first time you've come to Lijiang?

Steve: Thanks, Da Liu. Yes, this is my first time in Yunnan. I just arrived here from Kunming yesterday. Yunnan is really a great place. Are you a local here? You are so lucky to be able to live here!

Da Liu: I'm not a local. I came here for travelling seven years ago, and, after arriving, I didn't want to leave. Later, I quit my job and moved to Lijiang.

Steve: What did you do in the past?

Da Liu: I used to work in Shanghai, a typical white-collar employee. The job seemed decent, but in fact, there was too much pressure. I often suffered from insomnia. At the time I wondered whether that was the life I really wanted. When I came to Lijiang for travelling, I suddenly experienced the pleasure of enjoying life. I asked myself: why not change my lifestyle? I really hated my previous life.

Steve: I see. I once interviewed a teacher, who had also given up the life in Beijing and moved to Inner Mongolia.

Da Liu: So you are a journalist. Are you here to interview people?

Steve: I'm here for a holiday. I heard long ago that the scenery in Yunnan is like a postcard and that it is a paradise for photography buff. Clearly it lives up to its reputation.

Da Liu: What do you think of Lijiang?

Steve: Lijiang is a very beautiful little town. However, it is more commercialized than I imagined. I haven't thought about where to go next. Do you have any suggestions?

Da Liu: You have asked the right person! Wait a minute, and I will go to get a map. Then I'll tell you some places you don't want to miss!

Steve: That's great! I will buy you a beer afterwards!

❖ Reading and writing

Yeong-min,

I'm in Kunming, Yunnan Province now. It's as warm as spring no matter what season it is in Kunming, so it is also known as "Spring City". In the picture is the famous "Stone Forest". There are a lot of delicacies here, and the one I like most is Dai food. Dai is an ethnic minority group in Yunnan, and their peacock dance is very beautiful. The Dai also have a musical instrument called the cucurbit flute, the sound of which is very distinct. I'm sure you would like it.

Steve, in Kunming, Yunnan Province

Wang Yu,

Is everything going well with you in the States? Currently I'm in Lijiang, Yunnan, a very small and ancient town. Life can be very slow and lazy here, and time seems to have stopped. If only you could be here too, we could enjoy the sunshine and daydream together…

In Lijiang I met group after group of young people from the big cities; they often mentioned a phrase "man shenghuo" (slow life). Have you heard of this?

Steve, in Lijiang, Yunnan Province

Amanda,

I haven't heard from you for a long time, and I hope everything has been going well since you have returned to Brazil. I'm now in Shangri-La, Yunnan Province. Here everything is awash with Tibetan cultural features, which is quite different from the world outside. Tomorrow I'm leaving for Meri Snow Mountain, and I'm very excited about it. I hope this "holy mountain" can bring me good luck!

Steve, in Shangri-La, Yunnan Province

Mark,

I have been in Yunnan for two weeks, and haven't had time to go to many places. Unfortunately, I'm leaving here today. What impressed me most was the trip on horseback to Yubeng Village behind the Meri Snow Mountain. Although in some places the road was very narrow and a bit dangerous, and my altitude sickness was serious, I thought it was worthwhile after I got to Yubeng. It is a Shangri-La, an amazing retreat from the world!

Steve, at Kunming Airport, Yunnan Province

Unit 9

❖ Vocabulary and listening

Wang Yu: Steve, you look thinner and have a nice tan.

Steve: Do I look more handsome?

Wang Yu: Haha, you look fine.

Steve: I just came back from Yunnan. Although the temperature was not high, the UV rays were strong. While at Meri Snow Mountain, my altitude sickness was so serious that I was nearly hospitalized. That's why I look thinner and tanned now.

Wang Yu: Fortunately you are OK, otherwise the trip wouldn't have been worthwhile.

Steve: It would still have been worthwhile even if I had got sick. I enjoyed Yunnan so much as to not want to go home!

Wang Yu: Then send me a couple of photos you're pleased with now.

Steve: I haven't had a chance to sort out the photos in my camera. I am sending you two photos from my mobile phone.

Wang Yu: The snow mountain in your pictures has a calming effect.

Steve: It's even more beautiful if you see it with your own eyes. But the quality of my photos this time is really good. Honestly, they could match those taken by a professional photojournalist.

Wang Yu: Really? Then you should try to submit them to a travel magazine.

Steve: Actually, I've been considering whether to participate in a photography contest. The theme is "Yunnan through My Eyes".

Wang Yu: What a good opportunity! Why are you hesitating then?

Steve: The closing date is coming soon. I'm worried that I may not have enough time to choose the photos. In addition, there are so many talented photographers, which definitely makes it difficult to win an award.

Wang Yu: Didn't you say just now that you are very professional? Why, are you afraid of failure and too scared to compete with them?

Steve: I'm not afraid at all. Winning or losing is not important. Participation is what really matters.

Wang Yu: Invite me for dinner if you win an award.

Steve: Only too glad to!

❖ Reading and writing

"Yunnan through My Eyes" Photography Contest Calling for Submissions

In order to provide a platform for photography buff to display their work, and to reflect the charm of Yunnan and promote tourism development, *Yunnan Travel* magazine and the Yunnan Photographers Association have decided to jointly hold a photography contest entitled "Yunnan through My Eyes".

1 Contest schedule

  1) Submission of work: From now until 31 July 2023

  2) Evaluation: three weeks after the closing of submission

  3) Result announcement: *Yunnan Travel*, the September 2023 volume

2 Submission requirements

  1) The contest is open to all photography buff.

  2) The photographs must be taken in Yunnan after June 2020, with no limitation on style.

  3) Each person can submit up to six photos, each of which must be accompanied by a title and information about the photo, including when and where it was taken and what the photo is about.

  4) Participants must send their printed photos by post first, and then send electronic files as required after being selected for the contest. The photos must be original images and should not have been altered in any way.

  5) The work should be original photos which have not been published before. All legal liability for the works shall be the sole responsibility of the participants. The participants must agree to abide by the above regulations.

3 Prizes

  First prize: one winner, with the prize money of 5,000 yuan

  Second prize: five winners, with the prize money of 2,000 yuan each

Third prize: ten winners, with the prize money of 500 yuan each

All prize winners will be issued with a certificate by Yunnan Photographers Association, and all volumes of *Yunnan Travel* magazine in 2022.

4 Submission address: "Yunnan through My Eyes" Contest, *Yunnan Travel* Magazine Press, Kunming, Yunnan Province, Postal code: 650000

All participants should provide their names and contact information.

Yunnan Photographers Association
Yunnan Travel magazine
15 May 2023

Unit 10

Vocabulary and listening

Yeong-min: It's nice and cool here. Let's sit down.

Xiaowen: OK. Yeong-min, about the topics for the speech and debate competition, I can only think of three. The first is "Why I study Chinese". This should not be difficult for the students of the summer camp, and they will definitely have something to say.

Yeong-min: Having something to say doesn't guarantee that they will be interested. Our topics have to be ones that participants are happy to talk about and the audience is willing to listen to. What other topics do you have in mind?

Xiaowen: The second topic is "The development of science and technology and modern life". What do you think?

Yeong-min: Isn't this topic too broad? Even if students have opinions on this, they may not be able to explain them clearly in Chinese. A more specific topic would be better.

Xiaowen: The third topic then is very specific: "The influence of the Internet on daily life". I remember on the opening day, several students looked quite disappointed after learning that there would be few opportunities to go online. Is this topic good?

Yeong-min: Yeah, it is better than the previous two, definitely. However…

Xiaowen: Ah, nothing works! If we keep going like this, we are not going to get a result, even if we continue this discussion for three days!

Yeong-min: Xiaowen, don't worry. Let me finish first. I think this is a very good topic for the speech competition, but as a topic for debate, it is not controversial enough.

Xiaowen: That's right. I've got a new idea! How about this: "Can money bring happiness?"

Yeong-min: There are many possible answers to this question, and no fixed conclusion. No matter what stand you take, you will always find something to say. I think it works!

Xiaowen: Really? Sorry, Yeong-min, I've got a bad temper…

Yeong-min: I don't think so. I think you are quite direct, and say what you think, which is really adorable!

Reading and writing

The Fourth International Summer Camp for Secondary School Students

Model composition: A Summer without the Internet

A Summer without the Internet

I used to think that the Internet was my best friend, with which I could do anything. For example, I watched sports programmes on the Internet almost every day. Every now and then, I would log in to social networking websites to update my status, and get the latest news about my friends. Before going out for dinner, I would check out the comments on the website. When going to a place I didn't know, I would check the map online in advance. Before leaving for someplace far away, I would also check the weather, buy plane tickets and book hotels online, etc.

This summer I attended a summer camp, where it was not convenient to go online anytime. I thought that this summer was going to be boring. However, when the summer camp ended, I found that, even though it was not easy without the Internet, there were some positive changes in my life.

First of all, I participated in many group activities, got close to nature and had more communication with the teachers and other students. This not only enabled us to develop deeper connections, but also helped me to improve my Chinese a lot. Second, since it was not convenient to log in to social networking websites, I sent my friend in the States typical Chinese postcards, which made them very happy because they could see my wishes to them written by hand. In addition, as I couldn't go online to listen to music and watch videos, I had much more time to focus on reading books quietly.

The experiences of this summer have made me realize that the Internet alienates people from the real world while making our lives easier. Now, although the Internet is still an indispensable part of my life, I will not waste all my time on the web. I will not allow the Internet to allocate my time, but will make it serve me better.

Comments:
1. Congratulations for stepping out of the virtual world and entering the real world.
2. The language is smooth, the structure is clear, and the main idea is definite. It is a good essay.
3. Not allowing the Internet to constrain our life, but making it serve us better - that is a very good conclusion!

Unit 11

❋ Vocabulary and listening

Steve: Wang Yu, I didn't expect you to come back home now. This is a surprise!

Wang Yu: It's a school holiday. All the students around were gone, and I was really bored being alone. It feels so good to be home! I can eat whatever I want, and sleep as long as I wish.

Steve: You must have found these six months very difficult, living abroad, away from home, by yourself.

Wang Yu: I couldn't get used to it when I first got there, and I cried a lot. Honestly, I could deal with the difficulties and pressure of life and study. The most difficult thing to overcome was the feeling of loneliness and of being isolated. Because of the time difference, I couldn't call my family any time I want. There was no one to share my happiness, and when I felt sad I often dealt with it by myself.

Steve: Actually you can call me at any time. Although I cannot give you any concrete help, at least I can be a good listener.

Wang Yu: I know. But the hardest time has already passed. Enough about me, how about you? Has the result of the photography contest been announced?

Steve: Haha, I have good news to tell you. I got the second prize, and I'm the only foreigner to get a prize.

Wang Yu: Great! Congratulations! Show me your masterpiece! … The photos look really nice. Why don't you put them on your blog?

Steve: It's not that I don't want to. The copyright of these photos has been purchased by a photo agency, and they no longer belong to me. Hey, we made a deal and I owe you a dinner. It can be your welcome home dinner as well. Tell me, what do you want to eat?

Wang Yu: I do happen to be hungry. In fact, I'm dying for hot pot now. Let's go eat hot pot! And it can be a celebration for you getting the prize!

❋ Reading and writing

Footprints

By Special correspondent Xiao'ai

In the Dai restaurant near Minzu University, I recognized my interviewee at a glance: Steve, a young man from London, UK, and the only foreigner to win a prize in the "Yunnan through My Eyes" photography contest. Nearsighted, Steve's wearing a pair of glasses, but his blue eyes were bright and friendly. Steve's handshake was sincere and strong. He spoke Chinese very well and at a moderate speed.

Steve decided to stay and live in Beijing after he graduated from university two years ago. During this period of time, he took a part-time job as a journalist for a British magazine while continuing his study of Chinese. What Steve likes to do most was to travel to different places in China, bringing along his beloved camera. The Yangtze River, the Great Wall, the Shaolin Temple in Songshan Mountain, the grasslands in Inner Mongolia… He took photos everywhere throughout these places. In his own words, he's recording his footprints through photography.

Steve told me he had not been confident enough to take part in the "Yunnan through My Eyes" contest at the beginning, and it was because of the encouragement of a Chinese friend that he finally decided to participate. Steve felt very happy about winning the prize. He fell in love with China, and Chinese people in particular. The theme of Steve's winning photos was the variety of people in different parts of Yunnan. The Yunnan trip also introduced him to many other friends who, like him, had fallen in love with Yunnan.

During the interview, Steve made particular mention of a British, H. R. Davis. Over one hundred years ago, this British scholar paid four visits to Yunnan in six years, using words and photos to record in detail the climate, geography, product, and culture of various places in Yunnan, leaving a record for us. "If the opportunity arises, I really hope I can live in Yunnan for some period of time, and not just be a passer-by who leaves after seeing the scenery and taking some photos." At the end of the interview, Steve said that he had one wish—to go to Yunnan again, following in the footprints of Davis.

Unit 12

❖ Vocabulary and listening

Yeong-min: Our last gathering was last summer, wasn't it? One year has passed in a flash!
Wang Yu: Yes. And everyone looks more mature.
Steve: I think we all have had some experiences. We should talk about them.
Mark: Me first. Actually you all know that I went to Shenzhen for an internship. Although occasionally I found it hard, I learnt a lot, and got rid of my bad habit of carelessness. The manager said that I would be welcome to work there after graduation.
Steve: Mark, that's great!
Mark: Stop it. You're really the great one. A few casual photos taken during your travels ended up winning a prize!
Wang Yu: Mark, I don't agree with what you're saying. Steve is not someone who takes casual photos. He has been trying hard to improve his photography skills. No pain, no gain.
Steve: Thank you, Wang Yu. It wasn't easy for you either, being alone in the States and having to handle everything by yourself.
Wang Yu: I often saw you all in my dreams while I was in the States, and felt lost when I woke up. But now here we are together again. Yeong-min, how about you?
Yeong-min: I feel ashamed to say this: I only went to help out at the school's summer camp. But I have good news: Xiaowen, who worked together with me at the summer camp, is now my girlfriend!
Mark: You've shocked us, Yeong-min! Come on, tell us how you go after the girl. Don't keep it to yourself!
Yeong-min: As a man, by being brave!
Steve: Great, Yeong-min! Why don't you bring Xiaowen here today?
Yeong-min: She's a bit shy. Maybe next time.
Wang Yu: It seems that everyone has gained a lot.
Mark: I think Yeong-min is the one who has gained the most!

❖ Reading and writing

Reunion in August

It is very muggy in Beijing this summer. It's already late August now, but the temperature is still high. It rained this morning, but it's finally cooled off a bit, with a taste of autumn.

Before I went to my friends' gathering today, my feelings were quite complicated. I was quite excited about seeing my old friends, but I felt sad when I thought of having to go back to the States soon, not knowing when would be our next meeting. During the get-together, some friends proposed that we would meet once every two years, and it could be anywhere in the world. This made me happy again. Yes, every parting leads to the next reunion, so why should I be upset!

It's not easy to study in the States, and I shed a lot of sweat and tears in the past six months. But whenever I thought of these friends, I had courage and energy. Several years ago when they first came to China, they were also alone. In addition to differences in language and food, they also faced various kinds of cultural impacts. But they all adapted to their new life quickly and well. M decided to work and live in China after graduation. S participated in a photography contest held by a Chinese magazine and won a prize. Y has found a Chinese girlfriend. Their Chinese all improved a lot too.

The best thing I can learn from them is their optimistic and open attitude, and their willingness to accept new things. For example, they all love travelling. During their two to three years in China they have been to many more places than I have been to. Even distant places like Inner Mongolia and Yunnan bear their footprints, not to mention big cities like Shenzhen and Xi'an. They also plan to travel all over China!

I'm very lucky to have such friends in my life, who inspire me to push myself incessantly and achieve more. From now on, I will be more positive and optimistic when facing difficulties and problems in my life. Even if I cannot go around the world, I will try my best to see more and travel more to broaden my horizons.

Comments:

It's so good for you all to get together! I miss you very much, and will definitely attend the gathering next time!

Amanda, we all miss you too! Maybe our next reunion will be in Brazil with you! ☺

Vocabulary list

WORD	PINYIN	PART OF SPEECH	MEANING	UNIT
A				
爱好者	àihàozhě		buff, enthusiast	8
爱上	àishang		fall in love	2
安排	ānpái	v.	arrange	1
B				
把握	bǎwò	v.	grasp, seize	5
白领	báilǐng	n.	white-collar worker	8
颁发	bānfā	v.	award, confer, issue	9
版本	bǎnběn	n.	version	5
帮不上	bāng bu shàng		cannot help	11
保密	bǎomì	v.	keep secret	12
保险	bǎoxiǎn	n.	insurance	3
保证	bǎozhèng	v.	guarantee	10
报告	bàogào	v./n.	report	4
倍	bèi	measure word	time (multiply)	3
必须	bìxū	adv.	must	8
避暑胜地	bìshǔ shèngdì		summer resort	3
遍	biàn	measure word	(for actions) once through	11
辩论	biànlùn	v.	debate	10
表达	biǎodá	v.	express	1
表扬	biǎoyáng	v.	praise, commend	12
冰灯	bīngdēng	n.	ice lantern	3
并且	bìngqiě	conj.	and	2
补助	bǔzhù	n.	subsidy	1
不得了	bùdéliǎo	adj.	extreme	2
不等	bùděng	adj.	varying	3
不断	buduàn	adv.	unceasingly	12
不过……罢了	búguò… bàle		just, only	7
不见得	bújiàndé	adv.	not necessarily	10
不通	bù tōng		be obstructed	12
不限	bú xiàn		with no limit	1
不许	bùxǔ	v.	not allow, must not	12
不足	bùzú	adj.	insufficient	7
布里斯班	Bùlǐsībān	n.	Brisbane	2
布置	bùzhì	v.	assign	5
步行街	bùxíngjiē	n.	pedestrian street	3
C				
踩	cǎi	v.	tread on	3
材料	cáiliào	n.	material	5
参考	cānkǎo	v.	refer to	5
参与	cānyù	v.	participate in	9
惭愧	cánkuì	adj.	ashamed, abashed	12
策划	cèhuà	v.	plan	2
曾经	céngjīng	adv.	once	2
差点儿	chàdiǎnr	adv.	nearly	9
差异	chāyì	n.	difference	2
馋	chán	v.	be gluttonous; hunger for	11
产品	chǎnpǐn	n.	product	1
长城	Chángchéng	n.	Great Wall	11
长江	Cháng Jiāng		Yangtze River	11
长期	chángqī	adj.	long term	12
长袖	cháng xiù		long sleeve	4
尝	cháng	v.	taste	5
常用	cháng yòng		commonly used	4
场	chǎng	measure word	spell, period	12
成立	chénglì	v.	set up	1
成熟	chéngshú	adj./v.	mature	12
诚恳	chéngkěn	adj.	sincere	7
诚意	chéngyì	n.	sincerity	5

212 ❖ Vocabulary list

WORD	PINYIN	PART OF SPEECH	MEANING	UNIT
承担	chéngdān	v.	bear, assume	9
程度	chéngdù	n.	degree	8
吃不惯	chī bu guàn		not get used to eating	2
吃惊	chījīng	v.	be surprised/astonished/shocked	12
迟迟	chíchí	adv.	slow	12
冲击	chōngjī	v.	impact	12
充满	chōngmǎn	v.	be filled with	7
重	chóng	adv.	again, afresh	11
重逢	chóngféng	v.	meet again	12
重庆	Chóngqìng	n.	Chongqing	1
抽时间	chōu shíjiān		make time	2
出发	chūfā	v.	set off	3
出远门	chū yuǎnmén		go out on a long trip	10
闯祸	chuǎnghuò	v.	get into trouble	7
辞职	cízhí	v.	resign	8
聪明	cōngmíng	adj.	smart	7
从事	cóngshì	v.	be engaged in	1
粗心	cūxīn	adj.	careless, thoughtless	12
错误	cuòwù	n.	mistake, error	7
D 答谢	dáxiè	v.	express appreciation	6
打印	dǎyìn	v.	print	1
大巴	dàbā	n.	bus	3
傣族	Dǎizú	n.	Dai ethnic group	8
待遇	dàiyù	n.	remuneration	1
戴	dài	v.	wear	11
单独	dāndú	adv.	alone, by oneself	4
当	dāng	prep.	when	4
当前位置	dāngqián wèizhì		current page	1
导致	dǎozhì	v.	cause	7

WORD	PINYIN	PART OF SPEECH	MEANING	UNIT
倒	dào	adv.	nevertheless	5
道歉	dàoqiàn	v.	apologize	7
得奖	dé jiǎng		win an award	9
得意	déyì	adj.	proud, pleased	9
登	dēng	v.	climb	3
登录	dēnglù	v.	log in	10
地点	dìdiǎn	n.	place	1
地理	dìlǐ	n.	geography	11
地球	dìqiú	n.	earth, globe	12
典型	diǎnxíng	adj.	typical	8
电子版	diànzǐbǎn	n.	electronic version	9
订单	dìngdān	n.	order	7
丢失	diūshī	v.	lose	4
对于	duìyú	prep.	as to	11
顿	dùn	measure word	(for meals)	11
多次	duō cì		many times	2
多亏	duōkuī	v.	owe sth to sb	6
E 饿	è	adj.	hungry	11
儿童	értóng	n.	children	1
F 发表	fābiǎo	v.	publish	9
发布	fābù	v.	release	1
发呆	fādāi	v.	stare blankly	8
发言	fāyán	n./v.	speech; give a speech	4
发扬	fāyáng	v.	carry on	4
翻译	fānyì	n./v.	translator; translate	1
反对	fǎnduì	v.	object, oppose	12
反而	fǎn'ér	adv.	on the contrary	10
反馈	fǎnkuì	v.	feed back	5
反正	fǎnzhèng	adv.	since, as	6
犯	fàn	v.	commit (error, crime)	7
方案	fāng'àn	n.	plan	3

Vocabulary list ❖ 213

WORD	PINYIN	PART OF SPEECH	MEANING	UNIT
防晒	fáng shài		prevent sunburn	3
防晒霜	fángshài shuāng		sun cream	4
放弃	fàngqì	v.	give up	8
费用	fèiyong	n.	expense	3
分工	fēngōng	v.	divide the jobs	6
分公司	fēngōngsī	n.	branch company	1
分析	fēnxī	v.	analyse	5
分享	fēnxiǎng	v.	share (in)	11
丰富多彩	fēngfù-duōcǎi		rich and colourful	4
风格	fēnggé	n.	style	9
风景如画	fēngjǐng rú huà		picturesque landscape	8
否则	fǒuzé	conj.	otherwise	9
服务	fúwù	v.	serve	10
符合	fúhé	v.	accord with	1
俯瞰	fǔkàn	v.	overlook	3
辅修	fǔxiū	v.	minor	2
付出	fùchū	v.	pay, expend	12
负责	fùzé	v.	take charge (of)	5
附	fù	v.	attach	2
附件	fùjiàn	n.	attachment	6
富有	fùyǒu	v.	be full of	2
复杂	fùzá	adj.	complex	2

G

WORD	PINYIN	PART OF SPEECH	MEANING	UNIT
改掉	gǎidiào		give up, drop	12
改进	gǎijìn	v.	improve	5
干杯	gānbēi	v.	drink a toast	6
赶上	gǎnshang	v.	catch up with	9
敢	gǎn	v.	dare	9
感动	gǎndòng	adj.	be touched	7
感情	gǎnqíng	n.	feeling, emotion	10
感受	gǎnshòu	v./n.	experience; feeling	3
感谢	gǎnxiè	v.	be grateful	2
刚好	gānghǎo	adv.	it so happens that	11
高材生	gāocáishēng	n.	top student	6
高速	gāosù	adj.	high-speed	3
高铁	gāotiě	n.	high-speed railway	3
高原反应	gāoyuán fǎnyìng		altitude sickness	8
隔	gé	v.	every other; separate	10
各位	gè wèi		everyone	4
更新	gēngxīn	v.	update	10
工厂	gōngchǎng	n.	factory	7
工人	gōngrén	n.	worker	7
公布	gōngbù	v.	make public, announce	9
公司	gōngsī	n.	company	1
功课	gōngkè	n.	course	4
供	gōng	v.	provide certain support	5
恭请	gōngqǐng	v.	invite respectfully	5
共同	gòngtóng	adv.	jointly	6
沟通	gōutōng	v.	communicate	1
孤单	gūdān	adj.	lonely	11
孤身一人	gūshēn yì rén		all on one's own	12
鼓励	gǔlì	v.	encourage	1
固定	gùdìng	v.	fix	10
顾客	gùkè	n.	customer	7
顾问	gùwèn	n.	consultant	3
怪	guài	v.	blame	7
关键	guānjiàn	n./adj.	crux; crucial	9
管理	guǎnlǐ	v.	administer	1
广场	guǎngchǎng	n.	square	3
广大	guǎngdà	adj.	numerous	9

WORD	PINYIN	PART OF SPEECH	MEANING	UNIT
逛	guàng	v.	stroll	3
规模	guīmó	n.	scale	1
贵	guì	adj.	(your) honourable	2
贵重	guìzhòng	adj.	valuable	4
国际	guójì	adj.	international	1
果然	guǒrán	adv.	sure enough	8
过	guò	v.	pass time, over	6
过	guò	v.	spend time	10
过客	guòkè	n.	passing guest	11
过去	guòqù	n.	past	2
H 害怕	hàipà	v.	be afraid of, fear	9
汗水	hànshuǐ	n.	sweat	12
行业	hángyè	n.	industry	1
好好	hǎohǎo	adv.	make great efforts	5
好在	hǎozài	adv.	fortunately	9
合格	hégé	adj.	qualified	7
合理	hélǐ	adj.	reasonable	3
合作	hézuò	v.	cooperate	6
何必	hébì	adv.	there is no need	12
黑	hēi	adj.	dark, tanned	9
后顾之忧	hòugùzhīyōu		disturbance in the rear	3
后悔	hòuhuǐ	v.	regret	8
后来	hòulái	n.	later on	2
忽然	hūrán	adv.	all of a sudden	8
葫芦丝	húlusī	n.	cucurbit flute	8
互相	hùxiāng	adv.	mutually	4
怀疑	huáiyí	v.	doubt, suspect	8
环保	huánbǎo	adj.	environmentally friendly	5
回答	huídá	v.	answer	10
回顾	huígù	v.	review, retrospect	6

WORD	PINYIN	PART OF SPEECH	MEANING	UNIT
汇报	huìbào	v.	report	5
会议	huìyì	n.	meeting, conference	2
活力	huólì	n.	energy	7
火锅	huǒguō	n.	hotpot	11
火警	huǒjǐng	n.	fire alarm	4
伙伴	huǒbàn	n.	partner	6
获得	huòdé	v.	win, acquire	9
J 积极	jījí	adj.	active	4
积累	jīlěi	v.	accumulate	1
激动	jīdòng	adj.	excited	8
激励	jīlì	v.	inspire, encourage	12
激烈	jīliè	adj.	fierce	1
即日	jírì	n.	this very day	9
即使	jíshǐ	conj.	even if	10
急救	jíjiù	v.	give first aid	4
集体	jítǐ	n.	group, collective	10
记录	jìlù	n./v.	record	2
季节	jìjié	n.	season	8
既……也……	jì…yě…		both … and …	2
既然	jìrán	conj.	since	5
寄	jì	v.	mail	7
加班	jiābān	v.	work overtime	7
加上	jiāshàng	conj.	moreover	2
兼职	jiānzhí	v./n.	moonlight; part-time job	11
简历	jiǎnlì	n.	résumé	1
建立	jiànlì	v.	establish	10
建筑	jiànzhù	n.	architecture	3
将来	jiānglái	n.	future	2
讲	jiǎng	v.	tell, speak	4
讲稿	jiǎnggǎo	n.	speech notes, script	6

Vocabulary list 215

WORD	PINYIN	PART OF SPEECH	MEANING	UNIT
讲信用	jiǎng xìnyòng		keep one's word	7
奖金	jiǎngjīn	n.	prize money, bonus	9
奖项	jiǎngxiàng	n.	prize	9
降	jiàng	v.	lower, drop, fall	12
交朋友	jiāo péngyou		make friends	2
阶段	jiēduàn	n.	phase	6
接待	jiēdài	v.	receive (clients)	1
接风	jiēfēng	v.	give a dinner of welcome	11
节目	jiémù	n.	programme	10
结论	jiélùn	n.	conclusion	10
截止日期	jiézhǐ rìqī		deadline	9
解决	jiějué	v.	solve	7
届	jiè	measure word	session, class (for meetings, graduating classes, etc.)	4
届时	jièshí	adv.	at the appointed time	5
借口	jièkǒu	n.	excuse	7
今后	jīnhòu	n.	from now on	6
金钱	jīnqián	n.	money	10
尽管	jǐnguǎn	conj.	even though	2
尽可能	jǐn kěnéng		to the best of one's ability	12
紧急	jǐnjí	adj.	urgent	4
进出口	jìn-chūkǒu		import and export	1
尽力而为	jìnlì'érwéi		try one's best	5
近视	jìnshì	adj.	nearsighted	11
经济	jīngjì	adj.	economical	3
经理	jīnglǐ	n.	manager	1
经历	jīnglì	n./v.	experience	1
竞争	jìngzhēng	v.	compete	1
竟然	jìngrán	adv.	to one's surprise	8
镜片	jìngpiàn	n.	lens	11
究竟	jiūjìng	adv.	on earth, exactly	7
就座	jiùzuò	v.	take one's seat	6
举办	jǔbàn	v.	host, hold	4
举行	jǔxíng	v.	host, hold	5
具有	jùyǒu	v.	have (an abstract quality)	5
聚	jù	v.	gather	12
聚会	jùhuì	n./v.	gathering; get together	12
K 开场白	kāichǎngbái	n.	opening words	6
开阔	kāikuò	v./adj.	broaden; wide	12
开朗	kāilǎng	adj.	sanguine	2
开营	kāiyíng		open (a camp)	4
刊	kān	n.	issue (periodical)	9
看出来	kàn chulai		discern, make out	6
考察	kǎochá	v.	investigate	2
客户	kèhù	n.	client	1
课外	kèwài	n.	time outside class	4
口译	kǒuyì	v./n.	interpret; interpreter	1
苦	kǔ	adj.	bitter; hard	11
夸奖	kuājiǎng	v.	praise, compliment	6
昆明	Kūnmíng	n.	Kunming	8
困难	kùnnan	n./adj.	difficulty; difficult	2
L 来宾	láibīn	n.	guest	6
来不及	láibují	v.	have no time to do sth	8
来得及	láidejí	v.	have enough time to do sth	9
……来……去	…lái…qù		(doing something) over and over	10

216 ❖ Vocabulary list

WORD	PINYIN	PART OF SPEECH	MEANING	UNIT
懒	lǎn	adj.	lazy, sluggish	8
浪费	làngfèi	v.	waste	10
劳务	láowù	n.	(labour) services	7
乐于	lèyú	v.	be happy to	12
类似	lèisì	v.	similar (to)	7
冷静	lěngjìng	adj.	calm	7
离别	líbié	v.	part, leave, bid farewell	12
离不开	lí bu kāi		cannot do without	10
理念	lǐniàn	n.	idea, concept	5
力量	lìliàng	n.	power, effect	9
立场	lìchǎng	n.	stand, position	10
丽江	Lìjiāng	n.	Lijiang	8
例会	lìhuì	n.	regular meeting	5
联合	liánhé	adj./v.	united; unite	9
链接	liànjiē	v.	link	1
良多	liáng duō		quite a lot	4
凉快	liángkuai	adj.	nice and cool	10
亮	liàng	adj.	bright, shining	11
列车	lièchē	n.	train	3
零用钱	língyòngqián		pocket money	4
领队	lǐngduì	n.	group leader	3
留言	liúyán	v.	leave a message	5
流程	liúchéng	n.	programme	6
流利	liúlì	adj.	fluent	1
流连忘返	liúlián wàngfǎn		enjoy so much as to forget to go home	9
流眼泪	liú yǎnlèi		shed tears	11
龙塔	Lóng Tǎ		Dragon Tower	3
漏掉	lòudiào		miss	6
旅行社	lǚxíngshè	n.	travel agency	3
旅游业	lǚyóuyè		tourism	9

WORD	PINYIN	PART OF SPEECH	MEANING	UNIT
M 马虎	mǎhu	adj.	careless, sloopy	12
满意	mǎnyì	v.	be satisfied	2
忙碌	mánglù	adj.	busy	7
毛病	máobìng	n.	defect	12
帽子	màozi	n.	hat	4
美食	měishí	n.	cuisine	3
魅力	mèilì	n.	charm, glamour	9
闷热	mēnrè	adj.	muggy, sultry	12
梦	mèng	v./n.	dream	12
面对	miànduì	v.	face	12
面试	miànshì	v.	interview	1
面向	miànxiàng		be geared to the needs of	9
民乐	mínyuè	n.	folk music	6
名不虚传	míngbùxūchuán		live up to one's name	8
陌生	mòshēng	adj.	strange, unfamiliar	10
默默	mòmò	adv.	silently	11
母语	mǔyǔ	n.	mother tongue	2
目的地	mùdìdì		destination	3
目前	mùqián	n.	present moment	2
N 难熬	nán'áo	adj.	hard to bear	11
难得	nándé	adj.	rare, hard to get	5
脑子	nǎozi	n.	brain	7
能力	nénglì	n.	ability	1
拟	nǐ	v.	intend	5
年轻人	niánqīng rén		young people	8
弄	nòng	v.	manage to get	10
努力	nǔlì	adj./v.	hard-working; make an effort	12
O 哦	ò	interj.	oh (expressing understanding)	5

Vocabulary list ❖ 217

WORD	PINYIN	PART OF SPEECH	MEANING	UNIT
欧式	ōushì		European style	3
偶尔	ǒu'ěr	adv.	occasionally	12
P 陪	péi	v.	accompany	4
陪同	péitóng	v.	accompany	5
佩服	pèifú	v.	admire	6
配合	pèihé	v.	cooperate	5
批评	pīpíng	v.	criticize	7
啤酒	píjiǔ	n.	beer	8
品尝	pǐncháng	v.	taste	3
平台	píngtái	n.	platform	9
评价	píngjià	n./v.	judgement; judge	10
评审	píngshěn	v.	judge and determine	9
Q 期待	qīdài	v.	look forward to	2
期间	qījiān	n.	period	1
骑	qí	v.	ride (an animal/a bike)	8
启事	qǐshì	n.	notice, announcement	9
谦虚	qiānxū	adj.	modest, humble	6
签到	qiāndào	v.	sign in	5
签证	qiānzhèng	v.	visa	2
前辈	qiánbèi	n.	senior	6
欠	qiàn	v.	owe	11
强调	qiángdiào	v.	emphasise	2
亲近	qīnjìn	v.	get close to	10
亲眼	qīnyǎn	adv.	with one's own eyes	9
请	qǐng	v.	hire	7
请假	qǐngjià	v.	ask for leave	4
请柬	qǐngjiǎn	n.	invitation card	5
请教	qǐngjiào	v.	ask for advice	7
请示	qǐngshì	v.	ask for instructions	7
求之不得	qiúzhī-bùdé		more than one could wish for	9
求职信	qiúzhíxìn	n.	application letter	2
取长补短	qǔcháng-bǔduǎn		complement each other	6
全部	quánbù	n.	all, whole	3
全程	quánchéng	n.	the whole journey	1
全价	quánjià	n.	full price	3
全力	quánlì	adv./n.	(with) all one's strength	5
全体	quántǐ	n.	whole, all	5
群	qún	measure word	group, flock	8
R 然而	rán'ér	conj.	however	10
热烈	rèliè	adj.	warm, enthusiastic	6
人民币	rénmínbì	n.	Renminbi	4
人士	rénshì	n.	person, people (formal)	11
人文	rénwén	n.	humanities	11
忍受	rěnshòu	v.	bear	11
认出	rènchū		recognize	11
任何	rènhé	pron.	any	4
如下	rúxià		as follows	5
入场	rùchǎng	v.	enter	6
S 三分之一	sān fēnzhī yī		one third	3
伞	sǎn	n.	umbrella	4
散步	sànbù	v.	take a walk	3
色彩	sècǎi	n.	certain sentiment; colour	8
沙发	shāfā	n.	sofa	5
伤感	shānggǎn	adj.	sentimental	12
商量	shāngliang	v.	discuss	3
商业	shāngyè	n.	commerce	3
上司	shàngsi	n.	superior	7
稍等	shāo děng		wait a minute	3
稍微	shāowēi	adv.	slightly	10

WORD	PINYIN	PART OF SPEECH	MEANING	UNIT
设置	shèzhì	v.	set up	9
社交	shèjiāo	n.	social intercourse	10
摄影	shèyǐng	v.	take a photograph	8
申请	shēnqǐng	v.	apply for	1
深	shēn	adj.	deep, intimate	10
深圳	Shēnzhèn	n.	Shenzhen	1
声音	shēngyīn	n.	sound, voice	8
圣·索菲亚教堂	Shèngsuǒfēiyà Jiàotáng		Saint Sophia Cathedral	3
胜任	shèngrèn	v.	be competent at (a job)	2
剩	shèng	v.	remain, be left over	7
失败	shībài	v.	fail	9
失落	shīluò	adj.	feel lost	12
失眠	shīmián	v.	suffer from insomnia	8
失望	shīwàng	adj.	disappointed	10
十分	shífēn	adv.	very	8
石林	Shílín	n.	the Stone Forest	8
时差	shíchā	n.	time difference	11
实践	shíjiàn	v.	practise	4
实习	shíxí	v.	work as an intern	1
实在	shízài	adv.	indeed, really	8
食宿	shísù	n.	board and lodging	3
使	shǐ	v.	make, enable	10
世外桃源	shìwài-táoyuán		fictitious land of peace	8
市场	shìchǎng	n.	market	7
事情	shìqing	n.	matter, affair	5
事物	shìwù	n.	thing, object	12
事项	shìxiàng	n.	item, matter	3
视频	shìpín	n.	video clips	10

WORD	PINYIN	PART OF SPEECH	MEANING	UNIT
是否	shìfǒu	adv.	whether	1
适应	shìyìng	v.	adapt to	2
室内	shìnèi		indoor	3
手表	shǒubiǎo	n.	watch	4
手忙脚乱	shǒumáng-jiǎoluàn		be in a rush	7
手写	shǒuxiě	v.	write by hand	7
守则	shǒuzé	n.	rules	4
首页	shǒuyè		home page	1
疏远	shūyuǎn	v.	alienate, become distant	10
输	shū	v.	lose	9
熟悉	shúxi	v.	be familiar with	4
属于	shǔyú	v.	belong to	11
顺便	shùnbiàn	adv.	conveniently, in passing	10
说不定	shuōbudìng	adv.	perhaps	12
死	sǐ	adj.	extreme	6
似乎	sìhū	adv.	seemingly; as if	8
松花江	Sōnghuā Jiāng		Songhua River	3
送货	sòng huò		deliver goods	7
搜索	sōusuǒ	v.	search	1
随	suí	v.	go with	2
随时	suíshí	adv.	at any time	7
缩短	suōduǎn	v.	shorten	7
所	suǒ	measure word	(for institutions)	4
太阳岛	Tàiyáng Dǎo		Sun Island	3
太阳镜	tàiyángjìng	n.	sunglasses	4
态度	tàidù	n.	attitude	2
谈到	tándào		talking about	2
探访	tànfǎng	v.	visit, investigate	11
趟	tàng	measure word	(used for a round trip)	8

Vocabulary list ◆ 219

WORD	PINYIN	PART OF SPEECH	MEANING	UNIT
讨厌	tǎoyàn	v.	dislike, loathe	8
特点	tèdiǎn	n.	feature	8
特色	tèsè	n.	characteristic	5
特殊	tèshū	adj.	special	4
特约记者	tèyuē jìzhě		special reporter	11
提到	tídào		mention	8
提纲	tígāng	n.	outline	6
提醒	tíxǐng	v.	remind	2
提议	tíyì	v.	propose	6
体会	tǐhuì	v./n.	experience	8
体面	tǐmiàn	adj.	decent, respectable	8
天堂	tiāntáng	n.	heaven	8
条	tiáo	n.	slip, note	5
听从	tīngcóng	v.	obey	4
听众	tīngzhòng	n.	listener	11
停止	tíngzhǐ	v.	stop	8
通过	tōngguò	prep.	through	4
通知	tōngzhī	v./n.	notify; notice	1
同情	tóngqíng	v.	sympathize	2
同时	tóngshí	n./conj.	same time; in addition	10
投稿	tóugǎo	v.	submit for publication	9
突飞猛进	tūfēi-měngjìn		make great progress	12
突破	tūpò	v.	break through	12
突然	tūrán	adj.	sudden	11
图像	túxiàng	n.	image	9
团	tuán	n.	group	3
团队精神	tuánduì jīngshén		team spirit	4
团体票	tuántǐpiào		group ticket	3
推动	tuīdòng	v.	push forward, promote	9

WORD	PINYIN	PART OF SPEECH	MEANING	UNIT
W 外籍	wàijí	n.	foreign nationality	11
外贸	wàimào	n.	foreign trade	6
完成	wánchéng	v.	complete, accomplish	4
玩具	wánjù	n.	toy	1
晚宴	wǎnyàn	n.	dinner banquet	5
网站	wǎngzhàn	n.	website	1
忘	wàng	v.	forget	2
旺季	wàngjì	n.	peak period	3
危险	wēixiǎn	adj./n.	dangerous; danger	8
唯一	wéiyī	adj.	only	11
卫生	wèishēng	n.	hygiene	4
未	wèi	adv.	not yet	5
胃	wèi	n.	stomach	2
温差	wēnchā	n.	difference in temperature	3
温度	wēndù	n.	temperature	9
温暖如春	wēnnuǎn rú chūn		as warm as springtime	8
文件	wénjiàn	n.	document, file	6
文秘	wénmì	n.	secretary	1
文章	wénzhāng	n.	article	2
卧铺	wòpù	n.	berth	3
握手	wòshǒu	v.	shake hands	11
无法	wúfǎ	v.	be unable	7
无聊	wúliáo	adj.	boring	10
午休	wǔxiū	v.	noon break	4
物产	wùchǎn	n.	produce	11
物品	wùpǐn	n.	article	4
X 洗漱用品	xǐshù yòngpǐn		toiletries	4
系统	xìtǒng	n.	system	5
下面	xiàmiàn	n.	following	4
下旬	xiàxún	n.	last ten days of a month	12

WORD	PINYIN	PART OF SPEECH	MEANING	UNIT
下载	xiàzài	v.	download	6
夏令营	xiàlìngyíng	n.	summer camp	1
相反	xiāngfǎn	adj.	opposite	10
香格里拉	Xiānggélǐlā	n.	Shangri-La	8
详细	xiángxì	adj.	detailed	3
享受	xiǎngshòu	v.	enjoy	8
想法	xiǎngfǎ	n.	idea, opinion	10
想象	xiǎngxiàng	v.	imagine	8
消息	xiāoxi	n.	news	8
销售	xiāoshòu	v.	sell	1
小伙子	xiǎohuǒzi	n.	young fellow	11
协会	xiéhuì	n.	association	9
协助	xiézhù	v.	assist	1
心情	xīnqíng	n.	mood, feelings	2
心想事成	xīnxiǎng-shìchéng		all wishes come true	7
欣赏	xīnshǎng	v.	enjoy, appreciate	3
信	xìn	n.	letter	7
信任	xìnrèn	v.	trust	5
信息	xìnxī	n.	information	1
信心	xìnxīn	n.	confidence	1
兴奋	xīngfèn	adj.	excited	7
行程	xíngchéng	n.	itinerary	1
醒	xǐng	v.	wake up	12
兴致	xìngzhì	n.	mood to enjoy	6
幸福	xìngfú	adj./n.	happy; happiness	1
幸运	xìngyùn	adj.	lucky	7
修改	xiūgǎi	v.	revise, amend	9
宣布	xuānbù	v.	announce	4
学历	xuélì	n.	academic background	2
雪雕	xuědiāo	n.	snow sculpture	3
寻求	xúnqiú	v.	seek	6

WORD	PINYIN	PART OF SPEECH	MEANING	UNIT
Y 沿着	yánzhe		along	11
眼界	yǎnjiè	n.	field of vision	12
演讲	yǎnjiǎng	v.	make a speech	10
阳光	yángguāng	n.	sunshine	3
养成	yǎngchéng		cultivate (habits)	2
养老院	yǎnglǎoyuàn	n.	home for the aged	2
药品	yàopǐn	n.	medicine	4
业界同仁	yèjiè tóngrén		colleagues	6
业务	yèwù	n.	business	6
夜宵	yèxiāo	n.	nighttime snack	6
一等	yī děng		first-class	3
医疗	yīliáo	v.	give medical treatment (to)	4
一切	yíqiè	pron.	everything	7
一下子	yíxiàzi		all at once	12
仪式	yíshì	n.	ceremony	4
以为	yǐwéi	v.	think, consider (incorrectly)	10
一眼	yì yǎn		at a glance	11
异国他乡	yìguó-tāxiāng		foreign land	11
意外	yìwài	n.	accident	3
引导	yǐndǎo	v.	guide	6
饮食	yǐnshí	n.	drink and food	4
应付	yìngfu	v.	deal with	11
营员	yíngyuán	n.	camper	4
硬座	yìngzuò	n.	hard seat	3
永远	yǒngyuǎn	adv.	forever	7
勇敢	yǒnggǎn	adj.	brave	12
勇气	yǒngqì	n.	courage	12
优先	yōuxiān	v.	have priority	1
友谊	yǒuyì		friendship	6
邮政编码	yóuzhèng biānmǎ		postcode	9

Vocabulary list 221

WORD	PINYIN	PART OF SPEECH	MEANING	UNIT	WORD	PINYIN	PART OF SPEECH	MEANING	UNIT
犹豫	yóuyù	*adj.*	hesitant	9	珍贵	zhēnguì	*adj.*	valuable	11
游览	yóulǎn	*v.*	tour	1	真诚	zhēnchéng	*adj.*	sincere	11
友好	yǒuhǎo	*adj.*	friendly	4	争议性	zhēngyìxìng		contestability	10
有力	yǒulì	*adj.*	powerful	11	征稿	zhēnggǎo	*v.*	solicit contributions	9
有限公司	yǒuxiàn gōngsī		limited company	1	整理	zhěnglǐ	*v.*	sort out, clean	2
于是	yúshì	*conj.*	thereupon	6	正式	zhèngshì	*adj.*	formal	1
雨崩村	Yǔbēng Cūn		Yubeng Village	8	证书	zhèngshū	*n.*	certificate	9
预防	yùfáng	*v.*	prevent	3	之前	zhīqián	*n.*	before	5
员工	yuángōng	*n.*	staff	5	支配	zhīpèi	*v.*	control, arrange	10
原创	yuánchuàng	*v.*	originate, initiate	9	值班	zhíbān	*v.*	be on duty	4
原来	yuánlái	*adj./adv.*	former; as it turns out	8	职位	zhíwèi	*n.*	position	1
原谅	yuánliàng	*v.*	forgive	7	纸版	zhǐbǎn	*n.*	hard copy	9
原始	yuánshǐ	*adj.*	raw, original, primitive	9	至于	zhìyú	*prep.*	as for	3
远道而来	yuǎndào'ér lái		coming from far away	4	制订	zhìdìng	*v.*	formulate	3
愿望	yuànwàng	*n.*	wish	11	制作	zhìzuò	*v.*	manufacture, make	5
云南	Yúnnán	*n.*	Yunnan Province	8	质量	zhìliàng	*n.*	quality	9
Z 杂志	zázhì	*n.*	magazine	9	致辞	zhìcí	*v.*	make a speech	4
在座	zàizuò	*v.*	be present	6	忠实	zhōngshí	*adj.*	loyal	11
暂时	zànshí	*adj.*	temporary	2	主持	zhǔchí	*v.*	host	6
藏族	Zàngzú	*n.*	Tibetan ethnic group	8	主任	zhǔrèn	*n.*	director	4
糟糕	zāogāo	*adj.*	terrible	6	主题	zhǔtí	*n.*	theme	4
责任	zérèn	*n.*	responsibility	2	助理	zhùlǐ	*n.*	assistant	4
窄	zhǎi	*adj.*	narrow	8	住宿	zhùsù	*v.*	get accommodation	1
展现	zhǎnxiàn	*v.*	show	9	祝愿	zhùyuàn	*v.*	wish	6
招聘	zhāopìn	*v.*	recruit	1	专门	zhuānmén	*adv.*	specially	1
朝夕相处	zhāoxī xiāngchǔ		be together day and night	4	专心	zhuānxīn	*adj.*	focused	10
召开	zhàokāi	*v.*	call (a meeting)	5	专业	zhuānyè	*n.*	speciality	1
照相机	zhàoxiàngjī	*n.*	camera	9	转	zhuǎn	*v.*	transfer	3
折扣	zhékòu	*n.*	discount	3	转眼	zhuǎnyǎn	*v.*	in a flash	12
					状态	zhuàngtài	*n.*	status, condition	10
					准确	zhǔnquè	*adj.*	accurate, precise	6

WORD	PINYIN	PART OF SPEECH	MEANING	UNIT
兹定于	zī dìng yú		scheduled for	5
仔细	zǐxì	adj.	careful	2
紫外线	zǐwàixiàn	n.	ultraviolet ray	9
自费	zìfèi	v.	pay one's own expenses	3
自己来	zìjǐ lái		do by oneself	7
自习	zìxí	v.	study by oneself	4
自由	zìyóu	adj./n.	free; freedom	3
总结	zǒngjié	n./v.	summary; summarize	5
总之	zǒngzhī	conj.	in a word	2

WORD	PINYIN	PART OF SPEECH	MEANING	UNIT
走遍	zǒubiàn		travel all over	12
足迹	zújì	n.	footprint	11
组织	zǔzhī	v.	organize	2
最爱	zuì'ài	n.	favourite	8
遵守	zūnshǒu	v.	abide by, observe (the rules)	4
作品	zuòpǐn	n.	works (of literature and art)	9
作为	zuòwéi	prep.	as	2
作息	zuòxī	v.	work and rest	4